# DEATH

## BOOK ONE

### SEEDS PLANTED

# CHRISTINE CONTINI

Winterwolf Press
Las Vegas, Nevada

# DEATH

## Awakening To Life

### Seeds Planted

CHRISTINE CONTINI

Printed in the United States of America

First Edition

ISBN: 978-0-9885851-2-6

The author has tried to recreate events, locales and conversations from memories
of them. To protect and maintain anonymity of people referred to in this book, in
some instances the author has changed the names of individuals, some identifying
characteristics, and details such as physical properties, occupations, dates, places of
residence, and other possible identifying information.

Although the author and publisher have made every effort to ensure that the
information in this book was correct at press time, the author and publisher do
not assume and hereby disclaim any liability to any party for any loss, damage, or
disruption caused by errors or omissions, whether such errors or omissions result from
negligence, accident, or any other cause. Likewise, the author and publisher assume no
responsibility for any false information. No liability is assumed for damages that may
result from the reading or use of information contained within. The author has been
told that this book contains highly emotional material regarding life and death, and that
it challenges core belief systems. Read at your own risk. The views of this publication do
not necessarily reflect the views of Winterwolf Press.

Books may be purchased by contacting the publisher at:

Winterwolf Press
8635 West Sahara Avenue, #425
Las Vegas, NV 89117
www.WinterwolfPress.com

Info@WinterwolfPress.com

Chapter art and Cover art by Christine Contini
Interior formatting by Clark Kenyon
Cover design © 2017 by Winterwolf Press
Chapter art © 2017 by Christine ContiniDeath: Awakening to Life

# Table of Contents

# Dedication

To those who have entered my life as willing participants, I thank you. Without your constant love and commitment, my stubborn and stoic beliefs would have imprisoned me and defined my life for eternity. Inspired by your faithfulness, I have pushed past my own skeptical beliefs and broke away from the things that kept me afraid of admitting who I was. With your support, I live as the full expression of myself, and I revel in the beauty my existence creates. You have my tremendous gratitude for being in my life.

If you and I are meeting for the first time, I welcome you. As a participant in this awe-inspired awareness, you will look at my life and realize that my need to share my story is directly related to your need to hear it. I invite you, while reading, to find the connections to your own life experiences and awareness. I encourage you, just as I have been encouraged, to come to a greater understanding about yourself, about life and death, and to enjoy a glimpse of the energetics that create humanity's existence. I thank you for joining this most excellent adventure.

# Preface

&ach day I wake with the idea, *I want my truth*. I desire to be aware of things as they exist instead of as they appear. Many of us struggle to break free from belief systems and habitual behaviors; one such belief is the idea that death is scary. Many people survive day-to-day, believing nothing exists past the moment when a person's heart stops beating, or their lungs are no longer functioning to move oxygen through their bodies to keep cells alive. Those who do think life after physical death is possible may still fear they are wrong because they have no proof that any of their hopes are real.

I have the proof many seek. I have more experience with death and dying than anyone I know. With my science-based mind *and* my belief that God is real, I have been able to examine my experiences first, as a skeptic and second, as a person of faith.

Although my journey to wellness has not been easy, it has provided me with the opportunity to better understand the vast workings of my universe. I wondered what life would be like if it were experienced from a place of balance—feeling simultaneously connected with everyone, yet also feeling a separate sense of self. As these understandings came to me, a state of existence was revealed. I called it *Energetics*.

Energetics is a powerful way of simultaneously experiencing awareness of the body, brain, mind, energetic components, and spirit as a harmonious system that functions as a whole. Energetics moves us towards the full expression of ourselves in every moment, putting us in control of every aspect of our lives. With an understanding of Energetics, we clearly see every interaction is an energetic exchange we share with another welcomed, willing participant.

As a young girl, I did not have this understanding. When I was four years old, my parents, who had separated from the church, awakened to the decision that my little sister and two older brothers and I needed religion.

Dad had been raised in a strict Catholic family who believed that attending mass was an important part of embodying religion. As a teen, he had considered becoming a priest and had gone so far as to attend seminary, where he learned Catholic dogma in detail. While my sister and brothers played, I often listened to my father discuss theology and humanity for hours with his friends.

Our return to the Catholic Church came one Easter Sunday. When we arrived, the priest encouraged my dad to shuffle us kids off to Bible study, which was the tradition. To my frustration, he said, "No, thank you." Instead, all four of us sat in mass—still, silent, and alert—perfect examples of what good children should be.

I listened intently in order to comprehend what the priest said about suffering, just as I had listened to my father and his friends; the bit about Jesus dying for our sins, well, that made enough sense. But the part about our daily suffering—that confused me. It struck me as odd that Jesus had already died to save us from suffering, but we were all still suffering. Somebody made a mistake!

I looked at the idea of God this way: if God was everyone's good Father, would he not have a way to solve all our problems? I had a good dad. Every time I had a problem, Dad had a solution. If this was so, God must also know how to end suffering. I could not accept that God was okay with leaving his children to sit in misery with no solutions. Maybe those stuck in unhappiness did not know they had a way out.

That is when I heard what inspired me to pray for death—when we die, we will spend time with God in Heaven, just as Jesus had promised the man on the cross next to him.

*If I can ask God about suffering, I can share his words with the world, just as the priest was doing for us,* I thought. After all, was that not the entire reason for going to church? They said over and over, 'Let us pray.' Each time they prayed for something, the reason was always to end some form of suffering.

At the age of four, I did not comprehend that death meant leaving the earth for good; after all, Jesus came back in three days. There were also family stories surrounding the moment of my birth. I nearly died from severe jaundice. I grew up hearing this story and thought how wonderfully dramatic and exciting it was. I did not fear death—with a beginning like that, how could I?

Praying to be dead seemed a reasonable way to get the answers that people needed to solve their problems and stop suffering. These answers would be my gift to the world. I had the idea that we all needed to look for our hero moment, that we could contribute something great to the world in our lifetime. *This will be my contribution!* I thought. *I will tell everyone how to live in joy.*

At the age of five I was saved from choking at the very moment my sight started to blacken. By age seven, when I still had not died, I assumed that I must not yet be worthy of Heaven. After all, I still got angry with my little sister and my older brothers. And other kids called me names and got angry when I beat them in games, so maybe I was not as good of a person as I thought I was.

I tried 'being bad' like one would try on a new outfit; I wanted to see how it fit. I wittingly helped a little two-year-old boy, who was too small for the monkey bars, get up to them; then I watched him hang there. He could not move on his own. Afraid to fall, he whined, so I helped him down. Then I helped him up again, and this time left him to hang even longer. His arms began to shake and his legs pulled up to his abdomen. I sat there without helping him. *Nah, this doesn't feel good,* I thought. I deliberately gave up being bad, helped him down and went right back to learning to be Christ-like.

When I was eight years old, I watched a week-long news series about ESP with my parents. This was the first time I had ever heard about psychic abilities and the idea of it fascinated me. It was exciting to think telepathy, telekinesis, and astral projection were possible. We kids had imagined such things while playing. Now, to consider them as real was thrilling. *And to think, all you need is your mind!* On the program, they said that awareness was the key to harnessing these abilities. I strived to be self-aware so I could move objects with my mind and have ESP and be psychic. My friends and I theorized what it would be like to have psychic abilities, eventually scaring ourselves to the point that we ran home screaming as if ghosts were suddenly real and sitting next to us.

On the final show of the series about ESP, I heard the commentator say that it was against most religions to believe in such things. When my dad confirmed the Catholic religion was one of the institutions that shunned these beliefs, I completely shifted away from wanting to have those experiences. Anything else I experienced as extrasensory or intuitive was shoved to the corners of my mind and explained away in an effort to hold a more important belief—that the church was my guide to salvation and that these psychic experiences would lead me away from my goal of dying and ending suffering.

At age nine, I was one of a handful of kids still standing in our school spelling bee. When I flunked out, I could hear my friends chortling and cooing over my imperfections. I reflected on their behavior. Even at this young age, I already knew the only reason my friends would ridicule me was because they were unhappy with themselves. Still, I caused myself pain by believing that being my best was the catalyst for their suffering; they reveled in my mistakes. They needed to make fun of me to feel better about themselves. My logic told me that I needed to make myself less than what I was or else they would suffer. I forced myself to take responsibility for their pain and it hit me in my heart.

As I sat seething with anger toward myself for being the catalyst of their suffering, my teacher's attempt to console me only made matters worse. She told me it was okay not to be perfect because only Christ would ever be perfect. There I was, doing my best to be Christ-like, struggling to be continuously better to be worthy of Heaven, and this woman of authority in my life was telling me that humanity was flawed, that only Christ would ever be perfect!

Five years after I began praying for death, I still had not gone to Heaven. My dad, who was enlisted in the Navy, was out to sea again and my mom seemed to be endlessly stressed with the four of us children always underfoot. My mother struggled to save money to buy our next house while dealing with her own loneliness in my father's absence. She missed the camaraderie of working as a team.

As a pre-teen, I suffered from severe asthma attacks to the point that I would black out unless I was given a shot to reopen my airways. With each of these seemingly purposeful experiences, not only did death seem to be invited, it seemed to be inevitable and seeking the perfect moment to happen.

After hearing in service that selfish prayers would not be answered, I stopped praying. I concluded that my prayer to die and come back with information to save the world must have been one of vanity. Perhaps it was selfish to desire acknowledgement of my efforts to save the world. I added 'be selfless without ego' and 'be humble through service' to my list of things to be. Being human meant I would never be perfect; therefore, being Christ-like was unattainable. I would not be able to understand this huge dichotomy until I was in my thirties. Not being perfect created a belief in me that I was not good enough, and it was because of this confusion that suffering became a permanent fixture in my life.

I was twenty-four before I realized I had been depressed for as long as I could remember. At age four, I had already recognized other people did not know there was a solution to their suffering; now, I realized I had followed the same path. I, too, had put my will and my ability to choose for myself aside and became mired in the perceptions of others, unable to see the truth of myself. I began to believe that if someone saw me as unkind or unfair they must be right, assuming they saw something in me that I was blind to. I accepted their opinions, making it my priority to change to meet their perceptions instead of remaining in my truth. My personal intention was to always love and help others. Once these outside belief systems were implemented, it deleted my truth from my thoughts, which only allowed me to be happy when someone gave me permission.

I had accepted the church's teachings, as instructed by the saints, that in order to go to Heaven I was required to follow a set of predetermined rules. I had unknowingly locked myself into this indoctrination, canceling my own intuition, leaving myself to wander without support.

For years, I drove down the freeway imagining someone would cross over the divider and hit me head on. I was unable to accept suicide as a solution because I believed that if I killed myself I would 'burn in hell' and leave my family to suffer needlessly. I hoped if I was killed in an accident that I could skip Purgatory and go instantly to Heaven. If I could just keep working towards Heaven, one day this suffering—this endless depression—would end.

I felt as though I could not meet the needs of others around me. When I changed myself to make someone else feel better, it worked, but then I would try the same method on the next person and it would fail, causing that person and myself to suffer. I felt exhausted and unable to move. Once I tried to satisfy everyone I could no longer see myself. There was no safe direction to go since everything hurt someone. I was blocked at every turn by my own need to serve others.

I could see that my wish to die had shifted from a place of great blessing, like I had experienced in my innocence as a child, to a deep wrenching pit inside of my heart as an adult. Eventually, I discovered that I wanted death because I had not made my place here on earth my own. I needed to learn what freewill really was in order to leave this depression and move toward my own happiness.

As I became aware that the only true religion was one found within ourselves, this revelation forced me to question my every action and every thought, leaving me to choose which beliefs were my truth and which I should leave to others to own without my participation.

My pursuit of wellness began in desperation. By the time I was thirty-one, my health had taken a turn for the worse. It was not unusual for me to spend eighteen hours or more a day in bed, completely debilitated. I was crushed when I imagined the impact my poor health could have on my children. I did not want them to grow up too fast as they helped me with daily activities rather than being able to play. Instead of meeting my imagined fears, they surprised me.

My middle son, Johnny, was only eight years old when he noticed how difficult it was for me to get up to cook. He volunteered to help and would cook by asking me at each step what to do next. Meanwhile, my nine-year-old son, Joey, kept a general eye on the two younger kids, Johnny and Syndell. He also folded laundry for me, since moving my arms to that extent caused severe muscle spasms and cramping.

Eventually, I was diagnosed with Relapsing Remitting Multiple Sclerosis. However, shortly before that diagnosis, I woke up one day feeling great. After that day, friends and family asked me, "What did you do differently?" *Strangely, nothing,* I thought, and yet, I felt perfectly fine the entire day. The next morning, I awoke completely debilitated; my good health had lasted for only one day.

My dad had always shown me larger-than-life concepts. One of the concepts he encouraged me to believe was that once one human being could do something, it set the path for everyone else to follow. "Like the four-minute mile," he said. "If you start on the same path as others, crawling on your hands and knees, it is still possible to be the one leading the pack. Or," he added, smiling, "you can simply choose to stop when you feel you have arrived at happiness."

I repeatedly reflected upon that single day, my one oasis moment of being well. It gave me hope, just like the four-minute mile. Once experienced, I knew it must be possible to do it again and again at greater levels. Because of this belief, the idea of wellness, for me, kept expanding. Not only did I want to be free of Multiple Sclerosis, I wanted to be free of depression, guilt, and judgment. The longer I looked back at that single day, the more I believed I could forever be well.

Inspired, I somewhat uncharacteristically started to reach out to others. Driven by my love for my family and my need to be an amazing mom, I bravely talked to strangers and asked for details about obscure treatments. I downloaded people's personal stories, went to every seminar I could find on Multiple Sclerosis, and tried every type of therapy I could afford. I tracked down rumors about people healing from Multiple Sclerosis, cancer, and other fatal diseases. I looked everywhere to find someone who had been cured, only to find someone who knew someone who knew someone else who had healed from things seemingly impossible.

My search, although expansive, had not brought me any relief. I was still exhausted and unable to make it through an hour without collapsing. I continuously woke up in tears because the pain was so intense. At times, my body would involuntarily vibrate, as if I were riding in a truck with bad shocks on a bumpy road, even though I was trying to lie perfectly still. At its most intense, the episodes left me feeling as though I were a china doll that had been dropped. Upon impact, pieces of myself scattered everywhere, yet even though they were fractured and separated from my body, I still felt all the pieces. What I understood later was I had felt the energetic existence of myself. Pieces of me were energetically out of my body. They were literally not where they belonged because my system was broken.

Awakening at 2 A.M. experiencing one of these episodes, I was certain I was dying. I called my parents in desperation. I begged them until they promised to help with my children after I died.

Then my dad calmly said, "Find a Buddhist."

"A Buddhist? Really?" I was completely taken aback. *What good is that going to do?* I needed more than faith or a blessing. I already had those, even if they were failing me.

"Find one and learn to meditate," he continued. Up until this point, I had tried everything I could remotely imagine—traditional and otherwise. His suggestion had to be as good as any. In retrospect, it was my dad's wisdom that prompted my turning point.

The very next day, while mentioning this to my daughter's Girl Scout troop leader, I was shocked to find out that she was a Buddhist! Not only that, she was happy to be of service. The first time I went with her to a Soka Gakkai International Buddhist meeting and heard the chant of 'Nam-myoho-renge-kyo,' my body vibrated. It was a similar physical reaction that I had to the episodes that kept waking me in the night, except this experience felt joyous and was without pain.

Later, the chant leader explained to me, "Nam-myoho-renge-kyo is a vow, an expression of determination, to embrace and manifest our Buddha nature." Her gentle voice held my attention. "It is a pledge to oneself to never yield to difficulties and to win over one's suffering." She paused, looked into my eyes, and before she continued I believed she knew me both inside and out. "At the same time, it is a vow to help others reveal this law in their own lives and achieve happiness."

I could not have found a more perfect fit for my life; a chant designed to end suffering and help others find happiness! I was overcome with gratitude, and the ever-present ache of my body momentarily subsided.

Feeling my exposure to this chant was predestined, I continued chanting every day for months. Eventually, I moved on from Buddhism to experience other forms of meditation created within my own thoughts. Through each new idea I attempted to become aware of things I could not possibly know. I opened myself to the belief that limitations did not exist. Because of this, my practice developed organically through experimentation and eventually led to my complete relief from pain, which was a huge turning point for me.

My second largest turning point unexpectedly arrived in September 2008; I suffered a massive heart attack and died. The details of my near-death experience are contained in the first few chapters of this book. On my birthday, January 14, 2009, I had a second near-death experience during a test that was supposed to find out why my heart was unstable. I jumped at the chance to have this test, which was unusual for me, since I always maintained a strict policy against willingly participating in invasive procedures. Before I was revived from this second near-death experience, the doctor installed a defibrillator to counteract the life-threatening arrhythmias.

Later in 2009, I had a third, undocumented near-death experience in which I recalled begging the Angel of Death to allow me to live, presumably to make sure I would not forget that I wanted to be alive. Since that date, I have not needed to have the experience of death again. I now remember I am here through a decision of my own freewill, to stay and fight for the life I believe is possible for every living, breathing human being, and every living thing we touch.

Following my three near-death experiences, I continued to aggressively pursue enlightenment. Many months of daily meditation opened more and more doors before me. I thought at first that these doors were new. With experience, I began to recognize these doors had always been there. It reminded me of how our brains fill in so many blanks with habitual images—that we tend to miss the entire truth with our own eyes—like when the gas station up the street was suddenly there without my consciously witnessing the three months of construction it took to build.

With my readiness, I joyfully walked through each door and embraced each new experience. If I had been afraid, I would not have been allowed to move forward on my journey. My freedom from fear and my ability to simply observe during my meditations brought me the opportunity to experience unique levels of understanding. I clearly felt an internal connection to others as part of a universal awareness; they are connections we have all the time, but they exist below our conscious thoughts. I also met beings I had previously assumed only existed in myths and legends such as Ganesh, Shiva, Edgar Cayce, and Ohm. One of the most important things I learned was that wellness is a major contributor to acquiring the ability to have these experiences.

As I healed, I was able to connect to these abilities more clearly. Needing to free myself of beliefs that were killing my body, I had no other choice than to look at my life from different angles. I became aware that I was trying to control things that needed to be free to flow. I began to understand my responsibility in balancing my life, which affected my energy. I realized that I needed to trust myself before I could trust others.

Experiencing myself from this new and empowering place of personal truth forced me out of my comfort zone as my insights began to revolve around the supernatural—ghosts, Guardians, and Mother Nature. I pushed these revelations to the deep recesses of my mind until I came to a place in my growth and pursuit of wellness where I needed to acknowledge their existence so I could continue to find answers to achieve wellness.

Looking back, I now realize that I lived two-thirds of my life hoping to be dead; no wonder I achieved death at the early age of thirty-seven. Having continually imagined the freedom death would give me from suffering, it was only after experiencing my death and studying the deaths of many others that my opinion changed.

Death is not freedom from life; it is only the absence of a physical body. Everything we are in life, we continue to be after we die. Death is more like waking up on the first day of attending a new school; it is different than the old one and offers lots of new opportunities, but you are still you.

My experiences have made it clear to me how life can be lived with great joy instead of merely suffering through it. We can be free of pain and suffering *now!* It is not accomplished by a win-lose compromise or by stuffing down pieces of oneself or by being a martyr. Joyful balance is achieved through understanding and communication, by always making sure we are speaking and living our truths, and through accepting that others have the right to their own truths. Whether we learn these lessons at the moment of our death or become aware of them beforehand, death is our choice, made of our own freewill.

# Chapter One
# A MATTER OF THE HEART

## The Beginning

Las Vegas, 2008

For a while, I lived knowing my health required attention. Being a hard worker, a dedicated mom, and a selfless citizen was not enough to keep me well. In fact, it was being all those things while ignoring my own needs that put me in a place of desperation seven years prior. It was December 2001, on my daughter Syndell's sixth birthday, that I found myself in the doctor's office, thinking, *I got this, I can do this alone.*

I had already poured through a ton of research and felt fully prepared for what I was about to hear. Even so, when the doctor said the words, "Mrs. Contini, you have Multiple Sclerosis," I burst into tears. I desperately, wanted him to say more, to offer a solution that could free me from this nonstop, unbearable pain.

I was in a rapid downward spiral for the entire year following that diagnosis. My physical health was failing as I spent more than eighteen hours a day in bed. My disease was winning. For my family and me, it was tragic, but I held out, believing there had to be a 'cure,' some way to heal. I was certain I would find my way out of this; I had to.

For the next seven years, I tried everything from chiropractic, IV blood treatments, chemotherapy, steroids, and daily shots, to practically over-dosing on vitamins. My change in wellness did not occur until I finally understood I was in control of every aspect of my reality. Once I comprehended how the choices I made in every moment of every day affected every part of me, things finally started to turn around.

In the late summer of 2008, with strength gained through my new-found spirituality, I walked ten thousand steps, about five miles, every day. My depression lifted when I gained my understanding of Energetics and how to be well. Finally, off my last prescribed medication, I reached physical balance through diet and meditation that met my body's needs.

I stepped forward into each day with a commitment to show the world it was possible to be well. On this evening, I walked out the door with our two dogs, Raider and Raisin, and a spring in my step. My husband, Joseph, ran to catch up to us. I was happy, but within minutes of beginning our walk, that old, uncomfortable feeling that something was wrong returned.

I kept looking over my shoulder, convinced the flashes of light coming into my vision meant that a car speeding around the corner was heading right for us, but there was nothing there. Every twig that snapped or bush that rustled made me jump. Not being the gloom-and-doom type, this feeling of darkness creeping upon us was huge. I always believed the brighter side of life would offset the constant pressure of those looking to the darker side. But tonight...

Death felt imminent.

"Something's coming," Joseph said.

*He's not being himself,* I thought. "You can feel it too?"

His intuitive comment caught me off guard in my edgy state. He nodded. "Yes, I feel it."

*Strange that he's indulging me in this way since I'm the one who tends to know what's coming.* I assumed my ability to form predictions was singularly related to my intelligence and had nothing to do with telepathy. I enjoyed the feeling of being right, as I was seemingly able to guess the unknowable. *I am just really smart*, I considered. Yet, when people turned to me for more details, I had this way of minimizing myself; I was afraid of what I might imagine, and even more afraid when the things I knew without thought were correct.

"What do you think it is?" I asked, looking again over my shoulder. The feeling was manifesting into something tangible. *Maybe death itself,* I considered. My fears, driven by an instinct to survive, awoke my every cell; the hair on my body stood on end. I concluded this must be how dogs felt before a storm. *Hmm,* I wondered, *maybe it's not mine at all.* I looked at my two dogs to see if the feeling came from them. Both dogs seemed fine and peaceful trotting along beside me. I tried to shrug off the darkness.

"I don't know, but I definitely feel it," Joseph spoke in a low voice, looking down as he scratched the ground with a stick he had picked up.

Sharing that he felt something was wrong was definitely not like him. Gloom and doom were part of his character, but not the acceptance of premonitions as something that could be real. From there, we both drifted off into our own thoughts, silent for the rest of the walk.

Joseph went straight to the computer the moment we arrived home. He was intently focused on something in his own temporal universe. I could see the wheels in his mind as they began to turn. Hours later, he started spouting information about strokes and heart attacks. He shared what he had read in detail and for a great length of time.

"Why are you looking at all this?" I finally asked. I was frustrated after an hour-long litany as to how to recognize the symptoms of a stroke or heart attack. Suddenly it occurred to me. "Do you think this feeling of something coming is about your mom?" His mother lived with us and had been near death a few times already.

"I don't know; I just feel I need to learn this." He did not take his eyes off the screen, hypnotized as he scoured the internet for more information. Joseph loved learning details, but this time his effort was different. Night after night, for two weeks, he seemed hurried and obsessed as he continued his search for more and more information.

I wondered if he was rereading the same material over and over. After all, how much stuff could there be on this one topic without repeating itself? Occasionally, he would pull me back in with him.

"Did you know, after a person's heart stops they have twelve more minutes of oxygen left in their blood? Did you know that women don't have the same arm pain as men during an attack?"

I listened curiously with no attempt to retain the information. I could not relate to his fascination and I was distracted with planning for our annual family trip.

Three days before leaving for Lake Tahoe, I stood facing a mountain of clothes on my bed. Packing for all six of us would take a while. As I folded my way through the stack of swimsuits and t-shirts, suddenly the feeling of foreboding overcame me, it was even stronger than before. *Something is coming.*

Anxiety rose in my chest as an unfamiliar thought popped into my head, *I can't do this, I don't want to die!* I heard these words clearly, yet they did not sound like something I would say. I was still consciously looking forward to dying. I was looking forward to the day I would finally have a reprieve from the constant fight against depression and the release from the empathic intrusions into my life where I assumed the emotions and physical pains of others as my own. This behavior was an anomaly I did not understand. I prayed for freedom from the consumption of these burdens. I would not understand until much later that this unfamiliar voice telling me it was not ready to die was mine; it belonged to the true me and pushed through my unending depression to fight for my life.

Until this moment, I had only clearly heard the voices of my children in my head. Even so, I barely accepted telepathy as real. Moved by this thought, I looked at the shirt in my hands—it was my son Johnny's. I folded it, both fists across my chest. *Oh no,* I thought, sinking to the bed. All at once, my brain supplied the entire scene: the six of us in the van, rolling down the mountainside six thousand feet to our deaths. A tragic death was something I had imagined for myself, but never involving the kids. *What else could feel this big, this heavy?* I accepted the scene as a premonition.

The idea of my children dying was terrifying. I was willing to fight for them. *Is it going to happen?* I questioned, doubting my own fears. *If this isn't real, why does it feel so huge?* I pulled the shirt to my face, smelling the fabric as I used it to catch my silent tears.

Joseph came in; I was frozen with the shirt to my face.

"We can't go," I said as a matter of fact, raising my eyes to meet his. I was inflexible that way, immovable at times.

Always gentle with me, although a little impatient, Joseph was used to what he considered my overly emotional reactions to things. "Come on," he said, as he lifted me by my arms from the bed to hug me. "It's okay. We do this trip every year. There's nothing wrong." He released me and added, "Everyone is looking forward to it," as if he knew that my need to put the happiness of others above my own fears would change my mind.

The morning of our trip, I stood in the bathroom packing all the toothbrushes and shampoos. I felt anxious, caged-in even. I started pacing, my breath quickening. *This is a full-on panic attack*, I thought.

"I can't handle this!" I cried aloud as the panic became debilitating. I grabbed at the bag on the bed to unpack it just as Joseph walked in.

"What are you doing?" he asked, confused.

"We can't go!" I cried frantically. I was hysterical; I was convinced we needed to abandon our trip. *We are all going to die!* I screamed in my head to break the unbearable silence.

He grabbed me again, holding me tight, slowly pleading with me. "Christine, we talked about this." He paused, trying to think of what to say. "We want to go on this trip. Everything is going to be okay." We sat on the bed together until my crying subsided. Though externally silent, my internal struggle remained.

"Okay," he said. "You sit right here and I will let you know when we're ready." He figured if I did not move from this place—this space of appearing calm—I would be able to leave. I sat there, unable to understand the feelings that pressured my body, my mind, and my spirit.

He packed up the van as he always did. He had a meticulous need to load the luggage his way, a puzzle that only he could see, to make sure it all fit on the luggage rack. I was grateful for his efforts as I hated stuffing a bunch of bags around my feet. His work left the interior space free for bodies, handheld radios, travel games, and snacks. Although appreciated, it took more than an hour. The whole time I sat on the bed, feeling my impending doom. When he called for me to come, I felt like I was walking the plank. I put one foot in front of the other, all while feeling that I was walking to my certain demise, knowing I was going to die, and possibly that we might all die. The feeling was relentless.

I looked in the rearview mirror as we pulled out of the driveway. Something about being able to see behind me while also being able to see what was in front of me felt comforting. Instead of the panic and anxiety I had been experiencing for days, I suddenly felt calm. I was in a place of surrender. *Well, if we are going to die, it will be as a family,* I thought. The idea that my kids would suffer had evaporated. We were together, and in this moment, we were okay. In this moment, the future did not exist.

"Mom!" I squealed, excited as my mother swung open the door to her fifth-wheel trailer. I could easily see my dad's head above mom's, even though he claimed to be shrinking in his old age. It was a bonus to include a stop at my parents' house, and the look on their faces made the detour worth it. Because Tahoe was a long, eight-hour drive from Vegas, it was not normal for us to do anything other than stop for pizza.

I sat listening as my mom, waving her arms with unexpected enthusiasm, talked about her upcoming trip. "It's a water trip! I'll be on a boat," she exclaimed and shoved a book about birds into my lap. Much like the Cheshire cat, she had a cheeky grin, her lips pulled thin and turned up at the corners.

"What am I supposed to do with this?" I shrugged.

My mom, an avid birder, asked, "Can you tell me which birds I will see on the trip?"

I ran my palm across the book's cover. "How am I supposed to know? You're the bird expert."

Seeing the confusion on my face, she emphatically pointed at the book and attempted to find the right words to help me understand her excitement. "What about that brainwave trick? Can you try that?"

I sat staring.

Mom prodded, "You know, the one where you use the word game? Remember? You use something to trigger a word and then each thought triggers the next word."

She was referring to a previous conversation in which I had explained what I called the 'association method.'[1] It is where someone says black, and it triggers a thought that might be white or something else that might be associated with black.

With a huge, assuming smile, she pointed to the book again.

"How can I use a book to predict the future?" I asked.

Mom chuckled, "I don't know. You're the expert."

"Seriously?" I returned her chuckle uncomfortably.

Her silence, which felt like an energetic shove, forced me to consider the possibility. I thought, *What the heck? It can't hurt.* Without prior ex-

---

1. I had read online in Jad Alexander's *Book of Storms* that we use 'beta information,' basically any stimulus, to trigger beta waves in the brain. Seeing an item or hearing a word drives the beta waves like a search engine. This then finds and brings matching or supporting information to our conscious awareness. My reading gave me an idea—if I opened my brain and followed the beta signals to alpha, delta, or theta waves deeper into the brain while in a light state of meditation, I could use those waves to connect, receive, or communicate with others.

perience, I had no preconceived notion of the need to say it would not work, so why not give it a try?

"I need a paper and something to write with." I picked up the book and thumbed through it while I waited for her to fetch the items. Once the paper was in front of me, the book in my lap under my left hand and the pen in my right hand, I sat poised ready to begin. As I prepared to receive any information, I abruptly heard all the commotion around me that I had been blocking out. *Funny how that works, how a shift in our attention brings in more than we habitually allow.* I let go of my fear of being wrong as I overheard the kids and their dad making jokes to entertain the grandparents—all three, as my mother-in-law, Mary, had also come along on this trip.

Closing my eyes, I started the association—water, birds, none, blocked, fat, no birds, black and white, fluffy—then nothing. I waited to see if something else would happen or become apparent. Nothing. This lack of information flow was unlike any of my other experiences. Normally, when I performed the association method while not trying to predict the future, there would be a litany of words to decipher—twenty or more each time.

When I apologized to my mother, assuming my ability to receive extra-sensory information was not working, she responded, "That's okay, I was just excited to see."

I was puzzled. I had approached the association game just like I had for every other attempt. The idea that it had not worked did not sit well with me; I knew something was off. Yet, when I tried to follow the words to understand the story, all I saw was blackness. "Well," I said, "maybe it doesn't work for the future. Maybe it only works for the past." We both raised our shoulders in a synchronized shrug.

We wrapped up the visit with kisses, well wishes, and much love. It was always nice to see my folks, no matter how short the visit.

Later, when we arrived in Tahoe, I had completely let go of the idea that death was imminent. Since the only death I had considered was centered on a vehicle accident, I felt a release from the panic and anxiety that had been relentlessly plaguing me.

In fact, this was the smoothest trip we had ever taken as a family. The entire week continued free of a single hiccup and we could relax and enjoy the company of our siblings, nieces, and nephews. I laughed at myself a little for my drama-driven brain. *How silly I am*, I thought, as I enjoyed the close time with family.

On the last day of our trip, Joseph turned to me and said, "If this was your last day on Earth, what would you do?"

My conscious awareness perked up a bit, recognizing again how out of character this was for him. After all the anticipated death scenarios I had imagined, I decided this time to let it go. I shifted my focus to the idea that maybe he was just being sentimental. After all, with the kids entering their teens and increasingly wanting to be independent and active with their friends, this might be our last big family trip.

"My last day, hmm." I thought for a moment, and instead of thinking about my last day on Earth, I considered my last day in Tahoe. "If it were my last day, I would like to watch the sunset on Regan Beach where you proposed and where Joey took his first step." It was great timing too, since we were about to pass the road that led to that spot. We pulled over for a while, all of us happy to have the chance to soak up the last bit of sun for the day.

Sitting on my blanket, I reveled in the feeling that coming here was the perfect choice. Feeling introspective, I started a deep conversation with my kids. It reminded me of the ones I had with my dad when I was young. We talked about how important life and relationships were and what aspects of life have greater meaning than others. We discussed fear and how many people do not intentionally try to harm others but they do through acting out of fear. I wondered if the kids would remember me having this talk with them, like I had with my dad. Now that I was an adult, these memories kept me close to my father even though we were often a thousand miles apart.

The entire event seemed surreal to me. Before leaving, I shooed my kids and their cousins off to go run the sugar out of their systems from the ice cream they had just eaten before getting back into the van. I took off my sunglasses and stood up to gain a better vantage point of the sunset. I wanted to see it all. I wanted to feel it all. It felt larger than I could comprehend.

My daughter Syndell came over to me. She felt different, as if drawn to me. I pulled her into my arms, both of us hugging the other tightly. "Why don't you play with the other kids?" I encouraged her as we broke the embrace. I wanted her to make the best use of her time. She had time with me every day. "Enjoy your cousins." They were all running around, enjoying the kind of fun that only kids can have. "Tomorrow we leave for home. It's your last chance." My voice rose at the end in persuasion.

"No, I want to be with you," she said. The tone in her voice let me know her decision was final. Syndell and I stood alone, my arms draped over her shoulders, staring at the sky as it shifted from a light pink to a dark orange.

When the sun was behind the mountain, Joseph spoke to me, and again my senses picked up on some wording that was not his normal phrasing. "Are you okay? Are you ready to go now?"

"I want to sit with this feeling for a while longer," I said, looking over my shoulder at the kids playing, feeling Syndell in my arms. My attention was acute, a lump stuck in my throat as if I knew something was still to come. Then the peace of surrender again washed over me, as it had when I had looked in the rearview mirror. After a moment I said softly, "I am ready to go."

That was my last clear memory before my heart attack began.

# The Attack

Lake Tahoe, 2008

The heart attack started around 6:30 P.M. while I played Uno with the kids. I sat, seeing everyone's hands, but never felt as if I looked at their faces.[2] Their voices were louder than usual, as if I had candled my ears to remove wax. I had no idea what any of the other adults were doing. Except for the kids sitting on the floor in the circle with me, I had no peripheral sight, no sound, no sense of anyone else in the space.

I had been eating this zesty ranch cottage cheese dip my sister-in-law had made that I absolutely loved. It was weird, though—and this I remember clearly—I was eating far too much of it. The chips were especially greasy. I could taste the lingering oil that had been heated a tiny bit too high. I saw each grain of salt on the chips and even considered that this might be the reason why the dip was becoming more liquefied. I hypothesized that the salt was somehow mixing in the dip to change its consistency as I stirred it with each chip to get the perfect scoop. Even though I thought I was going to throw up, I continued eating ravenously.

The kids later told me I acted like I was drunk. During the card game, I would put down a card that could not be played. When they made me pick it up, I would laugh at myself, wondering why I could not convince them that the card was okay to play. I remember putting a blue skip on a yellow two. It made perfect sense; the next person had only one card left and if I did not skip them, they would win. My logic made sense; it just

2. Observing faces is a natural way to read body language. Those who do not look at faces are either avoiding the information or they are using extra sensory resources to get the information. In this case, I was using the latter, but because of the lack of oxygen to the body, my brain was unable to process the full amount of information. If the information had been completely absent, it would have sent a panic message to the brain, but because the information continued to come in, although distorted, no warning was signaled.

did not follow the rules. In that moment, I uncharacteristically prioritized winning over rules.

Even though I had been a childhood asthmatic, it never crossed my mind that I was suffering from cerebral hypoxia, a lack of oxygen getting to my brain. Nor did it register that I was having a heart attack or that the pain I felt in my chest as it tightened was not nausea from eating junk food. Even with all the research my husband had shared with me, at no point during this experience did it process in my brain that I was having a heart attack.

I remember returning to the motel and stumbling a bit. My daughter, Syndell, was staying in a room with my husband and me, while the boys stayed with my mother-in-law, Mary. *Something isn't right.* I was overcome with a need to get Syndell out of the room, completely fixated on the idea that I did not want her to see whatever was going to happen next.

As my urgency increased, I did something totally out of character for me; I cursed at Syndell. I told her she was selfish and I screamed at her that we needed our privacy. When she did not leave under that pressure, I called her an 'ungrateful bitch,' and used horrible words of manipulation. As a mother, the idea of harming my child makes this one of the worst things to recall, but in the moment, getting her out of the room was my priority. I had to accomplish the task and the method meant nothing to me as long as she was safely removed. Even as she texted me from the other room, asking for forgiveness, I gave her nothing. I needed her to be pushed away and separate from me. We had spent so much of our lives tightly intertwined; I needed her to feel pain in order to block our connection. *You cannot come with me on this journey.*

As soon as she was out of the room, I ran to the bathroom and began to vomit. Thinking I was done, I went to the bed, only to have my husband hand me a trashcan as I continued. My back was killing me. It felt like thousands of knives were ripping through each of my nerves.

The pain came in waves and took away my thoughts as I tried to listen to my husband talking on the phone with the nurse about our medical insurance. After all my dealings with doctors and medical staff during my experience with Multiple Sclerosis, I was very resistant to receive any kind of help. "I just want to go to sleep," I remember saying. "I am sick. I'll feel better when I wake up."

"Sir, your wife is having a heart attack," I heard the nurse say over the phone's speaker. Even with the nurse stating this as a fact, it had not occurred to me this was the moment Joseph had been relentlessly studying for. I was experiencing sudden cardiac death; a fatal heart attack causing extensive heart damage! In fact, Joseph knew the symptoms pointed to the kind of heart attack that only about six percent of the population survives.

With this awareness, my confused, agitated, knowledgeable husband did not seem to be able to hold the rest of his thoughts together. "You can't go to sleep," he pointed out, aggressively. "The biggest reason people die from heart attacks is because they go to sleep instead of going to the doctor!"

Joseph picked up the motel's phone again to call the hospital for an ambulance. Unable to focus on the address where we were staying, or even the motel's name, he dropped the phone into its cradle, deciding it would be quicker to drive me down the street to the emergency room. He knew exactly where it was, after all, Joey and Johnny were both born there.

I was topless. I had taken off my clothes, thinking it would reduce my back pain. After he helped me into my pajamas, he told me to wait while he went to fill Mary in on the situation.

Suddenly, things seemed to be so normal to me. All the commotion of feeling sick left me, and so did the pain. I felt very childlike. I remembered seeing my world this way when I was very young, before I was capable of purposely moving a single muscle. *What a strange thing to remember,* I thought. Completely fascinated by the experience, I began to think *I must be dreaming.* I remember watching myself put my shoes on to leave the room. At this point, I was not even real to myself anymore.

Outside, everyone around me was very upset. I could feel it. I kept Syndell encapsulated in her own little world. I separated her from me with my body language and with my thoughts. Still, I offered her nothing in the way of an apology. My usual thought would have been to make amends. I walked outside, my senses super sharp. This was ironic, considering I was now going on hours of my body having reduced oxygen, thirty-five minutes of which my body was severely deprived. I saw my son Joey's face. He had that blank expression that goes along with a fight or flight observation before the brain processes what is before it. Mary stood in the door, grasping her cane, full of responsibility as Joseph gave her directions.

As for me, I felt like dancing. I had lost all concentration on anything other than my feet. I could feel a physical distance between my sight and my body, as though I was in two places at the same time, all while logically knowing I was still observing my own feet. The separation of my senses from my body became more apparent as I watched my eyes travel to gain a microscopic view, leaving my body behind.

Suddenly, I could see the asphalts' atomic make-up with clarity. Even the space between the atoms was obvious. I was further distracted by my contemplation, viewing the pavement, seeing its life—when it was first poured, all its repairs and resurfacing—when a loud noise brought me back into reality.

The loud noise was my husband yelling. "What are you doing? You shouldn't be walking around!"

My thought: *He's angry that I'm having a heart attack.* Sighing, I looked up to see if I could see the stars, only to realize from the glow of the overhead lights that my astigmatism was now blocking my microscopic view. Only a moment earlier, I had experienced this microscopic view with fascination. I was confused as to why it was now gone.

He ordered me to get in the van as he jumped into the driver's seat. I wondered why he was so focused on himself all the time. After all, if I was the one having the heart attack, why had he taken the time to smoke and talk to his mom? And why had he not helped me get into the van instead of yelling at me? And why was he being so impatient when all I wanted to do was dance? On and on my thoughts twirled in my head as we drove, and then we reached the first stoplight.

Without turning to him, as my vision dimmed, I said, "The pain, it's coming again." I wished I had brought the trashcan with me. *How did I not think to bring it?* I was trained to be overly responsible, deeply ingrained with the need to always be prepared. This time, I had failed.

Instead of throwing up, I died.

My heart seized, and within a single beat, I was lifeless. This was the instant of my sudden cardiac death. My body slumped down next to Joseph in the van as he waited for the light to turn green. He saw my body sliding out of the seat, no life left to hold me upright. This confirmed the fact that I had passed. He pushed me back against the seat trying to get the seatbelt to hold up my mass of lifeless, dead weight.

Joseph's first instinct was to pull over and weep, recognizing that I was now dead. Instead of sitting there on the empty road at approximately 11:30 P.M., however, those two weeks of studying took over.

"Twelve more minutes of oxygen. Christine, you have twelve more minutes! Hang on!" Joseph began hitting my chest firmly, working my heart, guaranteeing oxygen would circulate through my body to keep my brain alive. He continued pounding on my chest for the entire five minutes it took him to drive to the hospital.

I was a thirty-seven-year-old female, reportedly in good health who had engaged in moderate exercise and meditation. I was medication-free, symptom-free, and a non-smoker who did not drink, use drugs, or indulge in a poor diet. With this history, the doctor could not figure out why I was having a heart attack.

"Clear!" It was the third time they applied the paddles to my chest. My heart had been locked in a battle with ventricular fibrillation, a fatal arrhythmia with chaotic and incomplete ventricular contractions. My heart was still fighting for my life, but no blood moved through it, making it impossible to register a pulse or blood pressure.

I was completely unresponsive.

The hospital staff completed their full CPR protocol which included a shot of epinephrine as they attempted to recover my heart rate and blood pressure to something manageable.

There was no change in my condition.

After a fourth shock, my heart converted to normal cardiac rhythm, but went straight back into ventricular fibrillation resulting yet again in the loss of pulse and blood pressure.

"Dial on three-sixty. Clear!"

California allows for a maximum of five shocks during resuscitation. If a patient is nonresponsive and further action will create no change, there is little more they are allowed to do. It was now the fifth time they applied the paddles. If I did not respond...

To the surprise of everyone in the room, my fatal arrhythmia was converted to a normal electrical impulse and maintained itself at a manageable rhythm.

I was alive.


Outside in the waiting area, I later learned, my husband stood facing the room where my body lay. Consciously, he felt my presence. He raised his hands and arms to the sky, praying stronger than he ever had in his life. "God, I want her alive. I want her alive, well, and healed!" This became his chant, his intercession on my behalf, "Alive, well, and healed."

Two doctors updated Joseph on my condition, which grimly pointed toward the only outcome worse than death—unresponsiveness.

"I want to see her. I need to see my wife."

"Sir, she's unresponsive," one of the doctors reiterated, as if Joseph should know it meant that they had no hope I would ever recover. In fact, with the forty-five minutes of oxygen deprivation alone they had no confidence that I could survive beyond a strict vegetative state of existence. Joseph pleaded to see me, but the other doctor emphatically refused, blaming hospital regulations. Their hands were tied.

"We don't have what she needs here. Your wife is undergoing preparation to be airlifted by the Flight for Life Helicopter to a cardiac facility. There's a small window before she is taken, when the pilot is doing his pre-flight checklist, where we can get you in to see her. It's a loophole where jurisdiction is cloudy."

The pilot, aware of the situation, casually went through the motions of completing his checklist, drawing things out to give Joseph time with me. Even though the doctors had no hope for me, it was clear that the next step on their cardiac plan was the required move to a critical care center. That meant I was going to Carson Tahoe Regional Medical Center, located forty-five minutes away by car, ten minutes by chopper.

"Christine, can you hear me?" Joseph took my hands, leaning in. Holding our hands together between both our hearts, he whispered in my ear, "It's important that you show them you are still here. If you don't let them know you're in there, they won't help you."

It was as if his words were magic. After all, this was the love of my life, the man I considered to be my one and only. In that moment, I swiftly inhaled, trying to speak, only capable of a gurgling sound. I remember attempting to bat my eyes at him, something I always did as an 'I love you'; only to barely open them as they rolled around in my eye sockets.

The pilot, quickly turned to the doctor and called out, "I thought you said...?" he dropped off from saying what everyone on the medical team was thinking. His entire demeanor and energy changed.

"She was!" The doctor was just as shocked as the pilot.

"Well, let's go, people!" The pilot commanded the room to life. "GO! GO! GO!" and in under two minutes we were in the air, headed for my emergency surgery.

Even though I had undergone surgery—primary angioplasty where they placed a stent in my left anterior descending artery—the doctors still expected me to be in a permanent vegetative state due to extensive damage and oxygen deprivation. They were in no hurry to wake me from the medically induced coma they had me in. The coma was supposed to give my body time to heal from the complications of the heart attack and some aspiration damage to my lungs.

I heard Joseph constantly in my ear. "Christine, you had a heart attack. You're in the hospital. You're going to be okay." They told him it would be impossible for me to break out of the medical coma. Still, he remained constant, vigilant for signs that I was still in there hearing his words as before.

I fought with all my might but was unable to push out from under the weight of the drugs to open my eyes. I opened to energetically feel the space around me. I could tell people were in the room but I could not identify anyone unless they were speaking.

With my mind, I looked for spaces between things. My meditation practices had taught me that finding spaces between things made room for the unexpected. Because of my experience with seeing the microscopic view of the pavement, I was inspired to look at my own molecular structure. Once I found the space between a molecule of the medicine and a molecule of oxygen, I began to push them apart, hoping to reduce the effects of the medicine. When enough of these were separated and with the strength of my will, I pushed out from under the weight of the medical coma to communicate.

The effort was exhausting, and I was only able to keep a clear conscious connection for fractions of a second at a time. Ultimately, my desire gathered more and more strength, and I willed my eyes to open, only to have them immediately shut with the loss of consciousness.

These moments I fought to achieve were not wasted. Joseph, knowing I was listening to everything, kept me up-to-date on my stats, encouraging me to meditate and to regain control when something moved out of the 'best' range. I remember him saying things like, "Christine, control your heart rate. It's one hundred and thirty-two, and it needs to be under one hundred to heal. You have to meditate." I did as he instructed and my heart rate came down to ninety-nine and stayed there. Joseph sat by my side for two days, making sure I knew every time something changed.

I remember trying to raise out of bed, using the leverage of my hands to pull myself up and away from the mattress, my mind pushing with extreme force, but I was too weak. All it took to stop my strongest effort was the gentle resting of a hand on my chest from whoever was present. Still I fought, periodically able to force my eyes open.

By the second day, my focus allowed me to gain some movement. Hating the unnatural feeling of oxygen being forced into my lungs, I kept reaching for the tube in my throat. The lack of full muscular control slowed the progress of my goal. Still, with each attempt, I became more coordinated. During my last effort, I grabbed the tube and started pulling, resulting in the medical staff tying my hands down so I would not hurt myself.

I started banging the bed with my tied hands, trying to get their attention since I could not speak. My right arm was locked down tight because of the IV. My left arm, held with less-restrictive binding, gave me a little more freedom of movement.

I tried to ask questions in sign language, a skill I learned from reading a book in elementary school. I grasped at every outlet I could to communicate, but I was unable to gain clarity of mind under the heavy sedatives. My effort was further complicated because I had to use my left hand, and I was right handed. One of the orderlies came through the room as I was making these signs on the second day. She chuckled, asking Joseph if I knew sign language.

"Why?" Joseph had asked.

"Because it looks like she does, but it looks like she's signing drunk!"

I heard them talking, but I could not comprehend anything more about what they were saying. I signed again, the best I could, asking for paper and pen. By the third day, they brought me some, but I was unable to recall the details of the urgent information I had wanted to make notes about. For one day, I had known the secrets of the universe, but by the time I could share them, the knowledge had disappeared.

Mid-afternoon on the third day, due to my constant attempts to communicate and my stable vitals, the medical team began the process of taking me off life support and the drugs that were used to induce the medical coma. My thoughts were foggy as I was still unable to fully comprehend conversations. Furthermore, I was unable to open my eyes, preventing me from gathering non-verbal information and cues.

My brain 'clicked' on as the medication reduced allowing me to realize that my body was being supported on both sides by nurses who were holding me up for extubation. As the tube began to shift in my throat, I went from being unconscious to consciously hearing.

"Exhale as hard as you can."

The words sounded like yelling in my head, as they were the first sounds I had heard in days without the dampening of drugs. Within a matter of minutes, my mind was clearing and I easily opened my eyes, pleased to realize the only thing preventing me from doing so before was the medication.

The doctor suggested that I not talk, indicating that my throat would be sore. I cannot remember smiling, which surprised me because I always had a smile when I communicated with others. I observed my family without emotion. They did not let the kids in to see me at first. Their decision left the children confused. They were unable to understand what was going on, and needed—more than the adults—to see that I was okay.

I sat there politely, staying awake to meet the needs of my visitors. I watched my mom with special attention. There was something eager in her body language. As she looked at me, I could see that her mind was somewhere other than focused on worrying about my health or recovery. As the others left the room, she sat waiting.

"Chris, you did it!" she exclaimed pulling a chair to my bedside. "You were right."

I stared, not following her excitement.

"Look how it all matched up!" She was jabbing at the paper on which I had written the association words during my visit. "Water, birds, none. See?" She looked at me as if her eyes could share with me all that she now understood.

"I was on the bird boat, getting ready to leave, when I saw all the missed messages from Joseph." She was not one to look at her cell phone very often and I knew she silenced it at night. She choked as she recalled what happened. I can only imagine how it must have felt to get that message, to have missed the call and to realize that her child had experienced a heart attack and had been rushed into surgery. "I got right off the boat." She shook her head, tears filling her eyes. "We came as quickly as we could."

I was still a little out of it, and waited patiently as she gathered herself again.

"It was just like you said—water, birds, I was about to go, then I saw none—my trip was blocked, your heart was blocked. They said that's why you had hours without enough oxygen; I bet it was blocked with fat. That's what you predicted!" She talked on excitedly. "You said you could only see black and white birds." She grabbed for her camera to show me what seemed to be the most exciting thing to her. "These are the pictures of the birds I've taken the last two days. Look at these…" She showed me about forty pictures of black and white birds, matching the description of what I had seen during the association—black and white, small, round, and fluffy.

"They're cute," I said.

"No, you don't get it." She paused for emphasis. "In two days of taking pictures there hasn't been a single bird other than this kind!" She was excited, punctuating each word as she spoke. For her, the confirmation was greater than I would have expected.

"You never see only one kind of bird for that long!" she said, shaking while letting the full impact of her revelation sink into my thoughts. *I had not gotten the message wrong, I had gotten it right!* I had accurately predicted her future.

This photo was taken about an hour before my heart attack. We are at Reagan Beach, South Lake Tahoe, CA.

Myself, Johnny, and Joey walking towards the sunset at Regan Beach. We stopped along the railing to look at the water and have an intimate conversation about life.

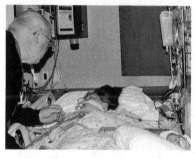

My father, John Stewart, offers me support while I am comatose. I am certain the love and care people shared with me during those three days made all the difference.

This is me shortly after extubation. My family and I talked at length about how different I looked and felt.

# *Awakening*

Carson City, 2008

When my first meal arrived, I was not inclined to eat. Still, I accepted the need to put several bites in my mouth to make the people around me feel better. I had a new awareness following my death and could recognize my behavior as meeting my social obligation to my family instead of meeting my own needs. Small changes in my personal balance brought my attention to these unhealthy behaviors, but without experience to show me the next healthy step I was left at a loss as to what to do different. Out of habit I took another bite.

The meal, to my relief, was interrupted when the kids were finally allowed in to see me. It pained me a bit to see each of them hesitant to come near me. I called each, one at a time, over for a hug. Syndell was the most reserved, still in shock following my treatment of her. I had to call her over for a hug several times before I could break through her fearful thoughts. She silently complied which was completely out of the ordinary for my bouncy, loud, beautiful girl.

"I think after I died I saw the Big Bang." Actually, I know I saw it, but while speaking to Joseph I minimized myself so as not to make him uncomfortable. Medication free, feeling well, I was still absorbing all the information and visions I had witnessed as movies in my semi-catatonic state over the last three days.

The head nurse was in my room wandering around. It seemed out of place for her to be here tidying up, and even though in general I attempted to minimize the impact of my words, while she was in the room I spoke with no reservations. "I saw this golden rock flying through space, not like refined gold but this dark gold. And it exploded! I was watching the history of the world."

I paused, trying to give a name to what I had seen. I felt a renewed awareness to my own energetic process. I was capable of consciously moving my mind further than the space of my brain. I could reach out into the surrounding information, into the thoughts of others, and return with a way to say what I was attempting to communicate. I remembered this feeling from childhood, from before my emotional blocks stopped the flow of awareness.

Finding what I was looking for in the thoughts of the nurse, I continued with the conversation. "It was the living library! I saw everything about Earth's formation, including the why. I could actually see the pebbles and minerals coming together to form larger and larger groupings."

During my medical coma, and for months following, I saw this information playing in my head as movies. At first, I considered that the electrical shocks had affected my brain, that they had reopened pathways and brought forgotten childhood memories to the surface. The first few movies I watched resembled places I had been or theories I had studied in grade school. After about thirty or so of these movies it became obvious to me they were not my memories at all, rather information being shared in the form of lessons, which held a new understanding for me. If I had no conflicting beliefs the movie became my knowledge.

When there was conflict between what I saw after my death versus what I had learned before dying, the new understanding was forced out by fear of the changes I would have to make. Letting go of the false beliefs I held was scary because it meant changing how I interacted with people. Each of those beliefs had been crafted to make sure I could not harm anyone. Without the safety of these beliefs, what would my life look like?

Until I reached an understanding regarding the conflicted lessons, I would experience each as movies, barely able to recall the details. However, some of the details would remain, picked up by my intuitive self, and held connected to a feeling of unrest. This unrest brought my attention over and over to the same replayed movie until I could grasp its content and it could be accepted.

I realized that before my death it was always like that—the first time I saw new information each foreign aspect would get pushed out. My strong conscious mind was unable to accept a new understanding if it conflicted with my currently held beliefs. I guess that is why we all need to hear something multiple times before it suddenly makes complete sense. Each time we experience something new, a seed is planted which allows for further recognition in the future.

I could feel the knowledge slipping away from me while I was under. For this reason, I had asked for paper to write down notes so I could remember the details. It felt unfortunate to lose most of what I had seen while I was stuck in the medical coma.

I paused my thoughts with plans to re-enter my conversation with Joseph as I shifted my weight on the pressure mattress that was my hospital bed. I was still moving slowly.

"I saw Earth's crust before water began to flow, and how she felt about the flow of water on her surface. That's where my brain froze. There was something in her experience about emotions, about having an experience similar to the emotions human beings have."

*Oh my!* This internal realization hit me hard. I was suddenly aware why Earth is so important to our universe. My awareness went to the lesson about Earth's creation of her surface. *It wasn't human beings that created emotions. It was her, Mother EARTH! She's the one!* The creation of emotions began when water, the first fluid moving across the Earth's crust with friction, redistributed her soil. I wished I could have shared my excitement of this understanding, how the motion over her first eon of existence produced the most basic experience, creating the energetic bonding process to our chemical structure, the basics from which modern emotions formed.

"Oh, and the Earth 'being a female,' I totally get it now!" I smiled, knowing the nurse in the room also knew what I was referring to. I understood that feminine energy is what supports our desire for relationships; feminine energy brings people together to work as a group.

I laughed as I realized my whole life I had referred to inanimate objects, including Earth, in masculine terms. What a surprise to realize and connect to Earth in her femininity. Previously, I had only reached up to the sky and into my core. I had always held myself separate from the earth. This behavior seemed to reduce the pain and fear I experienced while connecting to others. Reaching skyward strengthened my masculine attributes of responsibility and discipline and gave me a sense of safety. Unfortunately, without the support of grounding the Earth offered me, I found myself lacking in connection on a heart level to other humans, which left me yet again unsafe. I pondered these thoughts and shared bits and pieces as I made sense of them.

Everyone repeatedly told me to rest, but with these new thoughts my excitement grew. My family feared repercussions regarding my healing process if I did not slow down and rest; they shared with me warnings from the medical staff. The doctors had completely traumatized my family when they had told them my heart and brain would be destroyed from the lack of oxygen.

Despite the look of concern on Joseph's face, I persisted, feeling like I had too much to say to stop: "The most conflicting stuff I saw was about Egypt. It was confusing because I've always had a fascination with Egypt, and I assumed it was a majestic and prosperous place. But what I witnessed in my coma was nothing like I had imagined. The things I saw there were disturbing and unsettling."

I trailed off as I remembered the details of my historic vision. I could see that the fertile valleys far from the River Nile were just as lush and green as those immediately adjacent to the river. In this beautiful reality, people lived harmoniously with each other while maintaining their truths and individuation. Each person, independent and able, was separated by freewill and capable of meeting his or her own needs first and then the needs of others. There was perfect balance, everyone living with full embodiment from a place of internal truth.

When things changed, the harmonious community shifted from working as a whole to working as factions, each led by a prophet. The guiding Pharaoh asked each prophet to hand over his personal truth, attempting to unite the community again. Once their personal power was subjugated to the Pharaoh, he gained control over the freewill of everyone in the community. The Pharaoh, unable to personally embody each person's truth, could not completely understand the energetic information shared and fell into delusion. This destroyed the groups' natural energy of intuition and synchronicity.

It is important to know that these people willingly subjugated their freewill to support the goal of the community as a gift of devotion.

As devotion became obligation, the valley's rapid decline and the destruction of the landscape were obvious. Symptomatically, the destruction of the valley reflected the internal imbalance of each person.

I saw hundreds of people being sacrificed. They were being pushed off one of the pyramids onto wooden stakes and left to die; those who survived were buried alive. The most alarming part was those dying were okay with this method of sacrifice being the end of their lives. There was no resistance because devotion had changed to obligation. From their skewed place of balance and in hopes of saving many more lives, they used their freewill to override the desire to save themselves. It reminded me of my acceptance of the Catholic Church's teachings and how I believed there were rules to get into Heaven.

The nurse paused from her tasks just in time to see the confused look on my face—my energy was dropping rapidly. I was being forced out of consciousness by something outside my body. It pulled my awareness away from my body as if it were a separate thing that could easily be removed. As my eyes were on the verge of being forced to close, the nurse supported my thoughts with advice on meditation. Joseph, who had already spoken with the nurse at length, quickly told me she was a Reiki Master, letting me know that Reiki was a form of spiritual healing.

"Meditate on what?" I asked. I did not know how to meditate without a purpose.

I cannot recall her exact instructions; they reside in my memory as a jumble of words like a scene from Charlie Brown, "Whah-wha-wha

wha-wha-wah-wha, mwa-wah." I translated them to be: "Meditate on this space, from here to here." My vision, quickly fading, made it difficult to see her hands as she placed one at the bridge of her nose and the other just below her collarbone. "If you do that, you will have your answers."

Whatever was pulling on me was shutting down my bodily awareness so quickly it was as if I were being put under anesthesia all over again. I focused, filling my mind with the color blue for the throat chakra, the space the nurse had indicated with the placement of her hands. It was the only thing I could think of.

Unable to keep my eyes open a moment longer, they closed, but it was as if I had blinked and opened them again in a different world. All I saw in this space was open terrain. It was night, and a part of my energy was outside of the hospital. I felt the building behind me without turning to look. My physical size in proportion to the space would have put me at about the size of a gnat. I felt very alive and well. As I flew over the desert brush, I saw the ground in terms of its moisture. It was crisp in certain places, having lost its dampness, and dense in others, letting me know the ground had held water for a measurable amount of time. The space I was hovering over had taken three days to release its water. I realized my ability to know this information was a form of communication; I was versed in the language of nature! This part of myself could communicate with *everything*.

My attention moved to the top of what I would call a weed, but in that moment, it appeared to be more like a magic stick, shooting up high above its grassy bottom. The dried flower on the top held a sparkle that caught my attention. Suddenly, I felt the pull of a different part of my energy heading off into the distance.

As I share this experience, I must explain that even though I was out of my body as this gnat-sized expression of myself, inside my physical head I continued to focus my attention on blue.

Then, as before, I seemed to blink and open my eyes. This time, my entire view filled with only the head of a man. I was surprised to see someone so alive within the blackness of my closed eyes. Without his asking, I felt safe to accept his unspoken offer of support.

His presence, more solid than simply an image in my thoughts, filled up the entire space of my mind's eye. He appeared to be Native American, although I was not sure from which tribe. He was the embodiment of all tribes and none of them at the same time.

His face was oval. His deep, dark hair was pulled back, yet still loose from constraint. He had a slightly pointed nose that dipped at the end and a slightly smaller mouth than I expected based on his other features. His lips, though not protruding, were full. His simple eyes had little lash and eyebrow hair. His expression was calm, and as I looked, he engaged me with the gentlest of smiles.

His blue skin appeared weathered, and yet without texture. I had an uncanny ability to feel a person's age accurately. I would have guessed feeling him that he was older than one hundred and fifty, and yet he had no lines or marks to denote age at all. A single feather stood up from the back of his head and appeared to be about five inches long. It reminded me of the pigeon feathers I used to find in the yard as a child. Every little piece of him appeared unique, yet when observed as a whole he appeared nondescript, even common.

He communicated telepathically in strong clear words: *We're so glad you made it. We've been waiting for you.*

Outstretching his energy to me like reaching hands, he connected with my energetic system—a complete compilation of the different energetic layers of my being. As he merged further into my space, he engaged the layer of my energetic system known as the Etheric Template and planted a seed. This seed made it possible for me to both observe his healing of my energetic system and learn from the observation, allowing me to embody and adapt the skills for myself. Because of the seed, I would later understand that the Etheric Template is made up of hundreds of thousands of luminous green and blue lines that are the detailed energetic mappings of an individual's body. My vertices where the lines intersected were slightly brighter than my horizontal and vertical lines.

The vertices reminded me of a busy train station where many rails converge in one location.

The Etheric Template exists for the cells to draw information from and to enable them to organize into physical form. It defined my cells as uniquely me, encouraging my flesh to behave in a way that expresses my inner self. My Etheric Template delineated the lines on my face, the form of my muscles, and my experience of illness or health in each moment of this life depending on my frame of mind. All of my information was there.

This blueprint, my Etheric Template, had been with me before my physical life began. At conception, when the sperm enters the egg, that first initial explosion of light[3] creates the bond between our Etheric Template and the DNA material present. The bond is the creation and vibration allowing us to exist as physical life.

The Etheric Template also contained my historic record of every physical experience in this lifetime *and* my reactions to each of these experiences. When we die, the energy of this template leaves our bodies and stays with our consciousness. It is part of the reason the body no longer looks like us after we pass.

I watched as he lifted my Etheric Template away from my body. Only a master of energetics could have done what he did next.

He left with it!

I panicked, calling after him, *That's me! That's me! Come back with me!* It was no less traumatic than if a thief had stolen my child right out of my arms.

I watched in shock as he absconded with this very important layer of myself. I could feel it still existed; my ownership over this part of me remained a constant. His travel from one place to the next occurred in the space where time does not exist, therefore making his movement appear instantaneous and without effort.

---

3. The explosion of light is the ignition of strings into solid existence. Strings are the basic building blocks of existence.

By leaving my consciousness still connected to my body, his 'theft' made observation of my Etheric Template impossible. With that layer missing, my brain changed focus to observe my body, mapping out its awareness of my blood and every space in my physical form that my blood touched. My brain checked in with my remaining parts; it was unable to comprehend survival would be possible if this layer of myself was not present. The intuitive mind knew otherwise, so it stepped in and took control.

Unlike my brain, my intuitive mind was aware that the man had intentionally shown the layers of me how he had physically removed the Etheric Template. My intuitive mind rewound my awareness to just after the removal of the Etheric Template and before the moment he disappeared with it. We—my intuitive mind and brain—watched again step-by-step as the man pressed an electrical charge into us. We saw that our body did not respond. This action showed all of my layers that there was no physical connection remaining between my Etheric Template and my human body.

The mind—a combination of thought, intuition, feelings, and energy—could comprehend we were okay and relaxed with only slight internal pressure. The brain—a combination of thought[4], emotions, and body—could not see us as okay and so initiated our physical body's chemical release that accompanies emotions when in fight or flight.

Disregarding the mind's acceptance, my brain scrambled for a solution and, on cue, the other layer of myself—my spirit energy existing in its gnat-sized form—arrived.

My conscious mind spoke to my spirit energy, *Ha! You have come to my rescue. You can carry me!*

Spirit energy is responsible for communication between all layers of self, therefore, my spirit energy knew exactly how to find all the layers of me, no matter where the layers of myself ended up.

---

4. Thought in the brain is distinguished from thought in the mind. Thought in the brain is supported by the body, while thought in the mind is supported by the soul. It is because of this distinction that out-of-body experiences and other psychic phenomenon are possible, as the mind can travel without the body.

My spirit, ready for action, was not capable of jumping instantaneously as the man had. He had carried my conscious thought in its energetic form. For my spirit to carry my actual consciousness, it required us to travel. We moved forward by traversing the desert landscape. My very chatty conscious connection was experiencing excitement, as it was not used to being out of our body.

We moved quickly with this new focus. Feeling along the terrain, we raced over the rise and fall of the earth, as if riding in a vehicle. My energy kept an equal distance from the ground as we traveled. I could feel the air as it moved past, yet there was no air present. On an energetic level, air is experienced as a solid, the molecules as obvious as sand. Air, in this solid state, required our energy to travel on the molecules the same way my feet would experience walking on the earth.

We found the man easily. When we arrived at the cave, my conscious self was still very chatty. As my thoughts were communicated without words, they overlapped each other. I simultaneously observed and commented on everything from the angle of the sun, to the density of the dirt, to what the man might want with my Etheric Template, to how my body was doing on its own, to what my family was eating for dinner.

Even with all that going on, I still attempted to express to the man my line of sight, referencing I was six to eight feet above the ground, looking down at him from an angle. I knew this was a typical characteristic of an out-of-body experience, when both the consciousness and the spirit energy are moving as one. I wanted to share the excitement I had of my understanding in the moment and only stopped when I spotted my template on the cave's earth shelf, laying there, motionless.

*What are you doing with me?* He ignored my question and knelt next to my template, his hands outstretched over it. This only brought more questions. *Why are we here? How did you pick this place? Are you real? Do I still exist? Am I dead again? How come you are stable? Can I interrupt your concentration? Where do birds come from? How come life is like this?* and on and on…. these questions seemed to occur at once. It did not matter how many more questions I entertained, my asking still only took a single second. The difference was the accumulation of questions caused the asking to be experienced more loudly by the man. I continued adding my observations to the chat pile by talking about how I noticed he was now a full-bodied individual, instead of just being a head, as he had previously appeared. I felt excited to let him know that I knew his head appearing without his body was a manifestation of his spirit appearing before me without having his conscious connection with him. Now, as I observed him, he was an energetic being. This man's body was alive in the past, while his mind, etheric layer, and spirit were here with me in the present. I was thrilled as my awareness grew to recognize there were hundreds of years separating these aspects of him, and yet they were still acting as one.

This Native American man had made a personal choice to remain tied to Mother Earth as one of her caretakers. His choice allowed his energy and spirit to move more freely than her other inhabitants, both living and deceased, and gave him the ability to interact with the external environment even when not in his body. For his energy, time and space had no bounds, as he existed to meet Mother Earth's needs of safety and health.

That realization caused me to chitter away with even more happiness. The sound of my own questioning reminded me of crickets chirping, a noise that I find annoying when it is unrelenting. The man shushed me. Already engrossed in his work, he made no inclination to explain his behavior, respond to my observations, or answer my questions. As I watched his effort, my impatience to understand more continued as I started anew with my questioning—*What's that one? Why did you take that part out? How come those lines are connected now instead of the others? What made it get brighter?*

As I began to push into his space with this noise instead of keeping my distance, he shushed me again. Like many other energetic beings I have since encountered, he was absent of the common social human niceties we use to communicate, and without compassion he dampened me to remain a silent, passive bystander. I felt as if I had been tucked away in an observation room with double pane glass with no other choice but to follow his command.

Once quiet, the energy of questioning could release. I was still without answers when my awareness changed. In this quiet state, the endless looping of unanswered questions stopped. Instead, the questions left from me in a line moving away from me. Once in a line they were joined to the universe and would at some point find my answer and return to me under the law of attraction.

This release created a sense of peace and comprehension. Through observation, I could feel him. He felt whole to me, incarnated and connected to the earth. In fact, Earth was his sole support and gave him the energy to exist as life in that moment. I watched as he moved through each second of my life, examining my experiences. He opened my traumas and my self-inflicted pains first, to be seen with his wisdom. Then he rebuilt my experiences as aspects of me with his broader scope of understanding. He brought to my consciousness what he knew to be true that I could not find in myself because my template was broken.

Next, he pulled in the master body template, known as the Ketheric Template. Often referred to as 'God's Plan,' it is located about two feet out from the surface of our skin and surrounds our entire physical and energy bodies. Much like working with our modern computers, the Ketheric Template would be the master reset disk. When in capable hands, the Ketheric Template can be used to run all sorts of self-diagnostics and complete many repairs using nothing more than a person's own thoughts. When our interpretation of the Ketheric design into physical form is navigated, it must pass through the Etheric Template. If the Etheric Template has been damaged, it cannot be repaired by thought alone.

Since my Etheric Template had been damaged by years of forcibly holding the will of others over my own, he had to pull a copy of his own energy, gathered from his Ketheric Template, to be used to find the places in my Etheric Template to repair, making a full repair possible.

Before the heart attack, I had pushed myself to meet my perceived needs of what others wanted from me, afraid that if I did not I would somehow lose something—be it their love, their respect, or their approval. I had acted from a fear of loss instead of moving forward with the truth of love. Love, as an independent vibration, allows us to meet our needs first and then the needs of others. It was the belief I could harm others that held my energy in awkward patterns and eventually became damaging and self-destructive. It was things like not sleeping more than four hours a night so I could hand-make each of the kids the costumes they wanted after they picked something complicated at the last minute that added to this damage. It was not my desire to do things like this for my family that corrupted it with the energy of obligation, it was the way I stopped meeting my needs to meet theirs. Instead of all of us having a great experience I was exhausting my body, reducing my health, to meet their needs from a place of fear. Fear energy has a way of destroying the balance of our cellular structure.

With each of the adjustments to my energetic system, I could immediately feel the effects in my consciousness. His changes made it clear that it was the undulating energy that existed outside the physical body—the templates held in my aura's field—that drove my habitual behavior. The templates stored the observed information that my brain and body used to quickly respond to fight or flight impulses when triggered. For example, the template and habitual behavior I used to respond when someone lied, was to believe nothing I had ever experienced with that person was true; *everything* became unbelievable and had to be questioned. The pain I self-inflicted was more traumatic than the lie. This behavior totally obliterated my entire history with them, leaving me feeling unsafe and unloved.

His adjustments now made it clear to me that the habitual templates conflicted with my beliefs, and were incorrectly created by the way I perceived the beliefs of others. For example, after the adjustment of my Etheric Template, if someone lied to me, my personal truth was to know that the lie was about him or her. Knowing this, I could help him or her work through the fears and find a way of communication that did not require deceit.

Now, in this clarity, I remembered something seemingly small my dad said to me in passing: 'If someone lies about something small, what else will they lie to you about later?' This planted seed created the foundation of a concept that over time created my entire cascade of change. It led to my being unable to handle even the smallest of lies, assuming each was a personal attack on me.

The damage I caused by being out of my truth and holding the beliefs of others over my own blocked the flow of this energy. Not living my truth and blocking my flow of energy made it difficult, if not impossible, for my body to heal naturally. By repairing the damages, the conscious understanding I achieved allowed the energy to flow again. Disease and damage were released from the plan, making room for wellness.

When he was finished, the Etheric Template was reconnected to my physical form. The individual cells in my body recognized and followed the corrected blueprint, allowing the changes to fully take effect.

Although it was strange to be an audience witnessing my own changes, I was grateful. I felt it when he corrected my emotional responses, especially to pain. With these patterns fixed and now in alignment with my truth, instead of being aligned with the beliefs I had accepted from others, I could stop creating further physical damage whenever I had an emotional response to a situation. There would be no more driving the pain in so deep that it broke my heart or destroyed my heart chakra energy. I felt each wave as it washed through me and I reveled in my awareness as the changes to my perception occurred immediately.

I suddenly understood how to unblock my energy without effort. I had to let go of the judgments, attachments, and conclusions that pulled me away from the truth I enjoyed. These things created a false control in my energetic system that blocked the free flow I needed to be well.

Periodically, my consciousness, without the restrictions of my brain, looked at the whole of my existence. I was my own witness, seeing the effects as they rippled through all of space and time and released the obligations I had created to contain and control myself in my relationships with others.

From this larger perspective, it suddenly made sense that to heal something in myself was to heal it in others, and to change it in this moment meant to balance both past and future simultaneously.

After some time had passed, he gave complete control back to my body, and my conscious connection released.

When I awoke from this experience, all parts of me were present in my body and I was different, stronger, and well. I even looked different, brighter somehow. At my request, Joseph threw back the covers and helped me out of my hospital bed. I gingerly walked up and down the corridors without a problem.

After my release, we journeyed home from Tahoe on the fifth day following the heart attack. The eight-hour drive gave me time to think about what had happened. Although none of my nurses, doctors, or family had given me any reason to believe the things I had shared seemed crazy, my own thoughts left me considering that the entire journey beyond the body that I had experienced was not quite real.

In fact, if I had not already worked with energy and learned to leave my body during meditation, I would have sentenced my death experience to live in the cobwebs of my mind as some kind of psychosis. Yet, the medical facts, too, pointed to something more. In one hour, I had transitioned from being barely able to move, to being fully capable of walking on my own. My unexplainable rapid improvement was undeniable.

Still, the phrase, "We have been waiting for you," lingered in my mind. It had my full attention. The man's clear, telepathic statement made me question if my death was predetermined. Would there have been an easier way, other than dying, to make his acquaintance, or was death a necessary component for my success? And what about this miracle that I had recovered so easily after only a few days? *Could that be real?* This was no small feat, no lucky happening. *I walked a fine line and survived,* I thought, shaking my head. *Was it the energetic alterations by this man that had created this miracle? Was he waiting this whole time to return me*

*to normal, knowing this was going to happen? Or is this an elaborate way
for my brain to make sense of what cannot be understood?*

I felt the answers to my questions come to me. They pulled me toward a revelation—I would know what I had seen on the other side. The
thought of accepting what I knew to be true created pressure in my chest,
like a box of something that needed to be opened and unpacked. Afraid,
I instead chose to lean heavily in the direction of doubting my experience, allowing the veil to obscure what seemed to be so far out there that
it could not possibly be real.

Sifting uncomfortably through my thoughts, I considered all the times
I had questioned if ghosts only existed in my imagination. One time, I
woke from a dead sleep after witnessing my grandfather's life from his
point of view, seeing myself out of body as if I were him. It seemed like
a dream, but I knew in my gut he had passed hours before I received
the call. Oh, and the time I got the creeps when I felt my deceased aunt
walk right through me; she had lost a baby due to cancer two months
before dying herself. I concluded she must have wanted to visit my newborn son. Another time, I was certain Joseph's deceased father was in the
room while we were being intimate. He randomly showed up and would
not leave until Joseph convinced him to go visit our sleeping boys. This
was affirmed when I felt him leave and we heard both the boys talk in
their sleep!

Each of these experiences seemed real when they happened. Later,
my brain moved the parts of my experience that conflicted with my reality behind the veil.[5] My thoughts again fit what I had been told to expect
in this world—ghosts were not real, life after death cannot be known
while we are alive, and the only way to get to Heaven is through acts of
good deeds. When pieces popped up from behind the veil I would brush

---

5. A veil is a purposeful energetic block that separates the mind and brain. It allows the
brain to hold beliefs that conflict with what we know to be true at a soul level. This veil
separates us from a natural awareness of all of existence at the same time, and because
of this, we experience space and time in a linear fashion. This separation has us making
free will choices without knowing their impact.

them away. I told myself that the apparitions I had seen were merely the result of my fantastic imagination, instead of the factual experiences I knew them to be deep down.

Following my death, for two glorious weeks, I floated on a great feeling of euphoria. Born anew, I could clearly see joy in all things. In my previous skewed focus, I saw everything only from a point of suffering, but now the pain of others finally made sense. It was not needless!

As humans, I now understand that it is only comfort or discomfort which compels us to move. Experiencing suffering is a way to motivate us to change. It gives us a reason to fight for love, to learn, and to create, allowing our own freewill to light our paths, and to hear the guidance of our souls. I now understood how we as individuals drew all the events of our lives to us. I could see how we needed the difficulties we attracted so we could challenge our current beliefs and mindsets to set ourselves free to live in our truth.

However, during the third week, I was suddenly abandoned. The feeling of joy and support left me. It was not only that the door had suddenly closed; it was that the wall that held the door had vanished, too. Desperation enveloped me, looming heavy as a thick fog. I had spent so much time in the past maintaining this type of painful focus that it was my norm. Seeing the suffering in the faces and bodies of everyone I interacted with returned without effort. To be back here seemed natural, and the opposite experience—the temporary joy I had felt—now seemed to never have existed.

In the weeks that followed, I would be in a dark room with my eyes closed and for a second I would see lights, as if a car had driven past my house, its lights flashing through my window. This was not a brand-new experience. In the past, I saw infrequent flashes of light without investigating where they came from or what they were, having assumed the flashes were from the television or the kids moving things that gave off a reflection.

The difference now was that the flashes of light were happening more frequently and at all hours of the day and night. Sometimes, they would wake me from a dead sleep with my heart racing. I would grab my pulse oximeter to track my oxygen level and heart rate. My resting heart rate was usually sixty-eighty beats per minute (BPM), but I woke up to these lights flashing many times with my heart rate up to one-hundred-ninety-eight BPM. I was not having bad dreams. I had little to no stress in my life, and I was taking things slowly. With my family's help, I could rest and recover completely. So, what was causing this reaction?

I put up with the flashes for a couple of days, thinking that it was perhaps the new neighbor across the street making a turn into his driveway. *Maybe my heart can't handle the startle,* I considered as I got out of bed to investigate the source of the lights.

*Nothing. I see nothing.* I thought it curious. I checked multiple times and each time I could not find the source of the lights.

I attempted to block out the lights. *Maybe they are reflections bouncing around in an extreme pattern I can't follow.*

I sat in my room with the blackout shades drawn and all the doors closed. I had stuffed towels at the base of the doors just in case the light was coming from under them.

Contented, I lay there, all snuggled in, the room completely black.

*Now I will get a good night's sleep.*

I was about to doze off when suddenly there was a glow. I opened my eyes. Nothing, everything was completely black. I closed my eyes and there was the glow again.

*Okay...so I can see something with my eyes closed, but not when they are open. Hmm...Maybe I have some sort of neurological damage from the hypoxia. After all, that was a freaking long time to go without oxygen. What the hell! Who wouldn't have some kind of damage?* I laughed to myself.

I was resting with my eyes closed, unable to sleep, when suddenly there was a flash that seemed to zip past my face. This happened three times. I lay awake for at least another hour but nothing else happened.

I visited doctors to rule out the possibility of brain damage. I even got a second and third opinion, but each confirmed I was in surprisingly good health. In fact, I appeared to be doing so well that they went so far as to question whether I had been misdiagnosed with Multiple Sclerosis in the first place. They did not want to consider that I had simply spontaneously healed.

*Well, if it is not neurological and it is not psychological, then what else could it be? Why am I seeing these lights?* Still curious, I started looking for other options.

I repeated the experiment of being in the dark and watching the lights several more times and wound up with the same results: they just zipped by. I Googled what the lights could be and the only thing that offered any explanation was information about orbs. But that was not scientific, so I let it go with little consideration. After nearly a month of watching them, one finally slowed down and hovered near my face.

*Now, that is different!*

Months later, when my observations had yielded no answers and I was about to give up, another single orb stopped right in front of my face. This one was a little larger than a softball and had a pearlescent coating. The coating evaporated while I watched, which allowed me to see its inner workings. It reminded me of one of the more complicated elements from science class. Inside the orb flowed electrical currents. These currents moved independently between the smaller atomic pieces of matter.

*What are you?* I asked. Since childhood, I tended to talk to inanimate objects in my head as if they would answer. I often got a feel for things that seemed to reach past the obvious sensory perception. The only reason I did not ask out loud was because people would think me peculiar. Still, it surprised me when this one answered.

*I am an interactive global positioning device used to create and transfer matter from one place to another.*

*Are you sentient?* It was the gentle nature conveyed in the vibration of the telepathic response to my inquiry that compelled me to ask.

*No.* It sent a small electric current into my face and then vanished.

I sat stunned. It took a few moments for the surprise to wear off and then I realized I had new information in my thoughts regarding orbs. I was excited to be completely aware that orbs were information and support devices. The orange and brown ones originated from the earth, while the more common ones for me were the white, or light blue ones that came from out in space somewhere, and the new ones that were more like balls of undulating electrical current, those were energetic support, like food for the body.

For a while I remained conscious of their presence. When I asked for information using a specific frequency in my request, no matter the topic or the question, they would show up to deliver it. They also arrived unsolicited with information that would help a situation I had not even asked about, such as how to help family members with mental and emotional issues they were enduring. The orbs seemed to respond to more than my thoughts, more like my entire existence.

I realized while talking to others that my experience of having a massive heart attack and dying was not overly emotional for me. On the other hand, my entire family remained completely traumatized. They suffered from the shock that it had occurred in the first place and then were further shocked that I was able to leave the hospital alive and well.

I imagine their conflicting thoughts had something to do with the educational video the doctors asked Joseph to watch regarding the care and feeding of an invalid. Following my surgery, the doctor told him I would be in a vegetative state, unable to communicate. Under stress he had shared many details of this with Mary, my mother-in-law, details which the children overheard.

I see the doctor's behavior as an act of compassion, and I imagine it was done to give my family something stable to hang onto in this very difficult situation. In the world of medicine, a person does not go through what I did and survive without severe brain damage. Yet, here I was at home, laughing at my own jokes like I always did and walking around like little to nothing had happened.

Hearing my family speak about their experiences and what they went through was like listening to a harrowing tale of something I was not involved in. As I saw it, we did not have a shared experience. Joseph, especially, had a lot of trauma to move through. I found it necessary to make light of my own experience to balance his extreme emotions.

In a way, I could relate to his anxiety because I had saved Syndell from drowning when she was four years old. It is nearly impossible to have a detailed discussion about saving someone's life with anyone who has not experienced saving the life of another, especially a loved one. The hundreds of mental shifts that occur in rapid succession are indescribable—it is overwhelming! As humans, we do not have words to communicate completely what we go through in such moments. I think we save our loved ones because we have no other choice; not because we believe we can. The alternative is too hard for us to deal with so we MUST save them. After the fact, most people have a hard time seeing how it was possible. The brain seems to take over and move us past our fears without thinking. It is a big experience.

A few weeks after everyone had expressed the trauma they had endured and I knew they were on the mend, I gave myself a break from being the mom who solved everyone's problems. It became apparent I had some personal work to do when I found myself weeping uncontrollably while standing in a grocery store parking lot when I heard a helicopter overhead. The sound of the rotor blades spinning in my ears unexpectedly triggered the memory of my own Flight for Life ride. I stood there, realizing for the first time I had died—that my life had ended. I knew I was still alive, but for a moment, *my life had ended*! However temporary it had been, this realization was huge.

Once I allowed myself to accept this fact, my mind went straight to work, sorting and organizing thoughts about what it meant to be dead. I found myself worrying about how my kids would have been taken care of and how my family would have felt without me. The belief that I could, by dying, fail them in some way hit me in my self-esteem. I went to work looking for what I needed to change to make sure it did not happen

again. I felt that I needed to guarantee this was a one-time experience—
at least one that would not repeat itself until I was old and ready to die. I
was taking false responsibility for 'what I had done wrong.' Even though
I had not done anything wrong, I felt responsible and pressured myself to
control the experiences others would have by planning their futures. The
truth was, if I had not returned from the other side, my family would not
be spending time with me; they would have buried me.

I realized I had not taken time to grieve my own feelings of loss.
Confronting all the beliefs I had held about death was no small thing.
On one hand, I had every bit of information the church and society had
told me about life and death, and on the other hand, I had everything I
now knew to be true from my own experience.

My brain could barely keep up with the reorganization. For months,
each time I accepted another piece of my experience as being true, I also
accepted the necessary tools and personal growth to make changes to
what was humanly possible in this world. For instance, when I accepted
'pain is not reality and all pain is self-created' I was able to see where in
my life I falsely held pain as fact instead of as a choice of my own freewill. The very next time I had a headache I simply looked at it differently
and in doing so I could experience my life without it. I went as far as to
develop methods so I could help others live with the same reality I was
creating. I explained how our actions, beliefs, and obligations held us in
pain and kept us from relief. Awareness to these in conjunction to the
release of judgment, attachment, and conclusions then made the new
reality possible.

With these new truths, I could no longer hide behind the veil I had
used to create my reality. Life was changing rapidly.

Now, I would never tell you not to miss a loved one, or suggest that
you skip over grieving simply because I have shared what I know about
death. That would only be another form of denial. I would tell you to
mourn the loss of the physical instead of the loss of life. It is true when
the body dies, we will never have that exact contact again. When a loved

one passes they cannot physically whisper in our ears, yet I have heard many a whisper from beyond the grave. We will never again have the excitement of arriving at their homes for a visit, nor will we share the details of our lives, and yet, every day, loved ones who have passed on connect to us with the support, remembrance, and synchronicity we so earnestly need.

I have had people argue that once a loved one has passed they can no longer feel their embrace, and yet, I have witnessed and felt the physical embrace of a loved one from beyond. More is possible than many of us know and until you can personally experience this awareness, the grieving process is what will free you from your painful beliefs.

Once we are through our grief, we can live without being tied to despair, to the loss of hope, or to fear of any kind after the death of someone we love. We have a connection to them that will never be gone. In moments of need they show up, even if it is by encouraging others who are alive to step in for them. There is guidance at work. There is no doubt in my mind or heart that we are loved and cared for by those who have passed for eternity.

I have witnessed as others have mourned and have not released their connection to a loved one. By holding on so tightly they block their ability to reconnect to their loved ones on the other side. There is a bond, an unbreakable one, but it is not found through remembering a loved one's passing as loss. If we are looking outside of ourselves, wishing to see them, to hear them, to have them ever-present in a physical body, our own pain and the delusion about our perceived loss can be in the way of the very connection we crave. The way to connect to a loved one who has passed is to journey deep into our heart's center, into the very spark of divinity that feeds into who we are. That is where we can find them, at any moment, without fail.

When you find yourself missing the deceased, remember your experience of them is greater than their physical presence—you share a connection beyond the body, an energy that still exists. Instead of overindulging in the painful beliefs of loss and how your loved one's absence has changed your life, look at what the relationships brought you. Perhaps being vulnerable with your loved one was a space in which even being misunderstood did not leave you feeling unloved. Or your loved one pushed your buttons, which forced you to further express yourself to be understood.

Often, what you miss the most is not them, but the person you felt they allowed you to be. You let them see you for who you were on the inside, and allowed yourself the freedom to express the parts of yourself you hid from others while in their presence. With them you felt safe, secure and seen and because they loved you, you felt safe in loving yourself.

Though at times uncomfortable, their push gave you the freedom you needed to let go of your self-inflicted cage. The space they provided, the safety to fully express yourself, was a lovely gift you saw mirrored back to you when you were in their presence.

Giving yourself permission to be vulnerable and fully express what is uniquely you is a beautiful tribute to your loved one's life. Revel in that joy, that expression of yourself, secure in the knowledge that every time a loved one is missed, it is a reminder that you need to be that vulnerable and the full expression of personal truth again for yourself. I believe that when you honor your loved one who has passed from this place of love and remembrance, his or her energy will still support and guide you, making your life easier. The things you remember, whether beautiful or tragic, are about you and not about the departed.

I promise—and I make very few promises—that death is okay. No matter how many times I have witnessed the death of a living thing—be it human, animal, or plant—I am confident in knowing that life continues. Life is not only the physical. Death is not the end.

# Chapter Dedication

With gratitude to Joseph Contini for his support and his generous heart. Thank you for playing a pivotal part in my journey, making sure I stuck around to do the work.

To Kay Burnie-Stewart, my sister-in-law, for her support and strength, for helping Joseph keep his wits about him and making sure my kids had what they needed when I could not. Your unending commitment to being a witness to life and what is possible is a blessing to our entire family.

# Chapter Two
## AWAKENING FURTHER

## The Other Side

Las Vegas, Fall 2008

*E*ach time I looked at the moment of my death, I pressed up against a definable blank space—the space in my chest I had encountered on my trip home from the hospital—that box I had yet to unpack.

*My brain is blocking me from remembering what happened while I was dead. What's going to happen if I remove the veil?* The box was surrounded by fear, and I believed that whatever was inside would force a radical change.

To move past my fear and open the box, I sat down and prepared to meditate.

Taking one cooling breath after another, calmness washed over me. *Everything is for my benefit; fear is only a delusion.*

I chose the mantra 'show me' to reveal my greater will—my soul's knowledge.

Continuing my breathwork, fearful thoughts rose to the surface for release, reminding me that veils have a purpose. I had, through my first experience of removing the veil, nearly shattered my mind with the new awareness that good and evil do not exist. The realization that all things are equal, and the idea that good and evil are judgments, instead of facts, seemed foreign and took time for me to accept.

Pondering these ideas, I moved into a safety and released my fear. The absence of fear created an energetic space where I expanded my internal light[6]. With each breath I increased the quantity of light, which would be used to open the box containing the insight and awareness I was seeking.

I allowed my mind to remove the veil, to reveal my experience. My memory started with me being unable to see anything other than gray-toned hazy contours of my surroundings—completely contrary to the picture I had expected to see. I had assumed I would find a group of my family members standing next to me as I left my body; I was surprised to be surrounded by people I did not know, and so many more hundreds than I had expected. I could not see any of their details, but I could feel they were there.

My focus suddenly shifted. I became aware of being jostled around like the metal ball in a pinball game, bouncing off strangers and being guided by the crowd. We had all arrived at the same time and were seeking out whatever or whoever it was that would take us to our destination. I did not have the cognitive thought to ask questions; I simply followed my instincts. Feeling with my outstretched hands, I found an opening that led into a narrow corridor.

As I moved forward, I realized I was getting into a rollercoaster car. It felt like those theme rides at Disneyland, similar to Snow White's Scary Adventure. I was by myself in my car. In this busy place, with thousands

---

6. The internal light is light that has been adjusted to mirror one's identity, unlike external light which is a collective expression of light. Internal light originates from the Spark of Divinity.

of people spilling in and out of fully packed cars, I noted curiously that no one joined me. I departed alone into the darkness. I did not care that no one was going to my destination; I was excited to be on this journey.

The car edged forward. It rocked with a shock and a jerk, much like being dropped a foot to the ground in something heavy. Filled with anxiety at the thought that the car would stop, I was relieved when it did not. I realized later that this was the first time they shocked my heart, attempting to save my life.

I moved forward. The rail curved. I felt I was positioned on a straightaway, angled to go fast.

A second shock!

I deliberately ignored it this time, and to my excitement, I kept moving.

The rail turned abruptly skyward, my back pressed firmly against the seat. Pressure began to build inside of me. Feeling it as too much to bear, it pushed outward. Something heavy held me in my body.

A third shock!

The car fell away.

My conscious mind let go of the construct it had created to make sense of the experience. I had not been in a car after all.

Now, in a new awareness, and no longer needing the conscious constructs, I saw something not created by me—a tunnel.

I moved into the tube, flying. I looked up, toward the end of the tunnel. My body stretched like a rubber band. When it reached its maximum elasticity, it snapped and shot me forward. While still corded to my body, I flew like Superman beyond the sun as I left Earth, both arms at my side. Occasionally, I lifted one arm or the other to move in the right direction, which changed my angle of acceleration.

Excited, I knew where I was going. Moving faster and faster, I was on my way!

I stopped trying to see out of my eyes and instead I connected to everything around me. The surface of the tunnel shifted from a gray darkness to a now, living and breathing energy.

Immediately, I was distracted as I felt hands reach out from the wall and grab me. The tunnel was lined with the stacked and overlapping bodies of people. Their touch moved through me as if I were a liquid and yet I could not stand the growing feeling that those who grabbed me could somehow keep me from reaching my destination on time.

The fourth shock!

This whole time I had been moving further and further away from my body and this fourth shock had very little effect on me. I made my way through the people who grabbed at me and exited the tube.

I arrived on a platform, opening into a clear, light blue sky.

I did not know what to do. I had an expectation that someone should be here to greet me. I stood, blankly looking at the white platform. Then, as I decided the platform should be different, it transformed into a planked wooden pier—something one would find on a weathered dock next to the ocean. The only thing missing were the seagulls. I looked to the air. Its glow was different than what my eyes had seen when alive on earth. I knew this was not really sky. Before I had a chance to process what it was—air, water, jelly—I began to see motion. It was just a dark haze at first, becoming more and more solid as it moved toward me.

From the haze, a woman dressed in a dark green gown with long black hair materialized before my eyes. She glided, rather than walked, onto the platform.

I sensed her familiarity and realized that the family I had left behind on Earth paled in comparison to the depth and breadth of this connection. My feeling for her was immense, greater than any feeling I had ever had for anyone before.

*You are Love*, I said to her. I knew I belonged to her, and she to me. I realized we were speaking telepathically when I became aware of her name—Alma. She hugged me. I was elated, free of all the cares and woes of my existence. I had arrived at my destination.

After our moment of embrace, she held me at arm's length. The look of love on her face was sublime.

The fifth shock!

This shock was different. I did not actually feel it; it was a distant echo—an after thought reminding me of a life lived long ago.

Even though my energy was physically out of my body acting on its own it was still connected and affected by the restrictions of space and time regarding my physical form. This shock was a distant echo, and yet it had a dramatic effect on me; it reminded me of my family on Earth. That was enough to destabilize my desire to stay in this beautiful, loving embrace and the elastic connection to my now alive body was tugging me back.

I grabbed at Alma's arms to hang onto what was in front of me, unwilling to let go. As her arms dematerialized between my fingers, her expression changed.

She raised a single finger and wagged it side to side, like one would do when silently telling a child 'no, no, no.' I felt my eyes grow wide and my mouth opened in shock as I realized her intention.

Alma materialized again, and with one finger on my chest, she pushed with the force of a thousand pounds. Unable to resist, I was pushed back into the tunnel from which I had arrived.

As I journeyed back down the tunnel, my dismay left me. I returned to thoughtless observation. The tunnel was cold, the air like ice around me. There was no color and no light. All the people who had grabbed me before seemed to be in a deep sleep and I continued to fall past them with no inertia.

As my recollection ended, I sat up in bed. I sat in silence without thought for a long time. While the veil was still pulled to the side I allowed myself to accept truths from my conversation with Alma.

Alma enlightened me by momentarily raising the kinetic activity of the light content in my body; it displaced darker beliefs like others can harm me, I can fail, life is hard, and left me only with things that are my personal truth such as light is love, I always have what I need, all people are amazing, and it is my right to express myself. This expansion allowed me to see how my options and my choices created my world; how they were fashioned from my identity, my heart, my love and my compassion for all. When I stepped out of my truth into a belief like 'others can harm me' I created an energetic obligation. Everything from my choices, to the law of attraction, to the way people reacted to me, were now driven to support this belief. When existing in my truth, life was held as joyful. My choices, habits, and what I attracted were the reflection of me.

Alma laid before me ideas that would change my life and all of life on Earth.

My realization was loud in my head as each thought happened simultaneously. I saw humanity putting an end to all disease. I saw people who had significant healing abilities working in the medical field to save lives, using vibrations emanating from their hands and minds to stop people from bleeding out while surgeons fixed body damage. I saw healers minimizing traumas during surgical procedures with their will.

In this split second of truth, I learned that it only takes one moment of 'I AM'[7] to change all of existence. Everything in life that I am destined to do was already existing in time. If I brought more of my essence into my human life, becoming more of myself, the world would change and suffering could end. Playing my part was as simple as being the full expression of myself. As such, I was capable of experiencing miracles.

My comprehension was not a special gift given to me because I had died; it was my re-awakening!

I questioned if the human ego could handle such change and decided to forcefully lock in to my thoughts what was purely my own identity—a clear copy of myself without the veil. This would prioritize my beliefs when challenged by others, reducing the chance that I could be swayed as I had in the past. In my attempt to not harm others, I had arbitrarily changed my own identity.

My taking this action brought back the lesson I had witnessed regarding Egypt. I clearly understood why it had been shown to me, how my own behavior of changing my identity was the same as the members of

---

7. I AM is the embodied awareness that we are all one in the same.

that society. Witnessing[8] this exchange with Alma and all the lessons I viewed as movies afterward, altered my life.

After I fell back into my body, I realized if I could not have seen what Alma had revealed to me, if I had not been open to this truth, I would have left this human life. I would have died. I had walked a fine line. Alma had shown me my world and the importance of my being alive. Without the internal support of self, the light of my soul would have been damaged.

The universe protects us.

The universe will not allow us to damage our light past the point of extinction; if I did not see my truth in that moment, then I would have continued my journey to the other side instead of returning to my body to support others with what I know to be true.

Up until this point, I had lived my life while holding onto fear. This created a reality without personal freedom. Once changed, I would be able to change the impossible into the possible. The prayers I had continually stuffed down in me could be answered if I was willing to be vulnerable and release them to the world.

Now, I aligned with my truth, my entire being moved toward these magnificent changes. With the veil pulled back, I searched for the missing pieces necessary to bring the changes into humanity's existence, into my own existence.

I focused on the belief that to complete this transformation I would no longer be able to indulge in the things that kept me weighted, such as fear, attachment, judgment, conclusions, and assumptions. I admitted that to live my journey of leading the world away from suffering—a choice made of my own freewill—I would be leaving my husband. All these behaviors had been included in the foundation of our relationship. They would have to leave my life to make space for my new existence,

---

8. Energetically, witnessing is more than just watching. It is the energetic participation in the energy of others that allows us to personally create copies, information loops, and methods that are stored in our systems beyond the brain, such as templates, auras, and individuation.

my personal truth. Our co-dependent, obligated relationship would be no more.

As time passed, Joseph habitually fought to hold onto our original reality. I could understand why; the life and relationship we had built was safety for him. The changes my choice required meant an end to his safety. Without change of his own, he would be unable to navigate the transformation. A new life, while holding onto the old, was impossible.

I saw into the future as I questioned the end of my marriage to Joseph. Apparently, we had achieved what we were destined to create together and would be moving along different paths now. This was confusing. If he was my soulmate for life and longer, as we had promised each other, why would I have to leave him? My brain fought against this crushing reality. In that first moment, I could not believe it. There was no pain in the realization; I just did not think I could accept it. Although not a practicing Catholic, I had still lived my entire life with the belief that marriage is forever. Living that belief left no room for this new knowledge to be true. I believed there was no need for me to let go of him. My whole life was planned and we were going to grow old together. What would my world look like without him? With all of these thoughts, the veil moved thickly in to protect my beliefs of how my family and life should exist.

Three years later, we would separate. Joseph and I became polarized in our relationship. The two of us had always had fundamental differences and we chose to no longer ignore them. After twenty years of marriage the end still came as a shock to us both.

In 2013, our relationship officially came to an end and Sara, Syndell, and I moved out. I needed to pursue happiness and save the world from suffering. Joseph, although angry, knew he needed space to exist without the guidelines I considered important to form a healthy life. Leaving one another guaranteed we could both continue our journeys of personal discovery in a way that met our individual needs.

# A New Beginning

Las Vegas, Fall 2008

The next year following my death proceeded somewhat the same, led step-by-step by something larger than myself. Except for the three hours a day I meditated, I tried to live a somewhat normal life. As a wife, with my marriage to Joseph still intact, I paid the bills, organized our schedule, and made sure dinner was ready when he got home from work. All the while, I hoped with encouragement that Joseph would open up and the end of our marriage could be avoided. As a mother I still carpooled, took the kids to the drive-in with a pile of friends, grocery shopped, helped with science fair projects, threw amazing birthday bashes, and read Harry Potter to those who wanted to listen at bedtime.

But for three hours a day—when the house was quiet and everyone was busy with their own lives—I meditated. Upon awakening, I meditated on the night's adventures to gain insight and to set the tone for my day. In the middle of the day I meditated on methods of healing, followed by contemplation while I performed acts of service, like laundry or dishes that took no concentration. At night, I went to bed meditating, which released the trials of the day and set the tone for resting. I also posed intentions at bedtime to see where I could arrive by the next morning. Then I woke to do it all over again.

Contemplating what was possible, I turned my focus inward, craving a deeper understanding than society provided as to how and why my life developed as it did. Each day, my contemplation gave me space to live more and more in my personal truth. I began to notice when I reacted habitually to things that took me out of character, like getting mad at the kids for coming in late. That was my mother's habit, not mine. With each of these moments of awareness, I chose my truth and replaced the old gathered habits of others with actions that reflected me.

I followed all my compelling factors as they guided me to meet others who considered themselves healers. Each time, I learned something new about energy, and each time I ended the acquaintance confused. It did not make sense to me that many of them were unwell. They all had these awesome abilities, and instead of working internally with their own issues and using their abilities to heal themselves, they focused on the external, as if by changing the world instead of themselves, they would somehow make their lives better. Seeing this double standard created doubt for me regarding their intentions, and it drove me to question if my own beliefs in self-healing were real.

*But I know what I felt!* I looked back on my experience of dying, of standing on that platform and being pushed back into my body, and later, of walking out of the hospital after only five days following such an unfathomable event. I was not ready to let go of the idea that self-healing was real. Instead, with the support of my family, I quickly separated from other healers to forge a path of my own design.

Distancing myself from those who did not live wellness as their truth, I continued to focus inward and found it possible to speak to my individual cells as if they were a community. I approached them as their community leader, asking what their needs were, how they felt, and what would make life work for them. I took that information, looked at my body as a whole, and figured out what it would mean to apply it toward my wellness.

My physical improvement was rapid. The damage to my heart corrected itself faster than the medical field currently agreed was possible. My doctors, who had previously questioned my medical choices, were now coming along. As they saw my health improve, they supported me instead of challenging me. Before long, I felt as good as new.

I could feel empathically how people stacked one belief on top of another and caused conflict in their energy. Prioritizing the beliefs of others as more important than their own caused them to look at things from a skewed place of being.

Consider this: I have the belief that it is okay to be late for school in order to meet the needs of my children. The school system has stated that a late child's arrival is disruptive to the class and shows disrespect for both the teachers and students.

As a parent in a moment of distraction, when I chose to stack my beliefs instead of seeing all things as equal, my fear of harming others gave the school's tardy policy urgency. Out of fear, I lost sight of my most important priority—my want for my children to feel my constant love. Because of this skewed balance—believing the school, every student, and my own children would suffer—I found myself choosing to harass a sleepy Syndell to get her out of bed, and rushing a hungry Johnny to finish his breakfast, adding pressure to both them and myself.

Making external beliefs more important, I had shifted to a place of obligation, and under pressure, I chose to satisfy the needs of the others over my own. This kept me frustrated and misdirected.

The example I am sharing does not give me a free pass to be irresponsible. It simply demonstrates that when I am doing my best, I can give myself the freedom to be kind and loving towards others and myself. I can remember that life is full of options.

I reflected on how as a parent, knowing the morning habits of my children, I would wake them according to a schedule and guide them to prepare for the day. Most of the time, our system worked and the kids got to school on time. When it didn't work, however, I felt the burden of my false belief system kick in; it told me I could harm others. I would become frustrated and create undue stress and pressure on my entire family.

When I let go of obligation and chose to remain in my truth—that everything is always okay and I have the freewill to find the win-win in every situation—I found synchronicity. As a result, the pressures to perform according to someone else's expectations left me and I nurtured my children as they prepared for school.

Fully accepting that we could meet our needs from a place of balance, health, and wellness, we began our day with joy and ease. To my surprise, we often arrived at school on time. I realized that since we had moved more freely, without the energies of frustration slowing us down, we worked more efficiently and lovingly as a family unit.

I had not forgotten the school's rules of being on time. I simply gave myself permission to meet my needs first, while doing my best to also meet the needs of others. Living this way meant I could live a fluid life with varied experiences, which sometimes included delays.

What I observe in others is people tend to repress their needs altogether. Under the weight of their perceptions, they have difficulty seeing that it is possible to meet both the needs of self and others simultaneously.

Suddenly, all the years of watching, observing, and mentally recording the actions of others began to flip through my mind. It made sense! This was our needless suffering—meeting the needs of others while ignoring the need of self. Having finally recognized the process, with awareness, I could find the solution.

The next day, I started my meditation with the idea that the world and I could be well if we as a people found the truths we had hidden behind the veil. What I did not know was that by following this path, I was stepping onto a roller coaster.

I began experiencing huge energetic shifts. It was a process that would last for months, and seemed to be on a schedule. Each cycle would start calmly enough, then the pressure and mental stress would increase. For the first three days, anguish would build inside of me as I found myself in painful memories. I was reliving the past and becoming completely confused because I could see both my new awareness and my old beliefs existing in the same space; they resided side by side. My anguish resulted from my inability to clearly see which one was the truth.

At the apex of each cycle, I would reach a point where I was breaking. I felt incapable of handling the challenges of what I was thinking. Unable to bear my insights with the beliefs I currently held, I would repeatedly crumble, convinced I was losing my mind. I insisted I needed to see a doctor for my psychosis.

Thankfully, the cycle would conclude on the fourth day with a major release of old beliefs that brought clarity and identified the truth. I quickly dropped back to feeling normal, completely capable of understanding and seeing the blessings in my experiences and what it was I was trying to learn and integrate. By releasing the fear and the adopted beliefs from others, which conflicted with my own, the wisdom from the lessons was now mine without the delusions. I had found my truth.

I reveled in glee from the sheer awesomeness of my comprehension, until the fifth day, when the cycle began again. After about a month of this predictable, harried cycle, I stopped telling people I was losing my mind, confident I would comprehend my transformation following the apex. It seemed to go on for years, but when I look back, I see it only took eight months.

The revelations included:

- We are all equal on a greater level than I imagined;
- An intuitive understanding of quantum physics and string theory;
- An ability to see past the false barriers creating our illusion of privacy;
- The reality of ascension;
- That time is not real as we currently perceive it;
- All illness begins from energy;
- and on and on, the list seemed endless.

Every few days, I perceived these ideas with new comprehension. At one point, I did not think I could handle the pressure so I asked for it to stop. I had a break from the intensity of the visions for about five days then I started jonesing for the process again as if a greater part of me understood its importance. When I asked for it to return, it did. My acceptance of the process with less resistance allowed things to move at even greater speeds.

I reached a point where I had intense visions of what was to come, from a macrocosm or big picture version of the universe involving the earth and human evolution, to the microcosm or tiny little personal details of when my grandchildren would be born and what my future work would entail.

One vision showed me on a mountaintop. I stood watching the uncut grass sway in the breeze as I heard the telepathic conversations of people who were searching for me. They asked when would I awaken to guide them and wondered how they would find me. I had an undeniable peace and strength in the vision of myself, as first a handful of people appeared coming up the mountainside. I was willing to teach them, to guide them through the necessary steps, and even though they were not sure where the journey was taking them, they knew inside themselves I had information they were looking for. I would be an active participant in this new frontier, leading the force of change.

Other visions showed the complete overhaul of our medical and health practices, our learning to combine all things to be one created the journey of our wellness. I still remember the confusion I had when I saw myself writing a book to explain these necessary changes. The content had me linking each topic to another for comprehension. One in particular, regarding the ease of breath had at least fifty other thoughts I needed to combine to be one, yet they all remained on their own separate page. The existence of so many small overlapping concepts on separate pages was sure to create a book that would be confusing and impossible to read. The index for such a book would be a nightmare. I finally had to set aside my notes after I had more than one hundred and fifty pages of information on healing concepts and eight individual book outlines and no idea how to connect them all on paper.

It was following "The STUDY, Opening the Door", the first program I developed to study the energetic change in others while they learned the concepts I had found on the other side, that I realized the book I had been writing in my vision was actually an Internet website. In the original moment, I was without experience of such things. Tagging and linking sections with hyperlinks, referencing videos, and connecting to the work of others in detail were all new concepts I had not experienced. I had a good laugh realizing how confusing visions of the future are when we do not know what we are looking at, yet the facts are there.

Back in the reality of this world, the feelings of peace and strength from my visions quickly changed to pressure and obligation. I resisted this new calling of being a leader because I assumed this new experience would have the same pressures I had previously experienced in my life when in a position of authority. The assumed pressures left me afraid of how my life would change. I thought I was happy living my selfless, gentle, quiet life, so the intensity of the visions forced the skeptic in my brain to struggle. I did not know at the time this existence of being too selfless was essentially killing me.

Still, I could sense the visions were real. The seed had been planted and I had a feeling, an experience, to work towards. I considered what I needed to do in this moment that matched with the end result—to make the visions real. I forced myself to move closer to acceptance, breaking down the aspects of ego I feared. This huge, expansive feeling eventually overtook my thoughts and the skeptic was losing.

Even though I felt compelled to experience what I saw to be true, I resisted the level of vulnerability it would take to achieve it. *I don't enjoy being bold! I like having a small circle of friends and family to confide in and trust, and there is NO CHANCE I ever want to be responsible for the decisions of others.* I thrust my energy outward at the universe, pushing away what I had been shown, still in control of my own existence. Not knowing then that the decisions of others had nothing to do with me, I dug deep into that fear, the fear I had lived my life with—that I could somehow harm another human by being me.

My resistance set the precedence for my life utilizing the laws of attraction. A new direction was drawn to me; safely tucked away from my belief I could harm the living, I was given the dead.

A prerequisite for leaving Earth after dying is being able to comprehend our ability to be the full expression of ourselves. Whether we live our lives that way or not, it does not matter; it is the clarity that we have the ability to be the full expression of ourselves that counts. This, as a normal function of death, is why our lives' pass before our eyes to reveal the complete truth in every moment of our existence.

Because so many of us use our freewill from a skewed place of balance, most of us have damaged our Etheric Templates. The damage results from being conditioned to protect ourselves from vulnerability and prevents us from being able to experience our true selves without assistance. Vulnerability is our natural state of being. It literally allows us to be the full expression of ourselves in every moment.

While working with the dead, the ability to be vulnerable was required. The dead lingered and waited for me to change, to be vulnerable, because my example of this existence was the only way to help them move on.

Since I still questioned if most of what I was perceiving was only my imagination, it felt like less of a risk to communicate with the dead than the living, so I allowed myself to be more and more vulnerable more often.

With these experiences, my fears of my future were gently being pulled away, like so many layers of bandages. Underneath, I was raw and fragile. I needed constant support and confirmation to accept that my new reality was actually real. I struggled through my fears as support came from everywhere! I imagine the support was given to help me move forward and assist me in my continued development. I certainly would have given up many times along this journey if I did not have so many synchronistic moments[9].

For example, new people began showing up in my life. They spoke to me of the great things I would do with my work. The fact that they knew of the work I had yet to share was enough to give me pause. Their recitation of the life I had only heard of in my head gave me faith that what I had seen was not only possible, but probable; that what I was doing was indeed real.

---

9. Synchronistic moments are events planned on the spiritual level which occur in a person's life that confirm their path and/or show the support of others.

My friends started taking me to events where people were giving aura, tarot, psychic and other miscellaneous readings. Over and over, I was told my destiny was to teach and change the way our world views suffering and wellness. These readers confirmed for me through their own work that my wellness was real and encouraged me on my journey.

For a long time, I did not allow myself to see my actions as communicating with the dead. I kept a skeptical separation. The dead were not my only preoccupation. I chatted with entities who most people would consider to be aliens. I talked to plants, rocks, furniture, the sky, Earth, time and space—I found everything had its own voice, its own language.

As we all do, I was already intuitively speaking these languages, though I was not aware they existed on a conscious level. Finding a means to translate these energetic signatures into human vocabulary stretched my imagination. Whether I received information externally as a vibration or internally as pressure, translating this type of information so others could understand it seemed impossible at first.

*How do I even know I am right?* I thought many times. The only way I found to confirm my experiences was to ask questions, which required me to be in that uncomfortable vulnerable state, risking my ego.

Once, at a party, I heard a couple of trees talking about the homeowner. The trees said she sat under a particular tree in her yard to cry and another to laugh. The trees, pushing at me, would not let up until I agreed to ask her about it. To my surprise, she exclaimed joyfully, "Yes! I use the willow to support my sadness and the fig my happiness!" She wanted the fruit of the fig to multiply her joy and the willow that reached towards the ground to send her sadness back to the earth where it could be healed by nature. She said it would make the world a better place for everyone.

*Who does that?* I thought. Having been raised a strict, military Catholic, I had missed exposure to things many people considered to be common spiritual practices. My new openness brought me in contact with the most bizarre people. Upon reflection, though, I realized that as normal as I believed myself to be, I had spent the evening admitting I spoke to trees! I laughed and had to concede the fact that we all have our own internal worlds separate from those we share with others. Each of us creates our own definition of normal, fabricated by our personal beliefs and exposure to other people and circumstances. This understanding gave me inspiration.

I started branching out by reading the thoughts of others in an effort to understand what was normal for each of them. Learning to translate each unique individual's thoughts into words created a key, like the key of a map, making everything easier for me. I could then quickly read the thoughts of more and more people I did not know personally by using that key to unlock their personal translation. Although not infallible, it was very useful and efficient.

One day, while listening to some random thoughts, I asked my friend questions about what I was hearing. The person's thoughts I described were unmistakably that of her deceased relative. I had started doing most of my snooping of strangers' thoughts without engaging them. This moment helped me realize that sometimes what I was hearing were the dead in my space.

The more I worked to translate these energies, the more I realized that we all hear these words but we do not understand how to translate the language. I had been listening my entire life, and to my great awe, I had been hearing them all along! We all have these internal thoughts and conversations. The difference is, we do not realize our conversations are with more beings than just ourselves.

Moving the information across the gap from the dead to the living, the infinite to the finite, the telepathic to the verbal, took hours and hours of practice and many more hours of confirming what I understood with others. It was as great a task as was learning to speak my first words and then the entire English language.

The most important thing I learned from composing these translations was to recognize and withhold my biases. I followed every experience with the idea that 'I cannot possibly know what is true.' This openness left room for seeds of understanding to be planted and grown.

Having mastered the basics of energetics, I realized there was more, so much more, for me to experience and learn. Each time I became aware of a new twist or tangent concerning what I had seen expressed, it prevented me from locking myself into any false belief system. I accepted that it was possible to let go of beliefs that keep us from seeing our truths.

Today, as you read, you can be free of the burden of believing that ghosts are not real, that telepathy cannot possibly exist, or that life after death is a myth. Today, I encourage you to borrow my belief system, knowing it has been gained from experience. By the end of the book, you too, may remember more truths that exist for all of us.

# Chapter Dedication

With gratitude to everyone who kept me on my path, encouraging me to accept the challenges that then seemed so hard and that are now so easily part of my daily life.

# Chapter Three

# INSIGHT

## The Lighthouse

Las Vegas, early spring 2009

*J*f I were to pin down when I intentionally started helping the dead, I would have to say it happened one day when I had been running through the details of my near-death experience. In a light meditative state, as I reminisced about my death, the dead began walking directly toward me instead of how they had previously only wandered around me.

*What's different?* I asked, hoping one of them would answer. Before, only a few dead had shown much of an interest in me, choosing to respond to my questioning. Mostly, they seemed to be oblivious to my humanity.

A tired female responded, *I heard you. You were in the tunnel and I know I need to go there. You can show me the way.* Apparently, during my energetic questioning of my own experience, I moved into a state of being that made me more obvious to those who were currently dead. The difference between this questioning and my usual kind of questioning was the focused intent in the upper left part of my brain. *Interesting*, I thought, as I realized it was the same part of my brain I use to telepathically suggest control for others. It is always up to them to accept.

After about twenty minutes of discussing with this woman how she believed she'd failed, we were able to get things sorted out.

*Your life was supported by your experience of not getting your degree. If you hadn't been willing to leave and go away to school to study law you wouldn't have been the same person. I can see how later because of your brave decision you found joy by taking that job, the artistic one that allowed you to express your passionate self. Not becoming a lawyer was not a failure; it was the step that led you to your joy.*

I supported her without any preconceived notions as to how she should be experiencing her death. Using the gift of discernment bestowed upon me at the moment of my death, I observed her from the place of my compassionate self—with no judgment, attachment, nor conclusions. With this new understanding, she awakened to her truth. No longer self-victimizing, she released the belief of herself as a failure. She was immediately aware of the tunnel's location and left.

I was pleased with the outcome. Having taken the time to witness her life, I provided the support she had been missing. I simply helped her to see she had a right to exercise her freewill, and that coercion of spirit[10] made sure she found joy, whether she realized her life was her choice or not.

I was inspired; I had helped this woman let go of her perceived belief that she had failed. Further encouraged, I started offering the same kind of help to random dead individuals. Some did not need it, like the officer who died in a car chase near my house. He told me he was fine, that he and his wife had been prepared for this. Her love supported him as he moved on, and he was excited about the next phase of his existence.

---

10. Coercion of spirit is an act from the other side in conjunction with our spirit layer that works to make sure we reach critical truths.

I often opened the process for those who needed help by asking them about their lives. They would eventually share the painful belief that kept them tied to Earth, and once that was brought to their awareness with the support of compassion, they were able to untie and release the energy that previously held them bound. I realized more and more that these ties were simple connections to moments in their lives where they lacked awareness. My comprehending that there is neither good nor evil, and that all things involve our freewill choice, allowed me to see the choices of others and the events they attracted as blessings.

My initial discomfort with the dead faded. I confidently communicated with the ones who entered my space, helping them to move on. This new focus made me increasingly aware of their energetic presence. They were now as alive to me as my family. I found the interactions exciting and began pulling more and more of the dead to me to be helped.

I began finding them not only at my home, but also in my car, while grocery shopping, at the movies, and wherever they could sense me. I wondered if being near a few hospitals, rehab facilities, a long term critical care unit, and a major freeway where accidents were common had something to do with the quantity of dead I could pull to myself.

When I realized the work was becoming too much for me, they were already showing up in groups. My initial gift of service was to allow for twenty minutes to resolve a single dead individual's issues, but in short order, the time increased to hours every day to handle the groups. Overwhelmed, I made the decision I needed some rest, and chose to stop pulling them to me, believing they would then just stop showing up.

When I closed my eyes, thinking I had the answer to keep the wandering dead out of my space, I was surprised to find that they showed up even without my purposely drawing them to me. First it was one, then the next day another, and another, until they were again arriving in groups. They were now drawn to me by something other than my thoughts. Those arriving had more complicated issues than the previous dead I had attracted. These dead were desperate, lonely, and deeply confused. Their issues needed more than a little good cheer and a shoulder to lean on.

As I examined the snippets of the living library that remained in my thoughts, I began to realize that the excess of deceased wandering around is a more recent phenomenon, one that has increased over the last one hundred years or so. Historically, loved ones, shamans, medicine men, priests and the like were present to help with the process of crossing, to bear witness as the dead passed to the next phase of their journey.

I thought back to the Last Rites I had heard as a child. Back then, I had wondered why they were so important. Here on my bed, waking to the dead, I looked at this night's group as it swarmed around me, and it all began to make sense—until a person disconnected from what they had spent their lives creating, there was work to be done. The dozens of bonds connecting the energetic part of themselves to their physical lives needed to be 'untied.' Restricted, they were unable to move. Without this work, they could not cross.

Our prayers, our witnessing, creates an energetic change to assist this part of the process and their return to vulnerability. Once completed, the energy of the dead shifts, and support from the other side appears. The dead use the support from the other side to bridge the gap; it is the doorway needed to move on.

In today's current climate, due to the lack of knowledge and support along with the lack of conscious spiritual connection and the fear of loss, our natural ability to assist each other through the death process has decreased. The dead, abandoned, now wandered around, looking for someone to help them, someone awake to their reality; someone like me.

Having volunteered to meet the needs of the deceased and in my eagerness to understand the other side, I chose to give aid to those in need. I hoped my interactions with them would help me to clear up my fascination surrounding my own death. I looked at it as a win-win; I would supply support for those needing to cross over, and in return, I would have close contact with the dead, making it possible for me to learn as much as I could in a very short period of time.

## Insight

I was thankful the work was interesting and rewarding, and with each interaction I received a gift of knowledge. Every time I helped the dead, I could see why they needed help, what kept them from living their lives fully, and how they gave up their freewill to live for others. I could, after a while, find the energetic patterns in their systems that kept them heavy and unable to change. The process progressed from simple conversations to the energetic release of these burdens. These lessons turned out to be invaluable. They made it possible for me to see how living beings were blocking themselves and creating their own disconnect and pain. As time progressed, I saw myself as a sort of lighthouse. I imagined the dead scanning the horizon, hoping to see my light[11]; drawn to me as they weathered their own personal storms.

---

11. Every person has internal light that creates a unique glow. The dead are only be able to see the glow of people who are able to help them.

# The Door

Las Vegas, late spring 2009

I awoke to the strange sensation of a man sticking his arm through my shoulder.

*Whoa! What are you, new?* I joked, quickly shifting my position to get out from under the pressure.

The newly dead did not know how to control their push of energy, leaving me to catch them in my body instead of the usual respect of physical space the dead exhibited.

*Can you please back up? You're still in my skin.* My suggestion was aimed at the dead gentleman still standing two inches into my right side.

I yawned and added a telepathic visual of myself stretching awake. Having learned from experience that translation of telepathy took time, I used a more basic form with the newly dead. Instead of words, I communicated through clear mental images sent from the upper left side of my brain. This communication, more accurate than words alone, would show the newly dead that my intention was to wake up and be of service.

Still very interested in remembering my interactions with the dead, instead of allowing my subconscious to handle the effort, which is the method I use today, I would engage my conscious mind and wake up when their energy overlapped my physical space. My most abrupt awakenings came from the newly dead who walked through me, completely unaware of my existence. When they realized my presence from the interaction, they tended to turn around and walk through me again! The stringy, gooey feeling it gave me was very uncomfortable. I did my best to shrug it off. After all, these dead were lost. This particular gentleman had started his journey as many did, without a witness. He was unable to untie himself from energetic bonds, leaving him stranded here, confused.

Knowing they were lost did not change my situation. The demand for my attention was again growing, and the consistent sleep disturbances took a toll on my time and my serenity. I was constantly foggy, living a dream in my waking hours; the fatigue caused me to laugh at myself even when things were not funny. Out of desperation to feel normal, I began to follow the whims of my imagination, wherever it took me and the deceased.

Surprisingly, this openness seemed to give me a better overall connection to the dead, allowing me to witness their lives like a detailed movie playing before me. It was the only time I felt real. When I fought it, trying to separate what I assumed was fantasy from my traditional reality, I felt worse. Full of desperation, physical pressure pushed out from the inside of my body. When I accepted the new reality, I felt unable to fully stop the game or wake up from the dream. The dead felt more real than the living and I felt better. My consciousness still struggled a bit, challenging me to question if my experiences were the dream.

To get more rest, I tried to work with them during the day, but for some reason they were weaker and less able to cooperate than at night. I considered the possibility that the telepathic noise that bothered me from the conscious minds of all the people who were awake during the day may somehow affect the dead, too. During the day they resembled zombies as they moved and communicated without coordination, lacking the energy to show emotion and enthusiasm.

After months of late night hours and nonstop sleep disruption, I reached a point where I could not fully recharge. I considered my situation. I had set a precedent that allowed the dead to make themselves at home, possessing my living space. Because this now gave me a feeling of claustrophobia, I asked them to not hang out around me. The visual I sent them telepathically was one of me by myself, the space around me empty. Confused, instead of leaving, they started stuffing themselves into closets and other odd spaces to create the empty open space I had shown them.

I was used to certain social restraints observed by the living to feel safe in my own space; the ones that keep people from touching each other without permission or make it possible to stand next to each other without having to interact. The dead, as I currently witnessed them, were devoid of social manners; they were not conscious of such traditional boundaries. With the dead not needing sleep, their presence seemed never-ending. Regardless of the hour, or how much personal time and effort I put in, there were always more waiting. Now, I was physically uncomfortable and on edge. Something had to be done.

The way I experienced the dead differed from the way my daughter Syndell experienced them. I could look around a room and see nothing, yet feel something was present. By closing my eyes, I could see what it was I was feeling. Syndell, on the other hand, could see them as if they were as solid as you and me. For a brief period, her awareness was so acute that she was not aware that the people she was running into were even dead. More and more frequently, I would wake up to my daughter letting out a shout of dismay when she opened the hall cupboard to grab a clean towel, only to be greeted by several dead who had stuffed themselves inside, hiding out after I had pleaded with them to leave. She had run into my room, almost in tears, demanding something be done.

When it reached a level where my child was afraid and traumatized by their presence, I had to put my foot down. This one dead individual would go into her room at night, wake her up, and fill her mind with horrible details of how he had murdered his one true love. His jealous rage had ended her life and his guilt kept him from seeing the path to the other side.

His expression of that guilt was exaggerated by Syndell's teenage energy of drama and trauma. When souls come to a balanced person, the person feels them at their best. When they are drawn in by teenage energy, they can represent themselves as disturbed, often portraying the details of their egregious acts instead of looking for a way to cross. Both manifestations could be expressed simultaneously, so if this person were in the same room as Syndell and me, we would each be having a different experience of him.

I could not simply condemn the dead for their behavior and send them on their way, nor could I expect my child to understand how to share guidance while still so full of her own confusion. I rolled this around in my head for days. There had to be a solution, a way to help that did not compromise who I was or negate the experience of my child.

I reached for the part of me that is my full measure of compassion, not sure what I would find. It was a pleasant surprise to find my own heart center.

*Ah! That's it! The heart center is the spark of divinity, the truth of all that we are, prior to becoming a human being.*

I took a gamble and shared a deeper level of vulnerability; if I opened a connection to that part of myself, sharing my spark of divinity with the world, then something had to change. One of the revelations that followed from my death was that once something had been in contact with another, they were always connected. It was this concept that helped me learn I could reach others wherever they were located and in whatever time period they resided no matter where or when I was physically.

Convinced I could release Syndell from attracting discordant energy, I sat down and opened contact with the spark of divinity inside my heart chakra. Pulling from the place of source as I exist inside of divinity, I moved the energy into my physical body. Once the energy was both inside the spark and a part of me, I moved to fill up my entire space with this vibration and light. My child and every other energy in our living space were awash in my vibration. This energetic process effectively released the hold of Syndell's drama on the dead, leaving them docile. They returned to their original goal of crossing, which is why they had arrived to begin with.

The next time she ran into one of the dead in the house, Syndell laughed. She was joyful, able to see the energies as innocent and clean. All the trappings of their drama had fallen away.

Although their drama had dissolved, their presence had not. One afternoon, feeling especially smothered by so many dead invading my space, I pleaded, *Guys, I need you to back up!* They barely listened, giving me a few feet, but not much more. I was still uncomfortable.

I rushed into my closet to quickly change, but the overcrowded energy of the dead who had stuffed themselves into such a small space made it hard for me to breathe. It made me sick to my stomach, feeling the stress of obligation I had created when so many of them were waiting for help.

*You know what? It doesn't matter!* I finally said in frustration. *You need to get out of my house!* It was time for some boundaries. I used the same mama bear voice I used with my own children when I wanted to come across as angry and assertive to fully get their attention. Just as my kids could see through this voice and feel loved, so did these individuals.

Nothing happened. Nobody moved, nobody left. They did not change.

*All right, then,* I thought. What would any person servicing so many people need to do?

*A LINE!* If the DMV could line everyone up to wait hours for their turn, could I not do the same thing with the dead?

*Okay, guys, I've got it. I am going to put a doorway right here.* I pointed to the wall space that separated the bedroom closet and the bathroom. *Here's where the door is. You guys have to figure out some way to be here in this space without showing up in my bathroom or in the closet!*

I felt their confusion. They wanted to please me, but to them I was not making sense. They needed the telepathic visualization. While I quickly changed into a skirt and top, I slowed my thoughts way down and visualized a doorway. I pictured it with frosted glass so I could see if someone was there and still fulfill my need for privacy.

*There*, I said, satisfied with my creation. *Everyone needs to be in line behind that door. I don't care how it happens, just work it out amongst yourselves.* I energetically slammed the door, releasing my frustration. *The only time you can influence me is when I open the door.* I leaned against the wall as if leaning on a closed door. This was now real to me.

"When the door is closed, I don't have the energy or time to deal with the dead," I said aloud, "and when I have time for you, I will open the door and help; but only then!" I spoke with my mama bear attitude again, mentally waggling my finger. I knew this pressure was my own creation, and it was time to bring it into service for all of us.

Installing the energetic door moved me through lessons in controlling the connections, bonding me to my abilities. Having my awareness on or off became a choice instead of an obligation. I helped those in need, and in turn learned a new part to my own journey. A balanced win-win, both selfless and selfish in every moment.

Many walk away from this work because it is overwhelming and filled with uncertainty. We pull back, forcing our awareness into the corners, but it's still there, located behind our veils. The moment we can handle the truth, we allow the conscious connection to be obvious again.

Awareness is not something we can just wish for. We need to stop compartmentalizing our minds and understand how we use the veil to protect our brains from fracturing under the weight of our competing beliefs. The solution is to exist as our personal truth and release the beliefs of others.

Over time, I learned how to sleep and do this work simultaneously; giving my body much needed rest while my energy had the freedom to roam without the weight of my body. A large part of mastering energetics is managing body, mind, and spirit concurrently. It was the separation and focus on one of these pieces at a time that made it impossible to be fully aware. It was like learning to walk, talk, and chew gum all at the same time. The process to get there took years, but once accomplished, it was effortless.

# Tom

Las Vegas, fall 2009

After my heart attack, the doctors had taken me off birth control. It turned out Joseph and I fell into the two percent of the population condoms did not work for. We were suddenly expecting our sixth child. My heart doctor had impressed upon me the importance of not letting the ejection fraction of my heart go below forty, as anything less put me at risk for congestive heart failure. The fraction dropped from fifty-six to forty by the twelfth week of pregnancy. The OB doctors had said there was a seventy-five percent chance one of us would not survive. Determined to make sure both my child-to-be, Sara, and I would survive this pregnancy, I spent a lot of time resting in bed while doing energy work to maintain the health of my heart against the strain of pregnancy.

At five months along, I was relaxing into a meditation, nearly dozing off, when I felt a commotion behind the door. For the last two months I had been protected, the deceased kept at bay by sources other than myself, presumably for the health and safety of my unborn child.

*Don't worry*, I told myself, considering the commotion, *I'm not crazy...yet.* "Ha ha ha." I laughed out loud at my own joke. My family had reached the point where they had stopped reacting to my claims of crazy. Many of my visions and conversations with the dead were supported by confirmations from loved ones, and others were being factually verified by going to the source, such as funerals and gravesites.

I had been experimenting with creating and finding all kinds of interesting things to break the mundane beliefs that held me to the perception of my own environment, learning what was real and what was only my imagination.

An energetic plant placed at the bottom of a water source to create better tasting water—real.

Distance healing to mend bone, muscle, mind, heart and soul—real.

Crystalline plants to make a room feel more fresh—real.

Wormholes, astral projection, aliens—all real.

Money can mate to make more money—not real.

Dragons, leprechauns with gold to share, Lochness monster—not real. At least I could not find evidence of any of these living today in this world.

I tried to create little dust eaters to take over the chore of dusting, but that did not work. However, I had been able to create a lock for the energetic door. Its complicated construction was my strategic plan to stave off boredom one long day; I knew this lock to be impenetrable.

I sensed the commotion behind the door again. It seemed a stretch for me to allow the conscious connection to the dead after five months of them having been kept at a distance.

*And yet,* I realized, *someone is shoving his way through the line!* I took a deep breath and released into the experience. There was not a physical person doing anything, and I was protected against all things energetic by my own belief systems; still, I appreciated my mind's ability to translate the energy into something I could understand and play around with. I could be proud of my effort—it took a lot to reach this level of mental and spiritual control.

Sitting on my bed, I visualized myself placing an ear to the door, showing my intent to acknowledge who or what might be on the other side. I heard ruckus. These kinds of experiences used to bring me such emotional drama; I had made them seem so important and mighty. Now, as I remained calm, I wondered if my seeing these once spectacular experiences as mundane made life boring. Existing without the magic, my reaction to this was typical, the feeling no bigger than if the phone had rung.

BAM! My physical body lurched and although the sound was only heard in my internal thoughts, I instinctively surrounded my pregnant belly protectively with both arms in a surprised response.

*They tried to ram my door! Oh, you must be new!*

Everyone on the other side of my door knew me to be passive.

*Who would...?*

BAM! BAM! BAM!!

*Someone is! Someone is banging on my door!* I chuckled at myself as I tried to feel this experience as if it were my first of this kind, full of shock and awe, but it was no use; this was just another day of doing what I had become good at.

I settled back into my body to see the details of what was on the other side. My thoughts moved to the possibility of the dead fighting over something, but did that make sense? I had told them to work things out until I returned. Maybe this is what it took. Up until now, they had waited patiently or moved on to find help elsewhere.

*Why are you banging on the door?* I asked.

The noise came from a single energetic male, haphazardly fighting his way to the front of the line. I watched as a desperate energy, apparently recently deceased tried to push his way past the Jinns[12] who were protecting me. They allowed this man's passage only after receiving my permission. I thought it interesting that the intruder was still holding the energy of a living, breathing human being. He did not need help crossing over. He could leave this plane for the next simply by his own choosing.

---

12. Jinns are protectors assigned by Nature to take care of her inhabitants when extenuating circumstances require it. They are different from angels in that they have one purpose - to protect.

*I need your help,* he blurted telepathically. *It's my brother.*

I did not know the man in front of me at all, but the visual he sent was one I recognized as Tom. I could clearly see Tom in a dangerous situation in Afghanistan. It was not a biological brother he was referring to, it was 'a brother in arms.'

*I know him. I know Tom.* I acknowledged.

Tom, a student and new friend of mine had confessed to me his fears and his guilt before leaving for war. We had worked together to help him be okay with what he was being ordered to do. His highest energetic calling was one of protector, and yet, even though he knew this and felt this calling, he struggled with the idea that he was responsible for the deaths of many.

*What is it? How do you think I can help?* I asked, a bit shaken, knowing how impossible the task of saving Tom's life had felt before. It had taken everything I had to help move this man past the destruction of his own beliefs.

*He needs your blessing! He needs it now!* The man insisted.

*How's my blessing supposed to help Tom?* I knew what a blessing was. I had learned that things as simple as a kiss or a prayer and as complicated as an energetic construct delivered by intention were blessings.

*Look, he's going to die if you don't do this!*

I could feel the protection that had been keeping the dead back during my pregnancy start to push him back from me. As his energy decreased, he no longer had the strength to push through. I could feel the drain on my own system as I tried to reach out to Tom with only my mind to see what was going on.

With what I had learned about energetics, what this man was asking for could easily have been done. But in my physically weakened state, I was at best only fifty percent of my usual measure. I did not think I could use remote viewing; since I was pregnant, I did not think I could leave my body intentionally for any length of time. All my energy was currently being used to protect my damaged heart from failing both Sara and me.

I considered Tom's brother had fought past what others had not. He had forced his energy between time and space to ask me for this effort. I had to believe this meant something, that I could do something or he would not have asked me. Previously, when I helped Tom move past the desire to be dead and release the weight of his burdens, it had been done with prayer, through the gift of intercession. Now, faced with this impossible feeling, I did the only thing I could: I prayed. I prayed to be strong enough to help Tom without harming myself or my child.

That night, for the first time since I learned I was pregnant, I reached out of my body to help another human being. Tom gave me the feeling of being hunkered down in a war zone, which was actually only a battle in his own mind. Artillery exploded here and there. The lives of others rested solely on his ability to push a button. He was in a situation where he would second guess his actions, losing sight of what he needed to do, unable to move due to his guilt.

Since I could not maintain remote viewing, I joined Tom in a vision, which is more like virtual simulation. We worked symbolically through his issue as I sat next to him, untouched by the destruction all around us. I encouraged his confidence in this moment. I showed him how the beliefs that were causing him to remain frozen and motionless were not real. I reminded him he was a hero, releasing the positive powers of the human ego, using the kindness of his own heart to support his destiny. In that moment, he was no longer alone.

Next, I showed him how his inability to move, to not pull the trigger because of his fear, could lead to his death as well as that of many others. I showed this dear, patient man how he could use his own beliefs to navigate the self-destruction, to move between the beliefs—untying them so he could return to freewill. In the moment of need that was coming, he could choose to balance life even when faced with its destruction.

I held no judgment of Tom or his mission, acting only as a witness. My personal views and beliefs would not allow me to take the life of another, nor would it allow me to encourage others to do so. I did not tell him to kill, but I showed him how to be his truth. Others reach to me in these moments not to hear me spew my own dogma, but to support their efforts and beliefs, showing them the balance of themselves as they exist without fear. My ability to hold this balanced space is the reason for my success with helping others.

This was Tom's calling. My thoughts on the value of life and the need to always find a win-win to preserve it had to be released, allowing me to see the highest good in every moment, every action and reaction. Without this ability, I risked interfering in this critical moment in Tom's life. He would, with the touch of this button, take hundreds of lives. In this moment, he needed to be the full expression of who he was, the protector AND the annihilator; living up to a predetermined set of circumstances that led him to this place of decision. The universe was counting on his truth.

My support allowed Tom to see what his protection meant to the lives of thousands more, past the hundreds that would die. He could understand and see the circumstances and lack of balance leading to this moment, where so many pushed and fought in different directions. He understood that his actions would return balance. He would be an active participant in creating the solution for a greater good because of his faith in the value of human life. This was Tom. It was only fear that made him question that his action might be wrong.

Tom let go of the guilt he took on, concerned others would see his action as criminal or unforgivable. He again felt this calling instead of the focus on fear, compelled to action by something larger than himself.

In the end, Tom came home alive and whole. I cannot guarantee I did anything, or that I changed anything. I can tell you that my friend tells me he owes me his life, and I am eternally grateful for his experience and willingness to be his truth even when faced with fear.

# Chapter Dedication

To all the dead who chose to hold onto their pain long enough to match up with me for the win-win. As much as I know I helped them, if they had not been willing to find me, to be guided to me, I never would have opened up to these experiences. I would still be living a life of quiet desperation, hoping to die myself, destined to be stuck and unable to cross when my time comes.

# Chapter Four

# THE WEIGH STATION

Las Vegas, June 2009

*J* stood in the public library, looking at the Reiki beginners class listed on the calendar of events. "Hmmm," I mumbled to myself, considering what others had said about my work in the aura and electromagnetic field. "...hands off work is similar to Reiki. I wonder..." The work I was doing included physical movement of the hands above the body, working to adjust currents and align energetic systems. In a similar way, Reiki uses the body's own energy to realign itself.

The smallish woman next to me replied, not realizing I was talking to myself. "You do Reiki?" She gushed, and her excitement encouraged me to share.

The universe always made sure gentle people came into my life. They comforted me and enabled me to open up with ease.

"No," I shrugged. "But I think I might have stumbled upon something similar." I had been practicing the ideas I had picked up during my rollercoaster transformation for a few months. I had started practicing first on myself, then with all my friends, and now with their friends. I had experienced great success with each step.

Encouragement from the other side moved me to share my gift of hands-on energy work with more people. They instructed that waiting until I had perfected my skills was unnecessary and explained that the more I learned, the further from this beginning information I would move. I needed to get out there and expose people to what was possible while it was still fresh in my life. Doing the energy work created a synergistic effect for my expansion process. While I helped others, it was possible for me to learn from many different angles.

After an engaging conversation regarding her hip pain, which had disappeared while we spoke, the small woman led me to another, whose headache we removed, and then to another, whose questions about love we answered. By the end of the process I was, as usual, face-to-face with the person I needed to see, through no effort of my own.

I had a short discussion with the head librarian about her daughter's health. By the end of the conversation, the librarian encouraged me to put an event on the calendar.

"It's $250 an hour for the class space," she said, taking out some paperwork.

*Not going to happen*, I thought, dejected. That amount was impossible. I still considered my actions as more of a hobby than a calling, and calculated reasonable fees for hobbies at $25 an hour to fit my budget.

Seeing the expression on my face, she continued, "But, if you're willing to offer an event to the library as a donation, free of charge to the participants, we can host it for you."

Music to my ears! The words 'no charge' resonated as the perfect amount. The shine returned to my eyes.

As I filled out the forms, I came to 'topics to be discussed,' and it occurred to me I did not know very much. I shared my hesitation with the librarian as I was concerned I would not have answers to all the questions I might be asked, or perhaps I might not make sense to others.

She blinked a couple times, and shushed me. "It's your class. You control the conversation."

"Oh, I can do that!" How nice of her to empower me.

As I prepared for my first class the librarian told me to expect about five people. I decided to set up ten chairs, feeling optimistic, just in case the expected five people brought friends, or maybe they would not feel comfortable sitting next to each other.

Meanwhile, my family and friends had found it necessary to prepare me for a group of 'weirdos.'

"Why?" I asked.

Joseph answered. "Because that's what you attract with this kind of stuff."

I was excited and assumed they would all be just like me, eager to discuss wellness methods.

The librarian handed me a sign-in sheet. "This is how we justify the use of the room, by adding to our list of benefactors." A bunch of names on the list ensured that the library would be able to continue sponsoring events like this.

Five minutes before start time, the tenth chair was filled. Excited, I made my introduction without waiting. I talked in generalities about myself while I shared my past and my struggle with Multiple Sclerosis. I was nervous and attempting to hide my inexperience did not help. I picked up a paper so I would not wring my hands.

I smiled as another willing participant walked into the room.

"I better get you a chair." I pulled a chair from the stack while continuing to talk, excitedly welcoming each person to my world. Then in came another...and another...and another. I kept grabbing chairs for each person until a happy helper decided they no longer wanted me to stop in the middle of my sharing in order to get more chairs, so they took on the job.

When Trinidad, the librarian's assistant, showed me the sign-in sheet at the end of the class, we were both wide-eyed.

"Twenty-three!" she exclaimed.

Wow. I quickly calculated the numbers. That was more than a three-hundred percent increase over the librarian's estimated five.

For the most part, these were intelligent, curious individuals. Some seemed to have a personal experience with energy and what it did.

*Not a single weirdo!* I said to myself. *People really do need to hear this stuff and I really do need to share it.*

The second week, I walked into the meeting room at the library, happy to see a few of the same people and several new ones. This time, some of the participants had arrived early to speak with me. While awaiting my arrival they had set up the room for me. Thirty chairs were set out in tidy rows with a walking path down the center, just as I liked it. I strolled up the middle of the aisle and felt a strange new feeling…I was not just a person sharing what I had found; I was the authority in this room. I felt a new sense of responsibility to open people up to what I was feeling and seeing. This would no longer be a hobby.

This week, the people who believed they knew more than me seemed frustrated and impatient with my sharing. As I felt the frustration of these few individuals grow throughout class, instead of being in my mommy/teacher mode, I shifted into 'Zen goddess,' giving them insight into what this feeling I had been speaking on was all about. They now experienced first-hand what life could feel like when done with an open connection to intuition without judgment and attachment. Their frustration now gone with this amazing connection, I could see this energy was not only important to me, it was vital to the world and its effort to heal. Each participant continued to shift with me as I embodied my true self, and without effort, a type of resonance between us occurred.

I zipped through the material with very few questions, finishing in half the allotted time. With the remaining time, we began to explore other ideas together, adding in information about the hands-on component I had been playing with. From the demonstration, my first participant excitedly shared that she felt a sense of peace and wellness after the five minutes of effort I put towards shifting her energy.

My second participant, Mara, had struggled most of her life with her controlling family. She was literally flopping around on the table, appearing as if I were pulling strings inside of her. The room grew cold and people began to squirm. *This is new*, I realized, laughing internally. Up until now, I had brought people to relaxation and peace, or even tears and weeping, but this was an extreme response to this work.

Always the one looking for a reasonable explanation, I considered that perhaps Mara had watched too many movies and her subconscious was creating this reaction to make her feel in an obvious way something she had been avoiding. There was a sense that she was trying to break something in herself, and she hoped that this exaggerated experience would somehow make what it was clear.

"Were those demons being released?" someone asked.

Again, falling back to what I believed personally to be true, I suggested a less extreme idea. "Perhaps it's blocked energy in the body struggling to get out." I looked everyone in the eyes and shrugged. "I know it's not a very exciting explanation, but as I've said before, I don't believe evil exists."

"Okay, everyone, that about wraps it up." At the end of week three's class, I leaned against the massage table after the final participant returned to their seat. Each student had laid on the table to experience having their seven major chakras read and diagnosed using a pendulum. In addition, I had answered personal questions regarding their jobs, lovers, and money. We had also covered how to gather energy to their hands so they could locate fluctuations in the physical form of another person. The following week, we would work on how to use this energetic information to diagnose the physical form and prepare it for wellness. There was a hunger for this information and people pulled at me telepathically, calling for more and more details.

"Does anyone else have any questions?" I asked, clasping my hands together then allowing them to settle against my body. I hoped my closed body posture would bring the class to an end. Even though I was both mentally and emotionally enjoying this process, I had pushed myself past my usual limits to make sure each participant in my life that day received a reading. Fatigued, my insides tingled as they did when my spidey senses were turned on. *Why didn't I just say, 'That's all folks,' and wrap up the class myself?* Instead, an hour past the end of the class I was still answering questions, glancing from the clock to Trinidad, who was sucked into the conversation along with the rest of us.

"Take your time," she said, waving her hand. "I have a key to let you out."

Carla, a tiny little blonde in her fifties, had shown up for every class. With each session, I felt more and more that she was waiting for me to reveal something to her. Every time I attempted to telepathically check in with her, however, her very outgoing red-headed friend, Tina, would break my concentration with a comment or two. Tina was great, I enjoyed what she added to the discussion, but since I had not yet developed my ability to hold a fully telepathic conversation while in the midst of commotion, it made it impossible for me to listen and find what Carla was waiting for.

This was her moment. Carla, with a definite end game in mind, asked, "How can you tell the difference between your own thoughts, information, and an actual message or conversation from someone else?"

"Well," I began, remaining relaxed against the expectation that this would be something important. "When it's information about me I feel it in my skull." I pointed to the top of my head. "Different places are for different information. When it's a channel—information supported by the other side, my higher self, or the Akashic records[13]—I feel a pressure in my jaw line. The left is about historic energy, or the collective communication of all human thoughts known as the Universal Conscious Mind[14].

---

13. Akashic records are action based historic information independent of thought or emotions. It has details of all levels of existence, many things beyond what the human mind can comprehend. Inside these records exists something called 'The Living Library.' It is the addition of information as experienced on a planetary level and does include records of emotion and thought.

14. The Universal Conscious Mind (UCM) is accessed through the mind. It is the energetic collective of all thoughts and interactions involving all living things on Earth.

When it comes in on the right side of my jaw, I wait to see what a person has to say. It's more like a recording than telepathy, but if I have questions I can always move it into a conversation by asking."

I felt a pressure coming in. "Like right now I feel pressure moving down the right side of my jaw line." It was getting stronger and more persistent, uncomfortable even.

"Do you have a message for me?" Carla's voice was suddenly loud, holding my attention. She leaned forward, her smile became a thin line and turned down at the corners. She was trying to hold herself in. Distracted both by her body language and with answering her question, I had not realized the current pressure was indeed a channel waiting to be heard. Everyone moved in closer. My vision blackened as I listened for the words. The room disappeared even though my eyes were wide open.

With one hand up, I motioned for her to wait as I pulled in to listen. I did not know if I could channel in real time as this would mean being energetically with the speaker while simultaneously translating through my body. In the past, I had only written these communications. I had not shared what I felt coming in live and in color. As I reached a moment of no return, the pressure forced words into my mouth. Simultaneously, a great big, burly man appeared in the darkened space of my vision. He wore suspenders and a red plaid shirt. His overly dark hair seemed colored and his beard kept popping in and out of view.

"Tell her I am waiting," passed through my lips and my ability to see the room returned. Everyone stood nearly up against me without space between them. I was surrounded.

Carla burst into tears and grabbed for her friend.

CRAP! I heard myself saying telepathically. Uncomfortable with being so transparent, I wondered what I had done. I stood there, unable to move, unwilling to touch her. My feet were stuck to the ground and my hands frozen. More pressure was building in my jaw line. I felt a strong pull at my teeth, so strong I worried they would break under the stress. I spoke rather than let them crumble. My body shook from the adrenaline of fight or flight as I forced a refocus of my intention—I made sure

I cleared my ego and any assumed mental pressures of responsibility to this crowd—and continued.

"He says you have to stop rushing. He's really adamant about it. It's important to live your life, and he says not to worry—that he's there at the weigh station."

"What's the way station?" everyone asked in one voice. I noticed they had a different impression of the word than me. It was not the way station, as in the way to get somewhere; it was the weigh station as in seeing if you were ready to go based on your molecular weight. Burdens carry more weight.

He flashed me an image from my own personal near-death experience—the tunnel and then the platform.

*You touched me!* I said, realizing he had been there as I ascended the tunnel. *This is insane. Are you even real?* The skeptic in me was back, challenging this moment, trying to protect me from the crowd. *No, this is my active imagination. I am pulling in pieces trying to make sense of my own death.* I would have stopped there if not for the pressure in my jaw blinding my conscious thoughts. My intuition took over and I kept going.

"He says he will be there. He'll be there on the platform with you. He says you will cross together and he's in no hurry…so stop rushing to join him."

Carla cried even more at this. I could hear her thoughts. Simple and uncomplicated, she felt left behind and all she had to do was pack and catch up to him. Her goal was to join him in death, as though she were joining him in the past for one of his work trips.

"He's happy to wait," I eked out, squeaking as I said it, my chest tight, my heartbeat quickening. *If she could see your generous gift of waiting,* I said to him, *how you're offering support to help her carry on with her life, then maybe she could be free of this pain.*

Her desire to be with him caused her to continuously feel his connection. The understanding of this desire was blocked by her own fears, leaving her feeling empty instead of fully supported, and thus more driven to join him.

*It's a cycle!* I realized.

She did not see it—the bigger picture of how wonderful life could be with this new twist of fate and his loving support.

He spoke, *It's my turn to make her the center of my universe, just as she made me the center of hers.*

I wept internally as I felt his joy in waiting!

Coming back fully into my beliefs regarding humanity, I refocused on the fact that I was doing this in front of real, live people. Falling into my fear that others might judge my behavior and in turn, harm themselves with beliefs about my actions, the freewill of being in my truth vanished and I regressed to an oppressive sense of obligation. I was again timid with a need to retreat.

*Ugh! I want to move back in time before this happened and undo it completely.*

How strange it was to experience myself from one moment to the next. In my truth I was without fear, which allowed space for me to completely embody the aspects of my angelic self. Now, as I subjugated myself to the beliefs and assumed pressures of others, the density of this energy pushed those lighter aspects of self out of my body. I was no longer capable of holding the light I had absorbed only moments ago.

Tina, supporting Carla's weight as the only thing between her and the ground, sensed my shift. Offering energetic support, she looked me in the eyes. Transferring her support on a soul level, the light entered my body. I needed that comfort. Her angelic spirit aided me with compassion as I struggled with my own human existence.

Feeling naked and vulnerable, the added soul level support helped me fight the vibration of regret. I had risked my very ability to maintain my connection to what was becoming my work by allowing my mind to waffle back and forth between meeting the perceived needs of the group or staying in my truth. I held to the idea that I needed to trust; that my intention was for the highest good, and yet...I had in this moment reduced this adorable lady to a teary-eyed, crumpled heap.

She was transformed before our eyes, now fragile, shriveled, and gray.

Trinidad, seeing my strain, or maybe ready to go herself, rescued me by saying it was time to lock up.

I turned to gather my things. Getting ready to exit the room, I prayed loudly in my head, trying to block out Carla's deceased loved one. He rattled on about having seen me in the tunnel during my death. He was showing me the comparison between Carla's need to cross and my own in that moment.

*I understand,* I said to him. *But I can't make her understand!*

He wanted me to show her how I had rushed to be dead only to realize that I had more life to live. Her mind was already set. I could not see how my words would have any effect on her.

Realizing he might ask me to say more, I began to pray for him to shut up. With so many new experiences and the other side asking for things outside my comfort zone, I had an agreement with the spirit world. If something was necessary for the greater good and held more urgency than my comfort, I had a process for them to let me know. All they had to do was ask three times. Even if I had previously said no, I would surrender and meet their need whether I could understand why they needed it or not.

All those years of doing the right thing just because it was right supported me in such moments. *Thank you, God.* I thought. *Thank you for the military Catholic upbringing.* I had assumed those were the years that left me feeling damaged in my life, and now I realized they were, in fact, the years that taught me how to be strong under pressure. I would not have had the strength for any of this without them!

This giant of a man was now asking me a second time to talk to Carla further.

*No! Didn't you see the mess I already made of things?* I said, rushing and grabbing my papers, pens, pendulum, and stool while attempting to pack up my massage table as fast as I could. I did not want to be anywhere near her if he asked a third time.

Safely out in the parking lot, with Carla nowhere in sight, I said goodbye to the last of the participants. As I was getting into my vehicle, Tina rushed to catch my attention, and my good manners caused me to abandon my near escape.

"It's okay!" She wanted to reassure me and her urgency brought stinging tears to my eyes. "It's okay!" She hugged me and chuckled. Moving me to arm's length, we locked eyes, her angelic nature again rescued me from my own angst. "Can you wait? Carla wants to talk to you."

Back in my peaceful state, I was okay with waiting to hear whatever Carla might need to share. My fears pushed to the side, I was in my truth.

I watched as Carla exited the library. Her face was freshly washed and she was still clutching tissues.

"Can you tell me what he looked like, this man? Can you describe him?" She looked eager as she asked. This is the most common question I get when I share messages from the other side.

Nodding, I began. "He's a huge bear of a man. In my mind's eye, he came up and hugged me. I felt tiny in his arms, and his hands pulled me even closer. At first I was unsettled, but as he held me, I felt this joyful, light energy, like a puppy wanting to play." I continued sharing in detail how his eyebrows nearly touched in the middle, and his beard was darker than I expected. Reflecting curiously, I continued, "I don't understand the beard thing though; it kept vanishing and then reappearing."

Carla's laugh was surprisingly deep, with a little tinkle to it, like bells. "He liked it and I always wanted it shaved. He was coloring it because it was turning gray. I told him he could keep his beard after I died! It was a running joke between us for years." She laughed again at the memory. "I asked my friend to stop you because I have to thank you." She took both my hands and held them. "What you told me gives me hope." After a quick inhale, she continued. "I have been very depressed since my husband died and I have been daydreaming of ways to join him. I could never take my own life, even though I have been praying for death." Her eyes teared up again. "Henry always wanted me to move on if he died first, but I haven't had the desire to. If I know he's okay, I think I can try."

It was an interesting evening for all of us. More relaxed, we sat outside under the lamp post and continued to talk. Carla joyfully told me that Tina had been dragging her to these events to get her out of the house after her husband had passed, hoping to lift her from her depression. In the time before we met, she had held very little hope in the possibility that she could communicate with Henry. Tina was the believer and she had enough faith for both of them.

As we talked, Henry shared with me how his wife's love and pain touched him, how he realized after his death that Carla had given up her whole life to meet his needs. She was too selfless, keeping the house, waiting for him, leaving at a moment's notice to be with him, barely making personal plans because she might have to cancel them to handle a request of his. She adjusted everything in her world for him. Although it came from a loving place, it was completely out of balance.

As I translated between them, I realized his gift of waiting was a free-will choice on his part to correct this imbalance. While alive, he had seen his life as possible because of her generosity. Now deceased, he could see how her selfless giving had left her without support to create her own life, one that would meet her needs through growth and change.

The laundry list of symptoms Carla had experienced over the years was a direct reflection of her inability to meet her own needs because of her selfless behavior. She exhibited symptoms such as dependency, anxiety, and an inability to make decisions on her own. She'd lost her self-esteem and concentration. She'd had intestinal and gastric issues, weight gain, fatigue, headaches, insomnia, and more. These symptoms were all created by the energetic imbalance of being too selfless.

Henry wanted to support her in creating a life that met her needs and those around her instead of only his. He was excited, in fact, looking forward to being aware of her success and witnessing her release of these symptoms over time.

Carla, stuck in her selfless ways, was translating his energy into pressure, believing she still needed to take care of him. This created her constant desire to be dead so she could join him. While having this conversation with the two of them, we started to realize how they were still interacting and creating between one another. It was truly a beautiful romance that spanned further than the physical.

Personally, until that night I had not spoken with anyone who could truly answer my questions about my own near-death experience with any factual information regarding the tunnel and the platform where I had arrived. Not only did Henry know exactly what my experience was, he supplied me with the name 'weigh station,' and his own reason for waiting in the tunnel. I was grateful to have an answer to my questions about the people who had grabbed me during my ascent. These people awaited the arrival of their loved ones, passing time in and out of slumber. The grogginess with which they groped me was not as much a zombie style behavior as it was the difference of the speed and time in which we separately moved. Once I understood that they were checking to see if I, as a passerby, was their loved one, my memory of the experience changed to comfort. I liked thinking of the possibilities of their being able to continue together into their next adventure.

I laugh now, because if a guy who was alive would have told me the same things Henry did, I am not sure I would have believed him. How very generous of the universe to supply this skeptic with what I perceived as irrefutable proof.

With this new comfort, I could understand how Henry felt when he said Carla needed to stop rushing, he meant that she did not need to rush to her own death, but to live out the rest of her life in all its possibilities. I think this is the wish for all people who have left a physical body. Free from the burdens of being alive, they can clearly see how we create a labyrinth with our beliefs that traps us. This trap allows us to make conflicting decisions and ultimately be the creation of our own problems.

I continued to work with Carla. She had always wanted to attend a medical technical school but did not feel she had the mental capability to pass the strict testing required for completion. We worked on her belief systems, energetic connections, and trust issues. She was the first person whose brain patterns I followed in-depth and worked on to deliberately shift with my energy and focus. During her tests, I telepathically followed her brain activity, breaking blocks as they appeared energetically. Over time, her entire foundation of belief changed with our telepathic work without us ever having a verbal conversation about what her beliefs were. This was reflected in her actions, self-talk, and her increased levels of joy, which furthered my faith and trust that much of our lives happen without a conscious thought, and without requiring internal effort and awareness on our part to be whole.

From this experience, Carla learned to see her world from a place of joy and possibilities. She would later travel and do things on her own she never thought possible.

## Chapter Dedication

In memory of Henry.
Thank you for your generous conversations that provided my heart with continuity of thought and for helping me understand that living a fully conscious life does not have to end at death.

# Chapter Five

# UNTYING THE KNOT

Las Vegas/California, September 2009

"*I* don't know what else to do," Gia said, languishing over the thought. "I mean, it's been weeks, WEEKS of Nana going in and out of consciousness."

I could feel her roll over on the bed even though we were talking on the phone.

Gia shared her exasperation, "Everyone has been by to see her. I watched personally as each one held her hand and wished her a farewell."

*Deep breath to curb my frustration,* I heard her think. *I know it, they know it. We all know it's time for her to go, and yet she's still here.* Her words were long and drawn out.

I chuckled, feeling for my friend, loving her. It was great to be on this journey with her, to be connected as we were, knowing the thoughts that did not reach her lips. I liked to feel her breath. I had learned from her own meditation class that breath contains thought, emotion, and connection. In my imagination, the breath looked like spinning gears, connecting to things like gears in a clock, large and small concepts fitting together and working as one. Seeing how she applied breath in her own life created a new view for me of who she was. I gained a feeling of being intricately linked to her, as if I were one of those gears. Moving with each breath, I had knowledge of where her heart and head were focused all the time. This made it easier to know her truth in every moment.

"After all," she continued, "how often do you hear that people are ready for their loved ones to move on? We have done everything!"

It had been a long road for Gia and her family to reach this place of love and surrender, and now that everyone was here, Nana's steady progression towards death had been brought to a screeching halt. Neither the doctors nor home health care workers had any answers for them. No one had a single idea as to why this woman's body was still alive. She had a near constant heart rate of one-thirty-five and little-to-no nutritional intake for weeks. It did not make sense. The brief moments she was conscious, she would reference the conversations that had been happening around her, to the surprise of the individuals present, as if she were taking part all along.

"I have done everything you and I talked about and she just won't let go," wailed Gia. Her grandmother was now conscious for less than five minutes a day, sometimes skipping a day. Brain scans had shown she was not slipping in and out of a coma, and she was not sleeping, either. Instead, she was in a light meditative state, just below conscious level. She literally had no quality of life other than being in the presence of her loved ones.

"Christine, can you talk to her? Can you find out why she's still here?"

Before I knew I could do this kind of work, people tested me by asking me all sorts of questions there was no way I could possibly answer. Back then, I would simply guess and most of the time my answers were correct. Now, when someone asked me questions, my guessing brain drew a blank and forced me to look at things through a more intuitive connection. Unable to guess the answers to Gia's questions, I could not imagine why Nana was still here. Nana had spent years living alone, believing that she was not afraid of dying or leaving behind those she so dearly loved.

I found it interesting there was not a single man in this family group; each man had passed or been sent packing without a return ticket. The family group of women, twelve in total, had a close-knit bond, all centered around Nana, their matriarch.

"Okay, let's see what's going on with Nana." I took a deep breath, and as I had learned from watching Gia, I settled down into the base of my body. I pulled back the energy that tended to float up and out of my body through my head. Connected into the root chakra, I grounded to the earth. Grounding was not one of my favorite things because it increased my empathic connection to others and left me feeling vulnerable and exposed, but grounding was necessary to make it easier for me to translate the spiritual language I felt.

I began the conversation with Nana by introducing myself as Gia's friend.

*Oh, yes,* Nana accepted my introduction. *Gia told me of your work together. I am so excited for you both.*

This did not surprise me. I knew they talked on the phone a couple times a week.

*What can I do for you, Crissy?*

*Well,* I said, then paused to consider diplomacy before I started talking again. This was a sensitive subject. *Do you know where you are?* That's as good a beginning as any, I thought.

*I most certainly do.*

She flashed me a picture of herself lying on a double bed. I paid close attention to the picture in my head because after my conversation with Nana, I would share what I had learned with Gia; she would confirm or deny what I saw. Gia and I used her confirmations and denials to increase my accuracy and hone my skills.

*That's good, Nana. Do you know why you're there?* I asked.

*Yes, because I am too tired to go and visit everyone, so they are coming to visit me.* She seemed pleased with this arrangement, like a child would be if they had been given a special gift that was all about them and no one else.

# Untying the Knot

*Do you see that you are next to the kitchen? Does that mean anything to you?* I had hoped she would start to catch on, given that cultural reference. She knew that keeping a loved one in the midst of the commotion, instead of off in a bedroom somewhere, meant that her life was nearly at an end.

*Oh yes, it is magnificent. I can smell the sauce cooking. There must be a party because I can smell the meatballs too, and little niña*—as Nana referred to her daughter, Gia's mother—*never makes homemade meatballs unless there's a party.*

Hmm. This was going to take some work. She seemed to be dismissing everything regarding her approaching death.

*Nana, your family has been by. They have all said their good-byes and shared their memories. It's been better than a daytime soap opera, everyone having such great love for you. They've done their part; they have their closure. It's okay for you to let go.* It was easy for her family to let her move on knowing the extreme physical pain she had been in for the last few years.

*Yes, they have been by.* She showed me her conscious awareness of their visits, how her brain could process the conversations. She somehow held them in her subconscious as recordings of sorts; in the moments before returning to consciousness, she would recall these conversations which would trigger her to sift through the records of her own thoughts and remember her own part in each adventure.

At its essence, she was experiencing the process of seeing her life pass before her eyes. Instead of doing it in slow motion like those being held back by their attachments, or those who moved super-fast with assistance after leaving their bodies, Nana was doing it in real time from a place of conscious recollection.

This is something I have repeatedly seen in the lives of the elderly who have a ton of love and support. This review process is truly a tribute to the history of their lives, and a loving place to be. They travel through their life review without regrets or misunderstandings, unlike those without support who often become stuck.

Now, with my prodding, Nana referenced the last ten years of her life. Like many from her generation, she had begun to believe she was a burden. She had put up a block towards requesting help from her family because she did not want to be a weight around their necks.

As Nana's body had entered a state of deterioration, she gave up group outings with the women in her life—going shopping, eating at restaurants, and pampering herself. She passed up invitations to social events, and no longer hosted family holiday parties. She began opting for more casual, relaxed, and personal one-on-one moments. She noticed that the group began to separate without her influence.

Here now, keeping them all close, she wanted to relive the life they had so cherished together before the decline of her health. She feared their bond would end without her. Feeling this reconnection to her family, she was not willing to let go.

*I was worried*, she confessed. *I thought I was useless and I slowed everyone down. Now…*she paused.

The pause normally meant conflicting beliefs were present.

*Now, I am staying to keep my family together. Without me, they all move apart.*

I considered this thought with her for a bit, looking to see if there was any energetic truth to the statement.

*Oh, I see.* I watched as Nana showed me the interconnected cords holding her family together. Each cord from the girls was tied directly to her and a second cord connected her to each of them. This was how they had spent the last few years, directly corded to Nana instead of sharing a typical family connection that resembles a spider-like web. I watched in my mind's eye, my head slightly tilted as I had a tendency to do when considering something that might be out of place.

*Ah! The cords are all with you! I see. I am going to talk to Gia now. Thank you so much for spending this time with me.*

She gave me a kiss, extending to me its blessing.

"Okay, I know what has to be done." I began on the phone again with Gia. "Each person needs to be untied and re-tied to someone else in the group. Nana is hanging on because she is afraid to leave any of you alone."

I went on to describe the pictures in my head in detail. I described the gold metallic bed frame, the way the support of the open frame was made of balls and ovals instead of bars as I would have expected. "Is this right?"

"Yes. And the bedding?"

I described the dark blue, wool-lined blanket, the matching slippers just under the bed on the wood floor, the extra pillows with a bunch of little polka dots on them, and the bedside table with all its accoutrements.

"You got everything except the patterns on the pillows. They're not dots, they are tiny little flowers." I could feel she was rocking back and forth in her excitement. "Anything else?"

"There is something I think has to be wrong." I paused, still hesitant to trust things that seemed out of the ordinary. "I was expecting to see her with her gray hair, like in the picture you have in your kitchen window; but instead she has on a knitted cap that looks like one of those old-fashioned driving hats from back in the roadster days. And it's rainbow colored." This had to be wrong. I grimaced, expecting a correction.

"BINGO!" Gia jumped up, excited. She knew there was no chance I could have known this since Nana had just received it earlier that day. One of Gia's cousin had brought the gift, knowing Nana would have been horrified to have so many people see her with her hair undone.

After a bit of jubilation, Gia and I came back to the task at hand. I asked her what her plans were now that she knew what her grandmother needed.

"Aren't you going to do it?" She pushed.

"Do what?" I feigned ignorance, evading the question.

"Aren't you going to untie her?" Gia continued in a childlike voice.

"You want ME to do it? I don't have any idea how to do that." Panic, although insincere, was creeping into my voice. "You're the spiritual one. Don't YOU know how to do it?" We went back and forth. I argued that I was fine with waiting to see what happened. I did not need change. I was very comfortable simply observing Nana's life, whether she passed or not.

"Please, just try it!" Gia encouraged. "Let's just see. Ask someone else to help even; I know you've got connections." We giggled at the thought of my connections. Gia was convinced I had angels on my side.

"All right, all right." I smiled through the receiver. "I can ask for someone else to help," I said, finally accepting the challenge. "Let's do this. Let's meditate for thirty minutes and when it's done, we'll compare notes." We both set an alarm and hung up.

Even though I had been apprehensive about the specifics of the work, the actual calling of the guests for this next part was a normal action for me. Without windows or doors, the only way to get to my little room floating in the stratosphere was to be called by me to the space. My space above the earth had been acquired as a gift. It was designed to hold a proper energetic balance away from the constant push and pull of the Universal Conscious Mind. There, the work of assisting others to heal could be done. I called to Nana, Gia, and the family members needed to untie and retie the connections to join me. In addition to the guests, this time I called for something more; I called for universal support of something larger than the total energy of this group to guarantee we would have the means to accomplish the task at hand.

First to arrive was Nana on her bed. Then Gia appeared at the foot of the bed. I energetically placed myself within her body, making it possible for me to see through Gia's eyes.

A tall blonde woman appeared at the head of the bed. She had no humor. I could feel her as methodical and empty. Curiously, I knew she was kind, though I could not see it in her at all in this moment. As I looked at her there was a nagging feeling, some kind of sense pulling at my mind. Something familiar about her hair—the short curls, the shine that was not truly blonde, that my mind would not let go of.

*I recognize that woman. I totally know her.*

I worked to pull the memories into my conscious thoughts. She had appeared when I sought to define the higher self-energy. Another time, she had explained to me how to heal bone. Later, being faced with a life-or-death decision regarding my youngest child-to-be—as to whether to abort the pregnancy or risk both our lives—the woman helped me, always reflecting back to me my truth.

I found the oldest memory of this woman, one I had pushed to the furthest corner of my mind. I was twelve years old and unable to handle the pressures of human suffering any longer. I had spent the night staring in the mirror into my own eyes, trying to reach my soul, contemplating just how I would kill myself. Each method of death I considered had to be evaluated as to the impact it would have on my family.

Unwilling to bring them pain, I crawled into bed without the ability to free myself from suffering.

The sun was near rising as I called out in desperation to be saved from the weight of my burdens. My call for help had been different than any before. I felt a rush of energy in my throat—the energy of a thousand birds taking flight—which powered my ability to send out a deafening, telepathic screech. The screech was my attempt to shatter the bonds of suffering. My effort was unsuccessful. The pain of suffering cut further into the fibers of my being. In my call, my essence had expanded like a shockwave outside of myself and pulled something back to me.

At first, I could not figure out what it was, but with each day as the sun was near to rising, if I had spent the night in pain—carrying the burden of the world's suffering and wishing to be dead—the woman would come and pull the sadness from me, making it possible for me to keep going. As if stroking my hair, the passing of her affection would caress me, going deeper than the surface of my skin, cleansing me like water washing away the damage and debris.

I would see myself through her eyes, her clean, clear perception, without the distortion of my fearful beliefs. Our eyes would close and I would wake to the sun, feeling as if the previous night was just a dream and the sadness did not exist. This was her; this was the woman before me, ever-present with me.

Looking at this woman through Gia's eyes was like watching a movie. There was definitely something very unreal about how I was seeing her. I had never gotten such a detailed view of her before. I could see her tall, slender body as it showed easily through the one-piece suit she was wearing. Her boyish figure barely let on she was female. I somehow knew her outfit was made of a material that was not from here; it was indestructible and permanent. The suit showed no signs of wear or aging. The color, I also knew, changed with the level of her light energy to communicate the internal workings of her many energetic systems and the volume of light running through them. I wracked my brain to comprehend the color change, and then it came to me: right now, it had a greenish hue, representing her heart chakra's inner workings. It was different than the gentle, pale blue she normally wore when visiting me, which was used for compassionate communication.

I could see so many details of her, and yet the veil would not allow me to see her face. I knew she had an enigmatic smile, perfect skin with very little color to it, and a gentle, yet powerful set of light blue eyes. Still, knowing all this, I could not bring her face into focus no matter how hard I tried.

Five young ladies appeared at the head of the bed next to the much-taller blonde woman. They were excited, youthful women. Hair in pigtails, they were wearing white nightgowns. They appeared to be ready for a slumber party, all excited and full of joy and anticipation. The feeling was contagious.

I lowered myself from the level of excitement I was holding in my physical body. I was no longer only present in this space, I was the master of it. My point of view shifted from the foot of the bed to the head of the bed. I was now looking over the body of Nana as if I were the blonde woman, which allowed me to see the lights and energies inside of Nana's body as they glowed in the semi-darkened space in which we worked.

I watched through the blonde woman's eyes, completely entranced. Witnessing Nana in this way felt very natural. I had a knowingness about each step before it occurred. With my first-person perspective, I knew what she knew. Seeing this woman from two perspectives, Gia's and my own, I watched her teach the group of girls gathered around her how to untie their cords from Nana and select two other girls in their group to tie it to.

I felt the girls' intensity; their internal joy and enthusiasm was far greater than what I could see on the outside. My connection to them was gentle and kind, without reproach.

A light radiated from the suit as she/I worked, and the room became brighter. I could see streams of electric energy undulating against the ties that held the chakras' centers in Nana's body. Taking over completely, I urged the energy to untie and release the chakras, freeing Gia's grandmother from their bonds. The breaking down of her Etheric Template was mesmerizing and it took me deep into conscious speculation. I lost my conscious connection, even though I felt connected to the work still in process.

Even without the conscious connection to the group, I stayed in my meditative state, subconsciously assisting in the work from a distance until the alarm went off. It felt like more than an hour had passed. The reason we'd set our alarms for a half hour earlier was because we'd had similar experiences of distorted time before. As the bell rang, I found it harder than normal to pull myself back from the meditation.

I waited for the usual phone call from Gia, so we could compare our experiences. We always shared our first-person experiences in detail before we deliberated on what the other person's story meant in comparison. We were interested in how each of our perceptions shaped our individual experiences.

As I reached for the phone, it rang…"Yes, I'm almost back," I answered, still feeling a little out of it. "Give me a second, unless you want to go first."

"I do!" She took an extra deep breath, then rambled on. "You did it. I watched the whole thing. It was as if you cracked open the universe above her. Amazing!"

"Whoa, whoa, you skipped a bunch. Go back and start over."

Gia was not using our usual method, but more than that, her words made me uncomfortable.

"Start from when you arrived in the space."

"Okay, okay." Her breath was still coming rapidly, and she forced herself to slow down and reset. "When I arrived, my Nana was in front of me on her bed. We were the only people in the space and then you arrived. And you were amazing!" She caught herself getting worked up and slowed down again. "I saw my five aunts appear at the head of the bed with you. It was them, but it also was not them at the same time. Christine, it was the most bizarre experience. At times, you were in my head. I knew you were there when I had pressure behind my eyes. Also, your eyes glazed over. That's how I really knew you were in my body instead of yours. It was exactly the confirmation I needed."

She paused again to gather her thoughts. "Remember the phrase 'gossamer threads'? Well, these ties were like that—super fine, very flowy, undulating even, with this electric circuitry that they plugged into on each end of the thread. Not mechanical circuitry, but what electricity would look like if you could see it in action without the hardware, moving and connecting, transistors and switches and breakers and voltage meters all working together without actually being present! You were untying it all!"

It was hard for me to follow her words. The sound of her voice kept fading in and out. The veil was still too thick—my brain was trying to block out the experience.

"Each time you touched a thread, it would light up! Different colors. And the speed of the electric movement on the threads after you let them go, well, that was phenomenal. With each pass, the threads became brighter, and the light was flashing so fast it overlapped itself. I saw three and four flashes at a time in the same space. It was as if Nana's whole system was suddenly awake. Then you lifted the pile of threads up," she paused, speechless for a moment before she barreled onwards. "OH-MY-GOSH! When you let the whole thing go at once and it dropped into her body again…the sound it made! I cannot express that sound in any form of comparison. The best word I can give would be silence! Each cord had a sound and each conjunction had a sound, and before you knew it, all the sounds were happening at the same time and it equaled silence!"

She went on to tell me how the blonde lady and her aunts moved the energy from Nana's body to theirs. "They were building this web, each of the aunts taking a turn, following their cord to Nana's. Each released it from her body and tied it to a different aunt. Then the cord split and they tied that to a second aunt. It was such an intricate design by the end." She exhaled slowly. "And now, Christine, as I sit here watching the monitors, I can see her heart rate is slower. My mom said within fifteen minutes of us starting our experiment, the fever Nana had for weeks finally broke. Her body seems to be relaxed now."

I listened in a bit of a fog. My brain was not able to accept most of what Gia said. I found the whole thing to be very dreamlike. Gia soon shook me back to reality by asking me about my experience.

I proceeded to tell her my version of the experience without considering hers. After all, this was our process.

"So, what do you think? How do you feel about what you did?" she asked when I had finished. "Were you surprised you knew what to do?"

"I don't think it was me. I saw the lady with the blonde hair arrive. I was looking through your eyes, remember?" I struggled to resolve the conflicting information. After all, I had only recently accomplished the understanding that it took to help release emotional pain in another human being.

Gia and I had played around with astral projection. I felt as if I had very little knowledge and even less control over these experiences. Now, I had witnessed the actions of the blonde woman first hand as if they were my own. They were masterful, completely brilliant and creative, and far beyond what I had talent to enact. Yet, Gia was claiming that I was this otherworldly woman. I did not want to accept responsibility for being this person and my head began to spin. My brain struggled to hold my ego in place. All I wanted to do was settle down and relax with a cup of tea to observe the experience as an outsider and not a primary participant.

Gia said patiently, as if to a child, "Christine, it was you."

"I think we have to agree to disagree on this one," I said, cutting her off. To me, the conversation was over.

I felt her take a breath and then a deeper one, presumably to gain a sense of self-control. She tended to get angry with me when I downplayed what she thought was my role in things.

*And another deep breath.*

This must really be bothering her.

"Okay," she said eventually, and left it at that before moving back into a loving tone, "thanks again for your support."

I made a kissing sound and we hung up.

*I am not going to let this go. I am not going to let you have this one.* Her words in my head were very clear. She was such a strong telepathic sender! *I know it was you, and I know who you are.*

On the third day after untying all the cords, Nana passed, her energy evaporating into light. This was different than the traditional death process in which a person passes and then unties herself as she leaves her physical body. Nana's entire passing had been seamlessly completed, while her soul still resided in her living, breathing body. She used the three days to sort out the energetic bonds, keeping what was hers and returning the energy of her loved ones to each of them. Once this sorting process was complete, Gia's grandmother was ready to move on to the next plane.

Over time, Gia noticed in herself and in her family's lives how the bond between the aunts felt the same as when Nana had been connected to each of them. Loving and powerful, the connection gave them the space to release many of the little nitpicky arguments that had entered their relationships as they had grown apart. Now, bonded together in their new web, fashioned by Nana's commitment to family, they did not lose touch as they had when she was alive.

I did not need a call to know Nana had passed. I heard the whisper in my ear. The gift had been delivered. There is always a gift. I wanted to wait until later to open it because I was currently standing in the middle of a crowded room. Unfortunately, this gift came with instructions. It began to open against my desire to wait. The room began to spin as my mind fought to remain focused on the life around me instead of on the gift. I suddenly felt paranoid and unprepared, and the irrational feeling of 'being naked' in front of so many people overwhelmed me.

Just as quickly as the gift opened, I tried to stuff it to the back of my head but it was too late.

*Gia was right; the blonde woman I had seen doing the work—the one with the angelic presence—WAS me!*

I had grown up thinking of angels as beings in direct contact with God, without a human presence.

*And don't forget the wings. The blonde woman did not have visible wings.* I thought.

Nana was excited to be the one to present me with this next piece of the puzzle. Afraid of change, I was trying to control the gift out of fear. If I accepted this idea, what would my life look like? How does one wake up one day and say, 'Hey, I am an embodied angel, guys. My plan is to heal the world.' There was no chance any of this nonsense would make it out of my mouth.

Not until six years later did I allow myself to open this gift once more. The preponderance of evidence supported that I was indeed the blonde woman. I considered all the strangers who had added their two-cents regarding my angelic nature since assisting Nana—the support I had been given after my death that seemed super-natural. The church never covered this possibility and I struggled, not knowing what it would mean in my life.

Looking in the mirror, I attempted to accept the knowledge that my angelic self had ascended into this physical form. I examined my hair. Suddenly the veil disappeared and I recognized my hair as that of the angel who helped Nana, how it was shaped now in tight curls, colored by the sun and aging just as the woman's had been.

It took my brain a while to accept that I am in my angelic state of being. I realized how I needed the overlay of the suit back then to protect my mind against seeing the rest of me as I am. It was constructed from my memory and external beliefs of what something alien would look like, my brain filling in blanks to obscure what I could not yet accept.

I would later come to an understanding that in our lives we can focus on many things at once. Even though we all have this ability, our brains tend to focus on one main thing at a time, revealing our perception and therefore shaping our reality.

Unknowingly, many of us are constantly communicating below the levels of our conscious thoughts. Consequently, we are unaware of our subconscious involvement in helping others as well as helping Earth. We are so adept at utilizing the veil that it can be difficult to accept who and what we are in this world.

# Chapter Dedication

Thank you, Gia, more affectionately known as G. Without your enthusiasm and mind-blowing beliefs, I do not think I would have moved completely past the idea that 'it's all in my head.' Thank you for helping me to discover this reality so I can hold the door open for others!

# Chapter Six

# THE TEAHOUSE

Las Vegas, November 2009

*J* opened an email from my student, Daniel. "My wife's grandmother, Nancy, had an accident and she's not coherent today. She is speaking in slurs and we want her to be more comfortable emotionally..." Daniel shared that the family was disturbed by Nancy's inability to communicate clearly, and they wanted answers.

This is where I came in. I had become an expert of the dead and dying due to the sheer quantity of exposure I had to them. Increasingly, people had begun asking me to help with their still living loved ones, especially those unable to communicate with words.

To my surprise, even though only an acquaintance, I felt compelled to help Daniel, both eager and excited to see what this adventure would bring. His email went on to ask about the possibility of doing a spirit reading at a distance on someone who was not requesting it from me.

As my student, Daniel was aware of how my process worked. I combined meditation, channeling, visualization, telepathic communication, and the tracking of a person's energetics to form a complete picture of their situation. One thing I did not do was force my way into someone's private space and snoop.

"Yes, I can do a reading of Nancy even if she hasn't requested it." I had written. "My method allows me to communicate with her by making an introduction first through you. You might be disappointed though, because I won't force myself into her space, or lead her responses. I'll simply remain open to what she wants to comfortably share." Daniel said he and the family were eager and any support at all would be greatly appreciated.

Still floating on the excitement, I sat down to meditate. Within minutes of passing through Daniel to Nancy, I found myself invited to a teahouse as her guest.

I opened my eyes to look upon an empty table. Slow moving at first, my brain felt foggy, and my ability to concentrate seemed compromised. I blinked a few times, trying to wake myself up. As a heightened sense of peace moved through me, I could hear the joyful noise of clanking dishes off in the distance. Gradually my ears filled with the room's lively conversation until I was completely engulfed in the atmosphere. The early afternoon sun shined through the glass walls of the teahouse. I closed my eyes to adjust for the brilliance.

As I opened my eyes again, I saw before me an older woman—Nancy. She was wearing an oversized white lace hat with a slightly floppy, five-inch brim. My attention went to her face. The sunlight seemed to separate from itself as it moved through her hat's lace, breaking into crystals that floated in the air each time she tipped her head and sipped her tea. I sat watching her elbow-length satin gloves, which she had not removed, catch the light. The reflection of the light added the slightest bit of shine to her facial features. Again, as she raised her teacup to her lips, the two light sources danced on her cheeks, joyfully embracing one another.

Her movements were slow, graceful, and measured—very swan-like. She returned the cup to its saucer. Her lips remained slightly pursed as her gentle gaze moved to my eyes as if to say, "I am ready to begin." She was soft, lovely, and even at the age of ninety-two, I felt she was youthful.

A spur of excitement moved through me as she locked me in her gaze; I became further aware of myself. My heartbeat quickened to follow the rhythm of her own. She had me pinned tight. It made me think of a rocket ship when it connects to a substation in outer space. I shifted from the free flow of peaceful energy to becoming aligned with her rotation, under her control of gravity. For a moment, the rest of the room spun around us as we stood stationary.

Nancy shared her story as if she had been in conversation with me for some time, familiar as old friends. *I was seventeen the first time I came here. Father had been against my going on account of my attire. He said my friends would make fun of me because I didn't have the proper gloves. We were too poor, he said, and money mattered most.*

Her story was shared with gentle measure, comfort, and without regret. Clearly, this was one of the kindest, most even-tempered individuals I had ever met. I was witnessing her currently in her personal truth, a truth in which beliefs such as regret cannot exist. Even so, I watched as a look of longing crossed her face, barely noticeable beneath the dancing sunbeams. She shifted before me into obligation as she considered the needs she perceived of others in her life.

*I took it to heart and began to live with shame.*

Nancy paused to sip her tea and consider her choice of words.

*Of course, I had to get rid of that shame somehow, didn't I? So, I married Benjamin, a wealthy man, trying to erase my father's belief that our family was less in some way. My husband had been raised as a man of privilege. I believed he deserved more than my shameful feelings of inadequacy due to my being raised with less. He was at a loss to understand me. We often disagreed, both having married for the wrong reasons—he for my beauty and I for his wealth. Eventually, our relationship ended.*

She concluded her thoughts and we fell back into sync with the activity in the room. A waiter approached the table, asking if anyone would be joining madam for tea. He did not see me. My surprise at his lack of awareness of my presence was enough to shake me out of the connection.

Later, on the phone, I explained the scene to Daniel. He listened with interest as I described the experience of finding her in a teahouse instead of where her physical body lay.

"My guess would be that she's in a coma. Are you sure she's in and out of consciousness?" I asked, referring to the details of his email. Although he did not reveal it at that moment, she was indeed comatose.

Daniel hesitated to tell me anything. "My mother-in-law, Betty, doesn't want me to give you any details. She feels very skeptical about the idea of a spirit reading. She says some pieces may be possible and accurate, but most would probably be lucky guesses, plain wrong or even manifested. She doesn't seem to buy that you can reach out and connect to a spirit without being with them or knowing them personally. The people she knows who do this always use photos at the least."

"What does she mean, manifested?" I was not used to interacting with live people in the spiritual community. Self taught, I had my own words for things and the common spirituality lingo was foreign.

"She thinks you will make stuff up using your own imagination," he said.

I smirked at the idea of someone being more skeptical than me. Although I had begun to accept I was doing this work, I still held protective space for it to be my imagination, just in case.

"Ah, I understand. If I wasn't the one doing the work with proof right in front of my face, I wouldn't believe it either." Daniel and I both had a good laugh at that.

Betty's skepticism was a reminder of my past issues. The first time I had searched to identify a single person on the other side of the globe, I had been uncertain if such a thing were possible. Amongst billions, I found the woman without effort. When I told this woman on the other side of the globe what I could see of her both on the outside physically and on the inside concerning her situation, she confirmed everything to be factually correct and helpful.

Astounded that this was even possible, I asked God for an explanation. My science-based mind wanted to understand *how* I found and communicated with her, not just that I could. *Hey God, how can you tell each of us humans apart?*

Rarely hearing a spoken response from God, the slowly streaming words gave me such joy.

*I would know you anywhere, in any disguise, at any age.*

I was overwhelmed with a sense of unending freedom when I realized God saw and always had seen me for who I truly am. It did not matter how I disguised myself with beliefs or drama or in what time or space I chose to exist. I reveled in His clarity, feeling great joy from being truly seen.

I could now view myself completely from my truth, letting go of countless burdens that pushed and pulled on me. I was done meeting the needs and beliefs of others—things that were so clearly false in relation to my truth. This empowering revelation—the release of burden—led me to recall my ever-present connection to the divinity within my heart's center. In this moment, I comprehended how I had been performing my work; I accomplished it from my connection to the divine—the divinity within myself.

My ability to recognize a person's divine self was a blessing. My having the awareness to help them see it for themselves, well, that was an extraordinary experience. With that in mind, on the phone with Daniel, I offered my help. "I have no problem doing as little or as much as your family needs for support."

"Well, we want to make Grandma more comfortable. Can you tell us if she is in pain and how we can help her?" He added, "We'd also like you to ask her how she fell, and what she remembers about it."

As entertaining and as interesting as the teahouse was for me, it did not give me any of the answers Daniel was looking for. I needed, instead, to go back to before the fall to see how I could connect. Because I was doing this process using historic information that would be provided by the energy of the room, there would be more symbols to express the situation than there would be if I had witnessed her experience in real time. Sometimes, without the living and the dead to correct things, the translation of the energy would be wrong or had pieces wrapped up in metaphors.

*Okay, Nancy, let's see what happened to you.*

"I can see her now, drinking tea. There is an end table to her right. She is sitting in a well-stuffed, dark brown recliner chair. The TV is on, playing a game show. She is wearing a nightgown. My attention is pulled to dark blue slippers and there is a cat on her lap on a dark blue pillow as well." The pull I experienced during a reading usually indicated the object was more symbolic than factual. "She is smiley, but a bit achy. She has a headache that originates from the top of her head. Her leg muscles are tight and her shoulders, lopsided."

I paused to hear what Nancy had to add to the visual. Having already met with her in the space of the teahouse for our initial connection, gaining an invitation to step into her mind was easy. "She says she feels very dizzy and nauseous. She also says she has been experiencing the feeling that she was falling for a while now." Nancy felt as safe sharing with me as she would with a healthcare professional. I inferred from her thoughts that she had previously kept this to herself, not wanting to trouble her family.

Daniel jumped in. "She hit her head and it left a really big lump. She has been in and out of consciousness and we are guessing she is very uncomfortable because of her moaning." He paused to speak to someone else in the room with him. Coming back, he added, "Betty doesn't remember Nancy ever tolerating a cat, let alone holding one. I guess she could be remembering one from a long time ago," Daniel speculated.

I shared, "I think I know what the blue slippers and pillow mean. Blue is associated with the throat chakra for communication and expressing one's truth. My feeling is that her history of not speaking her truth has kept certain issues alive in the family and has not allowed her to move forward." We were now moving out of the incident into the energetics supporting the issues. Energetics control certain aspects of pain. If I could pinpoint the energetic blocks, her pain would decrease immediately.

I did some light energetic work on her head and could feel as the pain on the top of her head reduced. I continued to work, diminishing the swelling in her brain as well. Noticing there was still a little discomfort on her right side, I imagined the fall must have been to that side of her body. I gave Daniel suggestions for the placement of pillows and Nancy's bed elevation, which seemed to reduce her pain further, relaxing the physical strain on her aching muscles.

Later, I received another email from Daniel: "Thank you for a reading on such short notice. She has stopped her moaning and is resting quietly. A CAT scan has revealed that she has a huge clot in her brain that would take surgery to remove. The doctors think she would most likely not survive the surgery, so we are just trying to make her feel as comfortable as possible. Any support you can give on this is appreciated."

To my pleasure, that night, Nancy and I visited again. I spent time talking with her about what she loved. She showed me around the house I had visited during our earlier conversation and talked about how she spent her days. I was very comfortable discussing her habits and why she liked certain things. It was a very sweet time for us.

*My mother-in-law, Mary, has a similar habit of eating oatmeal every morning, too.* I shared to show her I understood. *Except she puts raisins in hers instead of strawberries like you.*

Before this experience with Nancy I had not understood why Mary would eat the same breakfast every day. I could not see why she did not choose something else instead of repeatedly complaining that it was all she ever ate for breakfast. Once I understood how Nancy's habitual behaviors defined her with joy, even when not expressed as such, I could see Mary more clearly and found myself appreciating her. Things that previously made no sense to me about Mary started to resonate as love instead of as confusion. For this change in my understanding, Nancy had my gratitude, which further increased our bond.

*Nancy, I need to be going.* I thanked her for the lovely visit. As I was leaving she invited me to venture back to the teahouse any time I could make it.

Following my visit with Nancy, I wrote an email response to Daniel about these experiences. I included my feeling that she did not have much time left, and how I was helping her handle her pain. I told him that when Nancy referenced her old fears about her family, with complete understanding of her own truth, she now had no regrets.

I added, "There seems to be nothing left for her to live for, so I think she is approaching death. My condolence to you and the family if this is indeed the case."

I felt brave in my sharing. I held my ego in check and trusted Daniel would see my experience was based in reality and not imagination.

At this time in my journey, I was still spending three hours a day or more in a meditative state, learning what I could about energy and what was possible regarding wellness. I sat down to meditate on the second day, the day after being in Nancy's home. I felt the door to the teahouse open.

"Oh, that's interesting," I said as I closed my eyes, remembering Nancy had extended an open invitation to me.

I found myself observing my teacup when I opened my eyes. The porcelain appeared to be thinner than what was possible. It was so delicate and so light I felt I could have seen through the material if it were not for the painting of the equally delicate pink and blue flowers surrounding the cup's exterior. As I looked past my teacup to my surroundings, I noticed conflicts in what I observed. Something I had seen on *National Geographic* regarding historic teahouses was inconsistent with what I saw before me. I realized we were not only outside of our current space in Las Vegas, but we were out of our current time as well.

*What year is this?* I asked Nancy.

She looked mischievously at me, peering past the rim of her cup. Her lips were pursed as she gently blew the heat away for a sip. I did not get an answer at first. Waiting patiently, I looked around. Realizing the teahouse had a life of its own, I saw it as a living, breathing entity.

The teahouse, completely a manifestation of Nancy's thoughts, was controlled by the woman in front of me; its very existence was a reflection of her thoughts and how she understood herself to be.

Its body consisted of the large rectangular room. It was constructed of columns too thick for me to put my arms around. I think perhaps two people could touch fingertips if they really stretched. These long, smooth, creamy-white columns held up the ceiling of what must have been a three-story high conservatory. The glass walls and ceiling allowed us to see the world outside.

Its breath was the wait staff who rapidly moved by with noise and flutter as they offered gifts of food and beverage to the hundreds of attendees, who were the lungs. The items served up satisfied the eyes as much as they did the palate.

Its heart was the large crystal chandelier in the center of the room, its soft glow steady and unchanging. Each crystal caught a different angle with its facets, showing how it personalized its connection to the room around it. Each crystal held its own perception, unique and separate from the others.

Its beliefs were mirrored in the customers, each one finely attired— the men in white suits and the women in colorful dresses. The children, also dressed in their finery, ran up and down the aisles while their parents sat occupied with their conversations. I found it interesting how the adults were capable of going on about their experience without being bothered by the children's behavior. The phrase 'paying them no nevermind' took on new meaning for me as I understood Nancy's ability to be surrounded by the complications of external life, yet still live internally with continuous joy.

Today, Nancy wore a fine, tight-laced, high neck, pale blue dress and white sheer gloves. I wondered what time period we had ventured into— the thirties? Forties?

*Oh, this isn't the proper year,* she said, as if reading my mind. *This would be the year 1910. I have regressed,* she said insinuating that not only had she gone back in time, but also had returned to aspects of her youth. She sipped again. Every important statement was emphasized with a sip of tea.

I looked around, surprised at the ease with which everyone experienced the commotion. I caught my reflection on a silver pitcher as the server walked by. I noticed I, too, wore a very pale, light blue gown. With only a quick glance, I saw I was absent of any adornment, although something shimmered around my back that reminded me of wings. My hair was again, as in other experiences, light instead of dark, held in tight curls.

Instead of a consistent movement of time, the outside changed dramatically from day to night, season to season, seemingly tied to wherever Nancy's mind wandered in the moment.

*Today we have cinnamon tea. It will help thin your blood in this blistering heat,* she said as she raised the steamy cup to her painted lips. I looked away to catch the sight of snow flurries just beyond the glass of the windows. The outside panes were slightly frosted; the inside air was hot, like a sauna.

*Why do you think there is such conflict here?* I asked, recognizing this process. I was beginning to understand her connection to the teahouse on an energetic level. The teahouse was her body. The interior of the building was her inner self, joyful and completely at peace, except when anger from confusion turned to blistering heat. The external events reflected her world, how she lived in confusion, not understanding the motivations or experiences of others in her life. She did not know how to enjoy her seemingly tumultuous external environment in connection to her internal peace. In life, she kept her confusion to herself, eventually expressing it to others as angry, frustrated outbursts. She pushed at them to create space so she could handle her own confusion, which caused her to appear cold to others. This was the opposite of the loving woman I knew before me.

*I don't know. I have lived my life with this type of contrast. Don't you suppose the opposites are inevitable? I like the distinction and I meddle in the mix,* Nancy said, eluding to the idea of how she controlled those around her, micromanaging everything she could. Her desire was to save them from the pain she had experienced in her life. If they were perfect, they would be safe. They would be loved. She sipped her tea again, giving me time to notice her pair of lorgnette glasses lying on the table, existing without lenses.

*Let me see,* she said as she lifted her stick glasses to the bridge of her nose. *You see, my cheaters have no glass. It's because I really don't need to see the world as it is. Here I can see the world as I wish it was.*

It took me a minute to realize cheaters were the nickname for her glasses, and yet, she had intentionally used it because of its double meaning.

*And my gloves...it is customary in the tea house to remove the gloves once seated, yet nothing compels me to cooperate with this notion. I simply don't eat. I would rather enjoy their glamour than remove them for the purpose of eating.*

Symbolically, today's tea selection served the purpose of cleansing. Nancy explained to me how cinnamon tea was good for stomach issues, breaking up belly fat, and controlling blood sugar, not to mention blood circulation and purification. The tea was helping Nancy to put her second chakra in order, which assisted the process of us being able to dive deep into this sacral information where we could work on her issues involving personal relationships.

We examined how she had created her own experiences by her thoughts and the deeds that followed them. As she stirred her tea, she stirred within herself an understanding of her own existence. Her awakening was this realization: nothing had been created for her, it was all created *by* her.

During our conversation, she appeared to me as a little girl, and then suddenly transformed back into her elderly state to speak. *I wasn't allowed the pleasure of being a little girl before. I was always working to support my family. I have given of myself when I shouldn't have. I had no personal boundaries to protect me from the wills of others and I lost myself in the process.* She paused. Under the fabric of her dress, the structures of her muscles rippled against her hold of excessive personal control.

She lifted her eyes to mine. Connected, I witnessed her reveal. Her thoughts mingled with mine. In service to her, I adjusted into my compassionate self, my gaze now had her pinned tight. My heartbeat guided hers to my rhythm, my knowingness slowing her nearly to a standstill.

I wanted her to see the beauty of her life as it was in truth, without the judgment and connection to these fears she had—her beliefs of harming her family with her control. As she addressed her concerns of how she had expressed anger, she let go of her guilt. She could clearly see without judgment how she had manipulated their every action. She did not want them to experience failure as she had. Reviewing her past, she realized that although she controlled her family, her love for them was true.

Nancy's fears released and she saw her actions of love towards others were without malice. She further released her belief that her children needed to be what she perceived others thought of as perfect. She prayed for her children's own perfection of self to be ever-present.

*Yes, they are loved. I was a good mother.* She began to realize they would be okay living in their freewill. The weather outside adjusted as well; flurries of snow stopped in mid-air, melted and evaporated.

*OH!* I considered further Nancy's connection to the teahouse and how she used it to move through her life and acknowledge her beliefs. In my presence, Nancy felt a connection to the compassion that I hold for others—knowing we are all always doing our best and that we always intend to help others instead of harm them. Using this connection, she managed to release herself from the cold, harsh feelings that tied her to the pain of her false beliefs.

I was very pleased as I witnessed Nancy see with her own eyes that she had not manipulated her loved ones out of selfishness.

As a witness to Nancy's process of release, I noticed the repeat of the same behaviors I had seen in others who were moving towards death.

As they rested in between sleep and awake, in a light meditative state just below consciousness, they could view their entire lives. Every single experience was self-witnessed. Nancy's process sorted out her human emotional responses from the deeper truth that occurred on the level of her higher self.

Every aspect of ego was stripped away, every false belief was recognized as an imbalance, and every moment of love someone else had for her was understood. She united the balance of all these truths and then combined them with the body's need to experience emotions. Going through the emotions instead of jumping over them would be complete once Nancy saw herself from the full understanding of true love. Not only did she get to re-experience her own feelings of love, she was able to experience each and every single moment when she was viewed with love through the eyes of another. She was capable of feeling their love in her own heart.

It intrigued me that in order for Nancy to embody the full expression of herself, she first needed to experience the truth of all the emotions she had avoided. Before this moment I had assumed that if we had originally avoided our emotions, there would be no need to revisit them once we understood the importance of their effects on us.

*Sigh. I was wrong.*

I could now see how our vulnerability—the honest and complete expression of our entire truth—was required for us to personally open the flow of our energy. This process of self-witnessing was how Nancy would release the unbalanced ties from her body.

I was pulled back from my thoughts to find Nancy suddenly very calm. Her gaze fell upon the cat walking along the benches outside the teahouse. A smile crossed her face and her eyes brightened. Her fingers gently fondled the edges of her fabric napkin as she drifted further into fond memories.

*Someone needs to feed my cat,* she said wistfully. Her face reminded me of a child's when they daydreamed of a pet they hoped to have. *I never really liked cats, until Tabby. Even though I tried to shoo him from the yard he kept returning. He needed me.* Nancy's willingness to love even the things she was raised to hate revealed her inner kindness. She was gentle and lovely through and through.

In a snap, Nancy shifted from her state of calm to agitation. The light in her eyes darkened, her soft voice now turned sharp.

*Be sure they check on my cat.* The tone of her words cut the air. These words were the strongest connection to Nancy's real life personality I had witnessed, revealing the personality she had created from pain—a woman who was harsh, controlling, and demanding.

And with that, I fell free from her presence, back into my own bedroom, back into my body.

"She doesn't have a cat? Are you sure?" I asked again, confused as I spoke with Daniel about the latest experience. "I know you said Betty didn't think she did, but Nancy was very insistent that the cat wouldn't be okay if someone didn't feed it."

He remained adamant that Nancy had never had a cat. I found this very strange and considered she might be delirious. Frustrated, I accepted the truth of the living, breathing human over my own experience in the teahouse where Nancy had shown such urgency regarding her cat.

That night, I was awakened from my sleep.

*Christine.* It was as if her presence shook me awake. Nancy continued, *It's been raining and it's too cold. I don't think that cat of mine will be okay in this weather if he doesn't get something to eat. Please tell them again.*

*Nancy, I told them. They don't believe me. They even said you hate cats.* Not always at my best when woken out of nowhere, I came across as impatient and uncaring. *They are very angry with me now because of this.* I was not worried about their anger—people often misunderstood their own pain in these moments and pushed their emotions at me as anger. What I wanted was for Nancy to be aware of her family's position.

I pleaded with Nancy, *Things don't always translate correctly so I could be completely wrong about this cat thing.*

Still alive, her emotions were more powerful than the emotions of the dead, carrying with them lots of attachments.

I released a heavy sigh, *All I am really trying to get you to understand is why I'm not telling them again.*

*Please! You have to fix this for me!* Nancy would not let her need go. *You are the only one who can help.*

Nancy was urgent, and since she had asked for a third time, I agreed.

"Okay, I'll see what I can do," I said aloud, half asleep.

I tried to ask Nancy for more details, but she had used up all her energy to wake me and was too weak to be of any further assistance. It crossed my mind that she might not be speaking about a cat at all, rather something that I interpreted as a cat. Referencing her home, I began my work by energetically duplicating her cat vibration. I hoped to find what she was so insistent about.

I placed myself energetically in her chair, the same chair I had seen her sitting in while holding the cat. I followed a compulsion and found myself wanting to look out the sliding glass door into the back yard. After a bit, I saw the cat walking along the yard near the tree.

*Ha! It is a cat! He just lives outside. Okay, what else can I find?* I wondered.

I switched from the vibration of the cat to the energetic signature of the room and watched as Nancy's image rose from the chair and walked over to the broom closet.

*Got it!* I exclaimed excitedly.

After the rest of the scene played out, I called and left a voice message for Daniel regarding the cat. I stressed how adamant Nancy was about his care.

"You can find the bag of cat food at the bottom of the broom closet." I added, "Nancy was very methodical in her behavior. Make sure you do it this way when you feed the cat: open the door slowly, then close it after you step out. Put the food in the bowl, then open the door slowly again, step inside and close it slowly."

I felt silly sharing these details about how to feed the cat with Daniel, but in the discovery this had seemed to be a very important part of getting the cat's attention.

I hung up the phone feeling confident that if there was a cat, he would be fed, and Nancy would be at peace.

On day three, I met with Nancy as we continued to converse through the various aspects of her life. Today, the teahouse was a place of immense comfort and safety for her.

*I love it here. I didn't get to come here but once, when I was seventeen, so I'm happy to be here now. I always wanted to come again, but I didn't seem to have the space for me to prioritize myself over the other distractions and necessities of life. Little luxuries seemed selfish.* She placed her gloved hands, fingers intertwined, in her lap as she said a prayer.

Then, as she did every day, she thanked me for coming.

With all the other tables full, it was interesting to me that I was the only guest at her table. I expected other members of her family to join us, but they did not.

Today, as we sat drinking our lavender tea—which she claimed was good for reducing anxiety, stress, and depression, while promoting restful sleep—Nancy shared a conclusion I had not heard her speak of before.

*You know, I've come to realize something. I have always shared a weighty responsibility with my children. In that, I've lost something of myself. It is like I've cancelled myself out by using my energy to control them instead of using it to feed myself. I finally understand the saying 'do as I say, not as I do.' All the control I forced was to bring them happiness and it brought me none; it brought them none.*

*What I know now is that I'm ready to let go of that guilt. I was so worried they would not have love and joy if they didn't make something of themselves in the eyes of others or if their manners were not always understood.*

*My new faith is that they will have what they need when they need it, and everything else is simply the understanding of the universe at work in our favor. I want them to forgive themselves for the wrongdoings that I obligated them to. Guilt weighed heavily on their hearts because my actions made them believe they were less than they were. They have always been amazing, they have always been loved.*

I watched Nancy brighten with each piece of her growing understanding. I felt her untie her crown chakra above her head.[15] Just as she was about to let go, I felt a downward pull on her head; instead of the expected release, she moved into regret, remembering, *I have invited my family here to come and witness my life, as you have each of these days. Not one has come. I am here alone in my death, just as I was in my life.*

*Ugh,* I thought. Nancy had seemed to finally be reaching an understanding of freewill and its importance when she moved into fear and closed her crown chakra again.

It was not that her family was unwilling, Nancy did not know how to be vulnerable enough to let them arrive. She still feared their judgment, what they might think of her if she were to be seen as her truth. She was making the decision for her loved ones, as many of us do, by assuming and controlling their responses from a place of her own judgment. This behavior does not allow people to use their own freewill. Having kept them at a distance in life, she was now repeating this pattern in her internal energy.

I could feel with each passing day that Nancy was coming closer to being ready to cross over and leave her mortal existence behind. I watched as she grew to understand the freedom she could have if she let go and let others live their lives. She needed to release the self-inflicted pain that resulted from the judgment she had placed upon them the few times they had attempted to become sovereign.

I wondered if the death process would be quicker if a person held no fear.

---

15. Untying the chakras is necessary. It is the release of our energetic bonds to the body, setting free the part of our self that is eternal. The person's order is dependent on their experiences; the crown is not always the last chakra to be untied.

As I awoke on the fourth day, I reached out for Nancy to see what the day's tea choice would bring. My love for her had grown with each of her stories, and I received a greater understanding about how I treated myself during my life. I could see how a slight change in perspective would alter my current existence. Each day my presence, my witnessing of her process, brought her to a place of joy.

Today, however, to my surprise, I could not find her.

I could not find the teahouse either.

I considered checking in with Daniel and resisted. After our conversation about the cat, Daniel had expressed the family was feeling great stress upon hearing of my interactions with Nancy.

Daniel admitted, "You know, I asked you to help them in this time of need. I did this. They didn't ask me to ask you. I did it for my own selfish reasons."

Daniel went into detail, explaining this was his need. He wanted to help with Nancy's crossing.

In that moment, his family was grieving. Because they had no way to know that the information I shared was true, it created more stress and confusion for them.

He continued, "I spoke to Betty, and it seems these issues are too close to her and she can't accept them at this time."

At 11 A.M. on the fourth day, Nancy arrived in my space.

*This is unusual,* I said, happy to see her. I had always joined her in the teahouse or her thoughts. Now, together in my space, her arrival inspired me.

*I want to take you somewhere,* I said, *I want you to see my world.* I had only ever taken people above the Universal Conscious Mind's influence for healing. Taking Nancy as my friend was a first for me. I held her hand, and in an instant, we were above the earth, wrapped in a blanket of stars amid the black sky.

Today felt different for us, full only of joy. We both had an increased lightness about us. Here, in my world, she was no longer her age. If I had to guess, I would say she was about thirty. We sat, talking about the self-imposed boundaries of life. She brought up the baby I was expecting, knowing there was an issue surrounding her birth.

*What is your fear?* Nancy asked me just as I would ask someone whose journey I was inspired to witness.

*I am afraid to give up my life.*

This statement had double meaning for me. I had been told by several of my doctors, for my own safety, to abort the pregnancy. The second meaning had a much larger impact. It was in regard to my being a full-time mom again. If I lived as I had with my other children, I would be giving up my new path. Instead of helping others learn to heal themselves—which was something I was very good at and was excited to continue—I would return to my overly selfless ways and have no personal freedom.

I could not imagine being a mother and not holding the needs of my newborn child above my own. These opposing beliefs held me in conflict. Even with the astonishing work I did, and having the understanding about how balance is critical for every aspect of one's mind, body and spirit, I was still unable to fully see how to live in balance when it came to my own family.

*More than that, I found out that the medicine I took for my heart before I learned I was pregnant could cause birth defects. My daughter might live her whole life suffering.*

I paused, torn between staying with the delusion of fear I shared with Nancy—one where I took responsibility for things completely out of my control—or letting it go. I chose the delusion; because it was familiar, I found it to be comfortable. I continued holding the delusion that it was my fault for having done this to my child.

*I will be responsible for her suffering.*

With the love of a mother, Nancy spoke. *I am grateful for the gift you have given me, for listening to me, enjoying me, and for sharing your love with my family and me.*

She had something foreign in her palm. She put it up to my heart as she held me still, her arm around my shoulders.

She explained, *They gave me this. They said I could choose to under-stand and give it to you as your witness or I could keep it for myself.*

As it opened, I moved into a vision. The vision was in my home. I was walking down the hall from my bedroom to the dining room, yelling to Syndell, "Hurry up or we will be late!" We were leaving for a lecture where I would be presenting my theories. As I exited the hallway, I saw her—I could see my soon-to-be born little girl—this would be Sara!

I had done it; I had chosen to have both a career and a child!

*It is possible.*

Sara was sitting in a high chair, eating carrots while I passed by her, readying to leave. As I watched myself, I shifted to guilt. *That! That's the feeling that has forced me to be too selfless. I believe my actions can harm her.*

The weight of my heart confused me. Suddenly heavy, it pulled on me. I wanted to be okay with someone else helping her, but all I could see was my abandonment of her.

When she would ask me later in life what kind of expressions she made when she ate carrots I would have to answer, *I don't remember.* I would not remember because I had not completely focused on her, locking into my memory every detail as she realized each new marvel of her world.

I tormented myself with the idea that she would resent me and feel less important than my other children when she learned I had given up my life for them, but with her I chose my work.

Sara had no need to suffer; I suffered for her, my heart breaking under the weight of my own guilt.

*How could I be so ungrateful?* I lamented. *If God gave me this beautiful gift, how can I put the needs of others over hers? She's mine!* I placed my hand over Nancy's hand, which rested over my heart in an attempt to release my pain.

That is when it happened. The item that Nancy held to my heart began to glow, replaying the very same moment I had witnessed with a different focus, the focus being from Sara herself.

Sara was pleased to be independently learning her world without the pressure of my observance. I saw her witness the happy energy between

Syndell and me as we rushed about, making sure not to be late. Sara was aware of the joy we took in our appearance, and the excitement of the souls we would be meeting with soon. Her point of view was totally different than the guilty one I experienced for myself.

It was obvious how much love there was between Sara and I, whether we sat face-to-face or moved to opposite ends of the city. My mouth wide open, awed, I finally understood.

*It's okay to live my life and not force myself to focus solely on gratitude.*

The way others believed that gratitude must be experienced with constant effort was not correct. Gratitude was innate for me, embodied and occurring every second, no matter where my attention was focused.

*In every instant, my gratitude exists because I am in my truth.*

I thought about my children who had come before. My thoughts had always been in conflict. I wanted to enjoy the personal focus of having a career, something about me, for me. Instead, I had given them all my time and attention, assuming I could have my life later.

*Everything was for them,* I suddenly realized. Whether it was the stay-at-home mom presence I created to meet their needs, or my gone-to-make-money for their needs persona, my focus was on them. They were always in my heart; they were always loved. I finally understood the tremendous weight I carried around, a burden of guilt that kept me energetically focused as if I were apart from them, instead of seeing that my love for them created every moment, every interaction of our relationship.

I was again amongst the bright stars.

Nancy spoke, interrupting the vision her gift had supplied. *This child that you carry will be a healthy one. Don't you worry. This is the right time for her to come into your life. You will both have what you need.*

As my focus left the vision, I was aware Nancy was different. I could feel her experience. With her understanding—her new embodiment of her truth—she was now choosing to hold the weight of my burden for me.

When she took my burden, it was different from the suffering she had experienced in life. In life, she was driven by obligation and what she believed her actions would bring her. Her actions were chosen because they supported fearful beliefs in a cause and effect way.

Here, in this moment, her action toward me was given because she loved me and could clearly see what I could not. Giving me this gift was truly an altruistic gesture. With this gift, I could see the same truth for myself.

I sat next to her—free.

I could still feel the vibrations of her words: *You will both have what you need. Your child can thrive in the environment that you are living and working within now.* The thought was profound and soothing. I understood the gift of freedom from guilt, seeing the truth that we all have what we need all the time.

I was surprised to receive a gift. I had simply wanted to help Nancy cross over with ease and comfort. Her choice to give me her gift was a lesson that was part of her journey.

The shift her choice caused was truly amazing. Giving freely without obligation was the piece she was missing to be whole. She had finished the lesson she wanted to experience with complete embodiment and understanding. Without consequential expectations, she offered her gift willingly, freely making the exchange to rescue me.

As these thoughts continued, I saw something strange open to the right of us. It was hard to see at first, appearing only as a space where the stars were not. I searched the darkness. The absence of stars bleeding into the inky blackness left me curious as to why this space was veiled, hiding its origin and meaning.

Then they emerged.

From the space of blackness, a group of shadows slightly less black than the black sky appeared. Cloaked in hooded garb, they floated smoothly towards us. They surrounded Nancy and gathered her up as someone would a load of laundry that needed to be ferried away.

In that moment, I did not have a thought. I only observed as they moved towards the dark opening with her. Just as she was crossing the threshold, she glanced over her shoulder at me. Her expression changed, giving me the feeling that perhaps she was not sure what she had gotten herself into by taking the weight of my burden as her own.

I strained to see into the blackness. Apparently, that was all I was going to get as the verbal response from the shadows was, *Stop asking questions. This is not your business! Stay in your own space.*

I could overhear the conversation these shadow beings were having with Nancy, but I could not make out their words. It was as if they were speaking in tongues—a language that I was not versed in—one far more complicated than the language of energetics, which to date was the most complicated language I had learned.

Within a short amount of time, they vanished, leaving me to my own conclusions. My mind filled with the idea that Nancy was moving to the side to continue this same lesson instead of moving up to a new adventure as I had helped others do when they passed. Perhaps this was how people repeated human life—they move to the side for re-education and then return for another shot. Or perhaps, this was purgatory. If she was capable of 'getting it' would she then move up to rejoin the process of life I had seen others attend?

"You won't believe this." Daniel began that evening before I had a chance to ask about Nancy's condition. "My wife went to her grandma's house to check on things because the power outage during the storm caused the alarm system to shut off. While she was there, she decided to look for the cat because of your last voicemail message. She didn't expect to find anything, but when she saw an empty bowl on the back porch she went to the broom closet to look for the cat food like you said." He paused as he took in a deep breath. "It wasn't there. No cat food."

"Ugh," I moaned. I had gotten so excited thinking Nancy's last wish for her cat was going to be fulfilled.

"But wait! What she did find was an empty cat food bag in the trash under the sink. So, then she looked through the rest of the kitchen and found some cans of cat food in the cupboard. When she went to fill the bowl, she did it like you said in the message about the door. You should have heard her. I was on the phone with her as she waited after closing the door. She screamed! She screamed with relief when she saw the cat. Once the door was shut, the cat showed up. He walked right up to the food and started eating."

Daniel choked up before continuing. "She was so relieved! She said, if the cat is real, then every other thing you said might be real, too, and knowing that her grandmother is still around..." He took a deep breath, and letting it go, said, "Thank you."

I could hear the release in his voice as he exhaled more completely.

*If the cat is real, then every other thing I said might be real, too. Wow!* It was powerful to think of him accepting what I already knew to be true as his new reality. The world around me was changing.

Nancy passed peacefully without waking again. Her time of death on the fourth day was 12:15 P.M.


Years later, I made the effort to check in with Nancy. I always felt she was okay, and yet each time I shared her story, people asked me how I could know.

*Are you still in the space where the shadows took you or somewhere else in the universe?* I asked. I wondered if she moved onto another life, or if that darkness was a place I still needed to learn about. Having been raised with the belief that hell exists left me wondering if the darkness had something to do with suffering.

*I am not there and I am not in outer space.* She did not mean outer space like amongst the stars where I had last seen her, but more like space without a body or without the defining characteristics of a form.

*So, where are you?* She gave me the feeling of being in the heart center, where the spark of divinity is located in the physical body. Not completely following her explanation I asked, *Are you with divinity?*

*No, I am divinity,* she clarified. With what I know about the divine, having been in its space to heal others, this was a most pleasant surprise.

The joy I felt reflecting on that information expands my heart light[16] every time I consider how glorious that reality is for her.

*I was worried for you when I thought about the look on your face as the shadow people took you away. Can you tell me where they took you?* I waited.

There was no answer.

I asked another question, not yet satisfied. *What was in the blackness?*

*I cannot talk about that.* There was no emotion. Her response was flat.

*So, what about those shadow people who took you?* I asked, trying a different angle. *Were they death?* I considered that the shadows resembled stories I had read regarding the Angel of Death.

*They were not death. Death cannot transport life.*

The more I pondered, the more my thoughts gave me pause. I felt a really strong truth here. I waited as the memories unfolded further into my thoughts. Nancy referred to her spirit as life.

Her out of body energy was still being referred to as life!

If this is fact, it also means the shadows are energy equal to life as well[17]. In order to move her, they have to be life! They were supporting her, not shuffling her off. This thought caused me to settle into myself, connecting more strongly to the earth.

With this new understanding, I considered releasing my beliefs about what life meant. I had always assumed living was only for things that could grow and change independently, like plants and people. The idea that a thing, although inanimate, could very well have a life of its own, suddenly made sense.

I thought about crystals and other inanimate objects I could feel life within. I had felt my own cells as if they were individuals living in a community, existing as a body, each with its own life. I considered my understanding of string theory, that all things are created from the same

---

16. This light is the expansion of the spark of divinity that is generally housed in the heart chakra.

17. 'Death' necessitates nothing, or absence, so because the shadow beings were not absent, they must be some form of life.

material, and how attention and focus causes strings to appear different to each of us.

The base component of all existence is alive; no matter how or what it forms, all things are life!

As I left my subconscious to ponder this further, I moved to another question regarding Nancy's experience.

*Can you tell me what happened to you once you went into the darkness?*
*Yes, I was no longer alive.*

*Really?!* This sent my mind reeling. Once dead and out of her human body she was still life, existing as energy, still formed by strings[18], but once in the darkness she was no longer life? I had to consider that once she moved into the darkness she was returned to pure awareness, the form in which we exist even prior to strings. It was a bit much to handle, so she continued showing me without words what happened.

When she entered the darkness, she gave up all energetic responsibility, a complete surrender of control, disconnecting herself from her own existence. Every vibration, the strings that were held as uniquely her, were now released and control returned to the divine. Our internal will holds the control of those strings as us, and her surrender of her will, which is not possible while alive, was made possible by being in the darkness. Her existence as pure awareness was a return to her original state. It was how she existed prior to her first thought and very first experience.

Nancy, as we knew her, was no longer holding space as a person with identity. Every path she had forged with belief could no longer be walked. As she was preparing to release her identity, all conflicts were seen from truth. The ideas she had, like loving a cat for its fur, its purr, and its warm presence, disappeared. At the same time, the ideas that made her originally hate cats, the counterbalance[19] of these thoughts, also disappeared.

---

18. Strings, of string theory, are the basic building blocks of every aspect of a human— body, Etheric Template, soul manifold (to be discussed later), and our light content. These exist separately from each other; they are not interdependent.

19. Every thought that is formed from judgment, attachment, conclusions, or assumptions has in our systems an opposite to hold balance or it could not exist.

Once balanced, there were no counterbalances to hold her identity and the energy returned to divinity, no longer held as her individual self.

Nancy still existed. She was no longer holding what her experience created as a unique combination. It was now held by divinity itself. She was a drop of water in the ocean and simultaneously the entire ocean, indistinguishable unless you know what to look for.

*This was a good thing?* I asked, trying to be free of judgment, accepting there were still things I could not understand from the space of my human life. As humans, one of our greatest fears is the loss of who we are after we have passed, and the assumption that this loss negates our existence.

*Yes.*

*Did you gain something from it?* I was still searching to suspend this wonder, wanting to know why this had happened to her. I hoped the answers would somehow stop the racing of my fearful thoughts.

*Yes.* Her response returned me to peace. Without effort, the racing stopped.

*What was it?*

*There is no death.*

# Chapter Dedication

With gratitude to my friends and fellow travelers, Daniel and his family,
for including me in their personal journey.
And to Nancy, whose gift gave me the strength to stop fearing the death
of my unborn child.

# Chapter Seven

# THE COMA

Las Vegas, winter 2009

*I* sat straight up from a dead sleep. *What the hell?!* I said in my telepathic push at whoever was now energetically in my private space. How did this even happen? Although physically still, energetically I was thrashing about and throwing a fit. *Didn't I put up those damn barriers?*

Were those curse words my thoughts? *Hmm, I think not. Something's different.* I was not prone to cursing and I did not have hostility anymore when the dead woke me up. I had indeed put in obstacles to eliminate spiritual interaction without my consent, especially since I was pregnant. For months, the activity of the dead had been held back while I waited for Sara, who was due to arrive on March 27, 2010.[20] Still, these thoughts were not mine, not completely. Someone was influencing me.

As an Empath, I found experiencing the emotions, thought patterns, and personality traits of others challenging. The dead, missing their so-

---

20. Sara was born six weeks premature, healthy, and loved by all.

cial filters, made everything more raw and obvious than the living. It left me feeling as if their impressions were impossible to separate from my own. In this moment it was difficult to tell the difference between them and me.

*Okay,* I thought, trying to remember what I had already learned. *I know the feelings and thought patterns you are impressing upon me are so I can help you. I must need to see things from your point of view.*

I was becoming someone else. My brain, my mind, and my ego worked together to point out how this dead person overlaid his personality over mine.

I gathered my wits about me, found my softer side, and called out to him, *It's not as easy as you think to suddenly not be yourself. If you're not alert you don't even realize it's not you until it wears off.*

By leaning more into the energy of this dead man and less into myself I could comprehend the information he was communicating. The side effect was that, instead of my usual calm, I flailed mentally. I felt as if I needed to strike out in defense of my life.

I demanded, *Who are you and why are you here? What's going on with you?*

I closed my eyes and when I opened them again I was no longer in the safety of my room. My vantage point was inside his storm, a storm on steroids.

*What the hell?!* I called again with false bravado, assuming this was how he expressed his masculinity.

His storm was loud, disorienting, and relentless.

*You must be under extreme duress for your energy to create something so drastic.* I stepped out of the storm and visualized myself reaching for the door I had created for the dead, hoping he would follow me through it and into the calmness of my space.

*Damn door! It should be here,* I said, mimicking the way he spoke.

There was a reason I had put up that door; I wanted to keep the dead from wandering around in my space, and to have a way to direct them when they were lost.

*I don't like it! I don't like the discomfort and I don't like being woken from a dead sleep with you in my head, my body, or my dreams, thrust into storms and other dramas that aren't my own. UGH!* I spat, carrying his feelings as my own.

Clearly, he was irritated and had a belief that the world was a burden. Keeping with his thoughts and beliefs, I grew concerned for my door. *What if it's missing or damaged? Where is that damn door?* I called out, picking up another piece of his puzzle—he had a fear of loss.

With months on bed rest, keeping both my heart and Sara safe, I spent hours a day playing with and building energetic constructions for friends and family. Finding my mental blueprint for the original build of the door would take a bit of effort. However, having this comparison would make it easier to understand what had changed.

The emotional and chemical bonding of this individual was different than my own and it left my brain in an altered state. I could not see my creations from the place of myself. I sifted through my memories to find the one I needed, as I held onto my template of self, which I had forcefully locked in my thoughts to hold my own identity. I wanted to make sure I could return to being solely me after this experience.

*Crystal tree: Ooh, I forgot about that one.* I cooed fondly at it, mimicking the gentleness of Mabel, who I had created it for. It was the first of its kind, used to continuously clean the air in her home, and so pretty.

*Wormhole, another nice one.*

Dang, it was easy to distract me today! This was not normal—another piece of his behavior.

*Door!* I was like a dog noticing a squirrel.

I struggled to focus and checked the door. *Still intact,* I called to my intruder, needing to justify myself—another of his pieces. My head started to ache; I was not sure if this was a piece of his or just the pressure from leaning so far into him and out of myself.

*Well, the door doesn't seem to be any different.* I peered past it, feeling like a peeping Tom with no self-confidence, as if I could invade the privacy of others—definitely his behavior.

*Yep, the line of people waiting is still there.* I confirmed for myself.

The process of waking up and checking all of this took about two seconds. This energetic stuff was definitely becoming more natural and easier than when I first built the door. In the beginning, this process would have taken me at least thirty minutes.

*What in hell's tarnation is going on here?* I heard him say. *Damn, this is a bit squirrely.* I felt that thought with an exaggerated southern accent and all.

*Creep much?* I pushed back at him with a response he might relate to based on how he made me feel. *Okay,* I thought, *if the door and the line are in place, then what's happening? How did you manage to pull me into your world?*

I reflected on the moment before I awoke.

*Run through list of speculation,* I heard myself say to him, but then my mind reminded me that I do not speculate!

*Okay, that's you.* I declared.

In general, I was no longer influenced at this level from the dead. Yet, his personality moved me and I continued to follow his method of speculation.

*Maybe you're different. I feel you more.* I shook my head, thinking of my suddenly poor manners. Then I remembered I was experiencing his way of thinking, not mine, *I don't have to worry; they're your manners anyway. You could care less. You don't hang onto socialized freaking niceties.*

I did not mind this part about the dead; their being blunt and abrupt was easier than the living's effort to be overly polite. Translating for dead was way faster and it took less energy.

*Manners!* I hollered. *They make us sentimental sissies.*

Despite being confused at how I was mouthing off to this guy, I questioned myself. *Why am I saying such things?*

Then it struck me.

*SARCASM! That's it, that's what you're doing to me. Got it!*

The overriding vibration coming from this guy was sarcasm.

I explained to him, *I don't do sarcasm. Without a counter balance, it could take me a while to overcome its influence.*

As the sarcasm continued to come in hard and fast, I was easily overtaken. My usual behavior templates, the habitual patterns that my subconscious used to create my personality without effort, did not slow it. Even my awareness of it happening was not slowing it down.

*Okay, think,* I commanded myself. *Before I put the door up, they found me from some kind of spectral glow over my house.* I checked the door again for leaks. *Nope, not that.* Feeling a little buggy from his influence, I lacked my usual patience.

*Hey, guy!* I mentally walked back into the storm to gain direct communication. The wind was so extreme I could not see past it. *What brings you and this mess here?*

The storm contained multicolor whipping winds. There were distinct edges between the different shades of blues, grays, blacks, and whites.

*What's the significance of these colors?* All the other storms I had experienced consisted of vibrant colors, but never any black or white. *Maybe it's how you see life?*

This was my investigative habit now. In the beginning, I looked for consistency in energetic situations so my mind would feel safe in its ability to comprehend the information. Once safe, I moved forward. Over time, I learned to look for the differences to see the issues I could not understand. If I matched stuff up that was the same, my mind tended to lean into my brain more and start making things up, instead of simply observing. By leaving every direction open, without drawing any conclusions, I could see past the brain's security and into the vast environment ahead of possibilities beyond my own thoughts.

*Guy!* I felt for him. *Do you know your name?*

*No.*

*Your response is only, "No?"* That was unusual. The dead were normally pretty chatty once they showed up at my door. *Well you're a wild one, a real festival of fun. Still sarcastic I see. Damn it!*

*Okay,* I thought. My brain was programmed to fill in a person's name. I used my own vibrational records to name them if they did not know who or what they were, if for no other reason than to give me a way to reference them later.

*Not that any of you are interested,* I randomly began speaking sarcastically to the dead in my space, *but I am also looking for a way to electronically communicate this information outside of the emotional and physical body into a method that would be universally accepted.* I kept talking, realizing that I knew what I was saying was not true at all, but still I carried on, looking internally for a reason I was acting this way. This uneducated rambling had to mean something.

*Currently, everyone translates energy according to their own energies, making the world into something like the Tower of Babel from the bible.* I was mumbling telepathically now, feeling a little drunk.

*HEAD INJURY! Did you hit your head?* I called to him. *That would explain a lot!*

I leveled out a bit with this conclusion; that is how it always works. Once I figure out what the overwhelming behavior meant, I could revert back to being me.

*Do you know how you got here?* I calmly asked him, feeling more confident now that I knew which direction to go.

*No.*

For all the influence this guy had over me, he was a man of few actual words. I wondered what kind of influence he had on others while alive.

I tried to make one of my normal intuitive jumps with this guy; it did not work.

*Huh! That's curious.*

It was easy to work with the dead; just pick up the pieces, make sense of them, and send the dead on their way.

*Something is still different.* I was compelled to continue a conversation with him, speaking as if we were colleagues working on the problem together. *You must have been a very keen observer.*

I could feel him in my thoughts. Watching me work through the process gave him something to hold onto. He was using it to reconnect splintered and fractured pieces of his mind.

I had got it, I understood what he was doing. *Pathways, you're rebuilding pathways. That's good. You'll free a lot of emotional damage that way.*

My process of talking things out with him seemed to help. *I'll have to keep that in mind to use with the living. Okay, time for the list so we can speculate again: You don't know who you are. You don't know how you got here. You don't know your name. You don't remember the head injury...*

*Aw, crap.* I realized he might not know he was dead.

I hate having to tell the dead they are dead.

I hoped I did not have to do that with this guy. Dead people, those who expire traumatically, tend to run around screaming in my space for days. *Please, don't let him do that,* I thought. Waiting for what seemed like a howling banshee to reach a moment of peace after days of shrieking was frazzling, at best. Under the influence of this guy's energy, I was unwilling to hear that non-stop creep show. I tended to lock myself into the human plane without a connection to the dead until those episodes were over.

Of course, I tried to check in periodically to give them compassion, but it wreaked havoc on my ability to live in the moment. It showed all over me—my face, my behavior, my ability to think. I was not myself during those connections. The energy was just too much for me to separate from. It was impossible for me to behave as me. My selfish need for sanity outweighed my belief that they needed support. There was not anything I could do for the would-be banshees really, other than bear witness to their suffering.

*How about a theory? Let's talk theory.* I wanted to change the subject. *Another phenomenon we experience with energies is association. Because I resonate on multiple levels with you, I can assume the vibrational existence as my own. That's what happened to us. You managed to get this hold on me by catching me by surprise, or maybe it is part of the message, still...*I trailed off as I started to form the visualization in the top left of my head to communicate more details with Bob. That was what I decided to call him—Bob.

I pictured reaching up and grabbing our next discernible piece of the puzzle—the *aha* moment I needed to understand how to help him—as if it were a solid thing. I pulled it down to a back-lit table in front of me to be examined.

*There isn't really a table here,* I told him in case he was more sentient than elemental and able to experience energetic reality, *it's just a large pool of light*[21] *energy that is in my core. I use the visuals to bring along my conscious mind in the process so I can communicate visually to others.*

I shared my process with Bob in simple terms. *I have found that keeping the spiritual froufrou to a manageable level by visualizing it as real animate things helps me focus better in my daily life. The process of realistic visualization allows for a consistency between my spiritual thoughts and my physical world. It keeps me from feeling scattered and pulled between the two realities. I feel more connected to life while being of service to others.*

I turned toward his energy. *You know, you have a very strong vibrational influence.* It was hard for me to focus and be me from the reverberation of his intensity. *But we need to put an end to how it is affecting me.* Oh! Of course. *I don't know why I didn't think of this sooner.*

With that, I imagined grabbing him by the collar and pulling him out of the storm into my space. I needed him in a place of peace and he needed to be more restful if he was going to be of any assistance, which from the influence he exhibited, I knew he would be at some point.

*What do you remember?* I asked him, once I pulled him into my room.

Released from the strength of his own storm, he could communicate more readily. *I remember riding around in my truck.*

I could see his big red dually truck.

Bob paused, unable to move his thoughts past that memory. *That's all I can remember.*

---

21. This light exists before thought, emotion, or awareness. It is not my internal light; it is light that has not been used.

Often in traumatic experiences the mind and brain separate, allowing the veil to take over to protect the brain from fracturing. The mind with its energetic connection can handle the information, but the brain, with its will and need to control and stack beliefs, can struggle to the point of breaking.

I wondered what was so extreme that forced Bob to need this protection.

I looked deeper into him to see. As I touched his trauma I immediately shut down telepathy.

"Fear of death!" I said aloud. I needed to keep the spiraling thoughts that followed internal. If I projected out to Bob in his current condition the results could be disastrous, taking him in a direction he was not prepared to handle. Knowing his fear, I could see his brain had tried to skip over the trauma and jump to the end conclusion that he would not survive. His energy separated to resist the shattering that occurs when the brain sees an unimaginable truth. Bob was afraid to die.

*That's what the entire overlay was for. So I could comprehend your situation.*

Still keeping my thoughts separated from his, I allowed my brain to process thoughts by speaking out loud, just under my breath. "Bob might not be dead at all." This was going to be delicate. Realizing he was afraid to die was not something I wanted to bring to his attention.

*Well,* I considered going back to our facts, *I am pretty sure you have a head injury, and you're out of your body, at some distance.* I paused, letting the idea sink in. *Do you think it's possible you were in an accident? What do you think about that?* I was being gentle. If I held the space for him to see what he needed to see, having no judgment or fear of my own for whatever trauma he encountered, I might be able to bring him through this experience completely. I waited as he fumbled through his thoughts, observing him for energetic cues. He gave me none.

*How about I help you with some of those connections? I will do the ones in the background of your thoughts and you keep thinking.* I repaired the broken thought patterns as I observed, supporting him where I could.

*Yes, I think*, he replied as my observations and support helped him to recall the circumstances of his trauma. His confusion lessened.

*Maybe what you need to do is realize where your body is*, I advised. *Where is your body, exactly? Can you see it or feel it?*

He offered no resistance to my suggestions, another sign of improvement.

*Yes, I can feel it.* He started to glow a bit with the recognition of his body. *I'm lying down.*

I did not want to freak him out, unsure of the condition of his body, so I made this a journey of discovery rather than jumping to a fact. *Are you lying next to your truck?* I asked, fishing for details.

*No.*

*Are you lying in the truck?* I was considering that maybe his body had not been found yet.

*No, I'm not anywhere near the truck.*

*Well, feel through your body what your surroundings are*, I suggested to him. I still wanted to avoid creating more trauma for him, hoping his spirit could reunite his mind and brain at his own pace.

After a while, it came to him. *I'm in a hospital room!* he said, excited that he had begun to figure things out.

I was already up now myself, getting ready to start my day. I looked around. His light had vanished from my room. *How do you know it's a hospital room?* I paused from picking out my clothes, hands raised to grab a shirt from the hanger, to listen. I would know from his answer if his energetic system had reached awareness and reunited.

*I'm standing next to my body!*

*Okay, good!* I rejoiced with him.

*I'm not dead*, he said again more relaxed, partially revealing his fear.

*Awesome! Congratulations. The next step should be easy then.* I said, realizing he was still not connected. *All you need to do is lie down and get back in your body.* I resumed pulling my clothes up and over my pregnant belly, feeling the problem solved.

*I bet you jumped out of your body thinking you were going to die and then they moved it while you were separated.* Experience had shown me that ordinarily, in instances of displaced energy, once the reunion is made with awareness, the two systems—physical body and energy body—will reattach. I paused again, as I did not feel this had happened.

*Lie down.* I encouraged, sending him a visual of what reattaching would look like. There was no literal need to lie down—it was just a mental translation to accurately communicate the feel of the process.

*I am! This isn't working,* he called to me. *I know my body is here, but I can't see it, and I can't get my head to fit back in at all!*

I gave his body a quick once over. I felt a sense of energy from his physical legs, but they lacked the feeling of wholeness I looked for in living beings. Just as he had stated, I felt the head had no connection, no energy at all. It reminded me of the headless horseman. I tried to hold back my chuckle and failed.

*Hey, it's not funny,* he said. *How am I supposed to do this?* He was breaking down, his workable energy reducing with each failed attempt to reconnect.

*I'm sorry. I wasn't laughing at your situation. I have this habit of trying to make light of difficult things. It makes it easier for me to think.* I paused long enough to feel him release his resistance. *My best guess is you have some type of trauma, probably to your brain. I wonder...*I was new to comas and did not yet have the faith in my skills to repair the brain at a distance. I could sense the location in the head where the healing of his physical brain was taking place. Maybe this was not a real coma. Maybe he was blocking his energy from re-entering his corporeal body for some other reason. Unsure what else to consider, I peered at his physical brain under the telescopic view of my connection and saw hundreds of tiny bleeds.

Suddenly, it occurred to me what I was missing! Love. The vibrational energy of love could do more amazing things than I could—maybe it could even stop these bleeds!

# The Coma

*Okay, here's what you're going to do*, I said to him. *Try to connect with someone around you. A nurse, a visitor, a family member.*

If there was some meaningful love connection between him and another human being, that connection would help him re-enter his physical body. I counted on his energy, that it would remember how to connect from the experience of apparent love. Then, with the connection, the body would have more power to fix those bleeds.

*There's no one here.*

*Just wait. Someone will show up, they always do.* I grabbed my keys. I had a twenty-minute drive ahead of me for my first doctor appointment of the day. Sara and I were constantly being monitored to make sure things did not go too far in the wrong direction.

*What do I do while I wait?* he asked.

I felt his confusion grow again and decided it was best to hang onto this one instead of turning him out on his own. I pulled him into a conversation to keep him close as I went on about my day. *Why don't you tell me what you remember about what happened?*

*I remember I was driving along Highway 15, out past the race track. I was getting pretty tired really fast.* I knew his exhaustion could have been from less oxygen reaching the heart, a block to the brain, his having pushed beyond his limits, or from just poor sleeping habits.

*Where were you going?*

*I can't remember that. I remember being nervous. I really wanted to go home and sleep, but there was something more important.*

Okay, his brain's need to focus on himself instead of external details was undoubtedly evidence that he had pushed to control himself while trying to meet his ideas of the needs of others. This was important for me to realize because it revealed, without a doubt, that he had experienced a traumatic event because the short-term visual memory of his environment was missing.

*Okay. What do you remember next?* I asked.

*Next thing I remember, I was wandering around in a dark forest, expecting to stumble. I could sense rocks and trees, but the ground was level and smooth.*

This was a complete separation of his energetics—no physical or conscious connection was left or he would have moved with the terrain.

*Hey, Bob, do this for me. Look at yourself. Look and see if there is a cord between you and your body in the hospital bed. In fact, look to see if there are any strings outside of either you or your body.* There were not actually physical cords for him to find; I wanted his thoughts to grab the energetic location and flow, thinking it might help.

*Yes. There is one on each body,* he reported seeing one on his spiritual energy form and one on his body lying in bed.

*Are they connected?* I asked, hopeful. It would mean an open energy flow to his body.

*No.*

*Are they glowing?* Glowing meant energetic connection, too.

*No.*

*Try tying them together.* I pulled off the road to concentrate with him and waited while he tried. I knew there was no control before he answered. He could not affect his physical body. This further confirmed my suspicion of his complete disembodiment of his energetic systems. I felt a slight sinking inside of me as my brain did the calculations of what was possible, knowing that death was likely.

*I can't tie them.*

*That's okay,* I said to him gently as I started driving again. I spoke like I would to a child learning something new, not wanting to discourage him. *It was just a thought. So, what else happened while you were in this forest?*

*I saw these little glowy things I think were fireflies. Although, I haven't seen fireflies in Vegas.*

*Me neither. They might have been orbs.*

*Then I saw this larger glow further out.* His tone shifted. *I had the thought that I should go there, and then I was there.*

*You didn't walk or anything?* I asked.

*No. I just arrived.*

This, too, was typical of energy existing without physical or conscious ties. Transportation and location are simultaneous to thought. It takes no effort.

*I saw this line,* he continued. *It was strange, though, like looking at a bunch of people through infrared vision. I could only see the red hue dimly, given off as a heat signature.*

*Oh, that makes sense. Since you're not dead you don't see the other disembodied entities as they see each other; you're not like them. That reminds me, what was with all the southern drawl and sarcasm and orneriness? You know you sounded like Yosemite Sam to me.*

*That? I always thought it would be great to be a cowboy in the old west, maybe even one of the bad guys.*

We both laughed as it all made more sense. He felt more human to me as we continued to talk, like we were kindred spirits. I felt my investment in him; his need to live slowly became my own.

*Then I saw you.* His voice softened. *I wasn't trying to reach you to ask for help. It was weird, I actually wanted to help you!*

*That's not unusual. Everyone seems to see me as fragile, that I need protection. It's gotten more so since I've been pregnant.* This change was true for both the living and the other side.

*It's not that I saw you as weak or needy, it's more like I felt the need to protect you for my benefit. It's important to all of us if you stick around.* He paused, lost in his remembrance of connecting to me, sharing the deeper feeling he had towards protecting me.

Previously, I had been irritated that everyone thought I was less or incapable. Bob showed me his experience was one of blessing, driven to protect my light from harm. I was finally able to experience this love as such instead of a hit to my ego.

*Then this storm started! I pushed past the line, trying to get to you and the closer I got to you the stronger the storm got.*

*Ha-ha, yeah, that happens, too.* I confessed. *One of my talents is to magnify people's awareness of their blocks so they can be released.* Because of my ability to witness without judgment or attachment or reaching conclusions, people release blocks in my presence with less effort. The storm is the energetic process of entanglement release.

*Okay, Bob. I'm going to go. I'm at my appointment. I'll be distracted watching the baby on the monitor*, I said as I turned off my van. *Let me know if someone visits and I'll do my best to help you out.*

It was hours later before I heard from Bob.

*There's a woman here*, he reported. *My mother.* His energetic separation from his body had disabled his ability to see his surroundings. His impressions were based solely on what he could feel. His third eye was non-functioning, which caused him to sense others in their most basic form. He saw everything as gray, with a sonar-type sensory perception.

*Is your mom touching you?* I asked.

*Yes…she's holding my hand.* He seemed surprised by this, sharing with me that they were not an affectionate family.

*Well, what do you feel?* I coaxed. *Can you focus on the hands, the touch, the energy between them? Can you feel anything through your body?*

I looked energetically at the two physical bodies, hoping for an apparent connection. The resonance needed to be there for him to do what I was asking. Otherwise he could not help himself.

*Ah, found it! I can feel a root chakra connection between you two.*

*What's that?*

*It's your connection to human survival. You know—food, clothing, shelter, tribal rules. It's values, principles, belief systems, and the ways in which we communicate. It's the seat of socialization. And it's right there below your seat.*

I laughed at myself, referencing the root chakra that way since it is located below the hip, butt, and groin area. Someone had to laugh; this guy did not get my humor.

*It makes sense that you hold this sort of connection with a parent, seeing as values and belief systems often start with them.*

*Yes! I feel that.* He moved to lie down in his body. As the connections ignited in the first, second, then third chakra centers of the body I noticed a defect.

*Oh no,* I thought—*the heart connection is broken.* I could see red and blue lines from the heart to the shoulders indicating an imperfect balance. *Oh NO!* The pathway connections in his energy we had created in the very beginning, when I thought he was dead, would no longer match with his Etheric Template.

"STOP!" I yelled out loud, to the surprise of the people in the bank line where I had been waiting to make a deposit. I excused myself and rushed off to the bathroom. There was nothing I could do. Too late, I slumped against the wall. With the pathway alterations, the variations in the heart chakra block were too big of a conflict to overcome.

*While you have been out of body, releasing energy that is not in balance with your soul, the body's energy has not changed.* I was trying to explain between gasps for air, not wanting to sob, feeling responsible for not stopping what I believed could be the death of him.

*When you laid down, you zapped the natural connection. It's like changing the polarity of a magnet and then trying to use it the same way. It will repel everything it previously attracted.*

My heart ached. How could I not have seen this coming?

*The beliefs you had about your mother, about her judging you rather than loving you, were changed in your energetic body when you realized that she was afraid for you because she loved you. But this didn't change in your physical body. So, when you tried to re-enter your body, the difference was too great, the match couldn't be made.*

This is why people who have extreme experiences often see their lives differently following the experience. It is the successful return to their truth. Those who cannot accomplish their return to truth move further into suffering.

*In that moment of reconnection, you tried to reattach without balance. Your ability to perceive your heart in a different way...well, it's now repelled. I think the break in your system is permanent.*

Tears streamed down my face as I finished explaining to Bob what had happened, certain I would never make this mistake again.

*No, that can't be,* he said, realizing the implication of my message. He wanted to contradict my belief that his life could not be maintained if he could not reconnect. *Watch.* He encouraged himself now, as I was incapable, momentarily caught up in the reflection of my own failure. *I can feel my body now,* he said, as he lay down again.

Each time the energy of the heart connected, he felt excruciating shoulder pain, forcing his energy to bounce back out of his body. To force himself past the pain would cause permanent physical and mental damage, most likely in the form of a heart attack or a stroke.

With the beliefs about his mom burned into his system, the reintegration of his energetic connection would be impossible. There was nothing we could do. I had not yet found a way to move past this type of issue in human existence. If he were in his body, we would encapsulate the block and move on from it until he was in a place to make real life changes to fully express himself. But he was not! Without his connection, from my place of limited understanding I could not see how encapsulation was possible.

*Damn,* I thought. *If there was more time or I knew other healers, then maybe this could be changed.* I sat in the bathroom stall, my face buried in my hands, my heart breaking into pieces.

As a child, I had been deeply ingrained with the idea that the loss of human life was the most tragic occurrence possible. My dad had said, "Everything else could be overcome with time, understanding, and change, but once the life was lost..." Bob's desire to live reignited this belief in me.

I wept uncontrollably, immersed in my own fears, remembering my attachment and desire for the lives of my own children. Two of my children had been in the hospital following major accidents. One time, my son, Johnny, had received third degree burns over eighteen percent of his body, including his face. It was touch and go, as we painfully waited to see whether his lungs survived the burning. And my step-daughter,

Stephanie, had been in a car accident where the car rolled over three times. She had been airlifted to the hospital, too critical for ground transportation. I knew how Bob's mother must have felt.

When my own emotional pain got to be too much during those two experiences, I had reached for inspiration. I was unable to help them, so I prayed for someone to intercede on my children's behalf. Someone had saved each child's life, and it was not me.

"Okay, Christine, pull yourself together." I adjusted my energy. *We can do this!* I stood and wiped away the sting of my tears, gathering hope from the idea that someone had helped my children, that lives can be saved. After all, Bob had found me amongst the more than six hundred thousand people in Las Vegas. If he could do that, I must have something for him.

*Can you move through this and make a change?* I asked Bob. We had been at this for hours. Each time someone entered his hospital room, he tried to reconnect. Each time, nothing happened. He was not giving up, though the drain on him from the effort was obvious.

Bob talked off and on about his life: he was a truck driver, and kind of quiet. He recently changed from long hauls to local driving as he studied to be a geologist. Given the excitement he shared about traveling together with his dog and seeing new places, I was surprised he had given up long distance driving.

*Why do you drive such a huge pickup if you drive trucks for a living?* I asked curiously. *I would expect you to want a break from it during your off-time.*

*I had a Jeep for camping but I gave it up for the dually because it can pull a camper. I was thinking of giving up deep woods camping for something more like lake sitting.* He seemed to have some sort of motivation, but he was not sharing. *Maybe it's love*, I thought.

*So, you fish?* I was fishing for details, holding back my chuckle at my own intended pun.

*Not too much, but I think I might change that.* He ended the conversation, giving me the feeling I was getting too personal. It was strange, because the dead, and even most of the living, found it easy to open up to me.

As the second full day of his ordeal dawned, I could feel his energy decrease. Bob had been energetically disconnected for more than thirty hours. The system can usually handle about three days of this—seventy-two hours—before a person begins their trajectory towards death instead of life.

*That's something to work against if you have a reason to live, Bob. We need to get this in check.* It was because of his desire for life that I worked so hard to help him maintain it. I follow the truth of the person seeking the assistance, never my own. Without his own desire, I would have been content to help guide him towards death.

I thought about paying him a visit in person, knowing my hands-on work had a greater effect on the physical form. It was not that hands-on healing was more effective, I was just more confident at that time when I could see things in person.

I could track him and find him. I had done it before; I had helped the deceased find their bodies when they could not let go on their own by visiting their grave sites with them. I always felt crazed, having to jump back and forth between where they were and my own body. Jumping between where their bodies were and where I was happened so rapidly that I felt myself in two places, aware of both. I was packing up to leave to go find him, not knowing what else to do, when I realized Bob was in critical care.

I placed my things on the floor and instead of leaving I stood still in my room.

*They're not going to let me see you.*

I had run into issues before when explaining, "Hey, I just want to put my hands on this unconscious person's body." Remembering those awkward moments brought on nervous laughter. I had tried to explain myself to the wrong people. The right people never needed an explanation; they often shuttled me to where I needed to go as if they were more aware of my task than I was.

I started pacing anxiously as I felt the transition. Bob's energy was decreasing even more. By the end of the day, I decided I would feel better emotionally if I were close. The only way to help him and to make the energetic shifts needed was to open myself to where he was by fully projecting out of my own body. This was different than some of the others ways I worked. Instead of just watching the energy like I had with Nancy, I would be creating energetic change in Bob. This required more of my energetic being to be present in his space. I had not done this level of work since I first found out I was pregnant.

Fully committed to helping Bob live, I told my family what I was up to, locked my bedroom doors to ensure I would not be interrupted, and began the method.

I concentrated on my hands, how they looked and how they felt. Then I looked at my feet to see where they were physically planted. I focused internally, knowing every truth that is my existence. I let go of all my beliefs and felt my feet on a cold hospital floor. I wiggled my toes, which was my habit, and once I felt the floor solid under my feet, I opened my sight. Now present with Bob, I laughed at something so irrelevant I almost lost the connection. His name was not Bob at all. It was Gene!

*Do you want your life to be over?* I asked him again, hoping to force his focus. It was time to get serious.

*No, NO! I know I have a reason to live!* he insisted. *I'm not ready to go.* He became frantic and worried I might give up. *You can't stop. I DON'T HAVE ANYONE ELSE!*

His usual energetic push was now applied physically to me, my energy in his space, as he put his forearm to my chest and his back to the exit in a symbolic attempt to keep me from leaving. He was moving beyond his previous abilities because of his strong desire to return to the living.

*Let's do this,* I said, recognizing his full investment, and moved to his bedside. I laid down in his body and pushed my heart center into his. By overlying my energy, I attempted to set up a template for him to release his mental and emotional blocks with his mother. *This has to be possible,* I said to reassure myself more than him.

As I connected, becoming Gene's energy for his physical body, I moved past his exaggerated sarcasm and brusque manners, converting to the very gentle and keen individual I had seen him to be at his core. My heart began to beat in rhythm with his. I felt my physical connection to both bodies, his and mine. I allowed my awareness of his gentle nature to spread. Little popping sensations occurred as the new energy flowed through thousands of tiny blocks stuck in his physical form.

These blocks were created over the years through self-abuse. It had started innocently enough with his observing his parents during a time that they had struggled with loving themselves and each other. When he was very young, Gene had witnessed his parents yelling and fighting, only to see their issues resolved by each parent turning away from the other, appearing cold and unfeeling. As a child seeing this, his observation was that resolution was achieved from passive-aggressive behavior. He embodied their patterns and templates and learned to hold back his own thoughts and needs. Gene continued these patterns into adulthood, not knowing how to stop the self-victimizations that were the norm for his relationship patterns.

I continued to blend my energy with Gene's body to create change, using the same method I had observed when the Native American had created change in me. As I focused on this task, the person I knew—the part that could not get back in his body—seemed to disappear. He was gone, just like when a magician makes something vanish in a cloud of smoke. I reached out to see where Gene went and I could not find him in a specific place. But I could find him in a specific state of being. His absence was like a baby incarnating and moving between the space of her body and then back to the source of her existence. The work I was doing took most of my concentration so I stopped my attempt to keep track of him.

Once the work was completed, I closed my sight again and felt the warmth of my socks on my feet and the pressure of my bed against my heels. I wiggled my toes and reopened my eyes. I was only me.

*Now, where is Gene?* He was not in his body. *God, why is this so hard for me?* I wondered, this being the most extreme experience of this kind I had ever encountered.

Unknowingly, I had fallen asleep, worn out from the experience. I was awakened by Gene's return. *Where'd you go?* I asked gently.

*I don't know where I was. It was even more confusing than before,* he said, visually referring to a recent storm he had experienced, one different than his own. *Another visitor is coming,* he said, seemingly without the energy to move to connect.

I had some vision left in which to see who approached Gene, having recently been in his body. The visitor's long, deep-red hair offset her brown freckles sprinkled warmly across her cheeks. She did not have on makeup, and the glow of her green eyes that had been crying were surrounded by short, wet eyelashes even though her face had been wiped dry.

*Well, let's try again. Go lie down in your body and see if you can connect with her,* I suggested. This visitor, the first one close to Gene's age, was clearly emotional. Her body language gave way to an intimate familiarity between them. Her focus was intense and revealed her selfless manner toward Gene. She existed without concern about how his situation would change her life, and she did not buffer against the ever-present vibration of orneriness that he held. This person accepted Gene as Gene!

*I don't recognize her,* he said in his exhaustion, still disoriented. Giving up, he said, *I don't feel any difference.*

*You're just worn out,* I repeated. *Wherever you went took a lot out of you.* I paused briefly as flashes of where Gene had been entered my thoughts. They were not coming from him but from the visitor. The storm he had been in involved mending things with this woman. The memories I witnessed were of intimate conversations, time spent laughing, and of moments her and Gene had planned for their future.

This was her! *You need to concentrate.*

She leaned in and kissed him. Regardless of his protest, it was apparent to me that he knew her. I felt a distinct change in Gene's vibration with that kiss. His body went from a smooth and even thrumming to a frenzied pulsation. It reminded me of how a person feels energetically when they have a fever, but a little different. I tried to remain calm, thinking this was the moment of change.

*This person feels different,* I told him again. *Lie down.*

As he did, his right arm connected.

*This is different!* he exclaimed, feeling bolstered by this sudden change. Thousands of tiny sparks lit up in his body. It was not just a single chakra at a time; it was every tiny aspect of every single chakra. He was absolutely open to her presence.

I watched the resonance between them. His hypersensitivity towards her, his rate of energetic exchange increased. This was not a passive relationship between friends; this was an active, caring connection. This was unmistakably love!

Suddenly, I was back in my own thoughts, no longer connected. I smiled, knowing this was what he was living for, having witnessed this deeper, cleaner love.


I lost contact with Gene for a couple of days while his energy worked with his body to repair the tiny brain bleeds. When we reconnected, I was glad to find him. *Not dead! Two thumbs up! Whoo!* I cheered for him. This time he laughed, appreciating my humor.

With his energy and physical body connected, we could communicate on a different telepathic level. Gene, who carried a ton of subconscious information about me in his body because of our connection, thought it interesting that he had ended up at a hospital in my area because of their cardiac specialties, the same hospital I had been in many times.

# The Coma

Later, I questioned the role I played in Gene's life, wondering how much of it was really necessary for him to be okay. After all, I believe it is love that heals. The whole experience supported a larger belief of mine—that we tend to work better in groups, even if we could go the road alone just fine.

The experience also supported another personal need of mine—a wake-up call. Having worked primarily with the deceased, I had grown complacent, assuming I could not create change in their human experiences since they were dead. Helping them still had not brought me closer to my goal of ending suffering on earth for the living. In hindsight, I thought my only task was to enlighten them, as Alma had enlightened me, and help them cross over to the next plane.

Gene reminded me of a truth I had embraced as a child—there is something unique and amazing in the power of the human mind and heart. We have in us the will to survive under the worst of circumstances. This strength is driven by a single vibration, known to us as love. If fully unlocked, love, in all its complexity, could stop people from passing at the very moment of death. I believe we have only just scratched the surface of this power.

With that in mind, Gene's adventure reinforced my desire to help others still living to find freedom from suffering like I had. I wanted others to awaken to this reality, to see how to move past their ability to simply survive and choose real living. I was now inspired to make sure others would understand that life is full of joy and light in every moment.

# Chapter Dedication

In dedication to Gene, for sharing your journey with me. I look forward to meeting you in person one day.

I am grateful for these experiences that have brought me so rapidly along this journey. I learned more in a short period of time than I ever could have imagined. In the moment, they were intense and sometimes seemingly unbearable. Your willingness to keep me company while I figured it out gave me strength. Your desire to live caused me to push my boundaries past what I thought was possible. The knowledge and understanding that followed our encounter is priceless. Thank you.

# *Chapter Eight*

# ECHINACEA PUPUREA, OR THE PURPLE CONE FLOWER

Las Vegas, winter 2011

*J*amie and I had become acquainted when she attended an enlightenment class[22] I taught at Whole Foods. As an artist, she would hit the occasional creative block, becoming incapable of manifesting the product necessary to make the financial living she knew was at her fingertips. After the class, we met a couple of times to see what could be done energetically to keep her artistic flow open.

During one conversation, we discussed how her mother, Mona, had struggled with breast cancer year after year. Her condition had recently changed.

"Can you see why she's getting worse?" Jamie inhaled rapidly. "Something must have changed that we can't find. She's had this condition for twenty years and managed to overcome it." There was another

---

22. In this class, I taught methods to increase one's own internal light content and to use it for one's personal benefit.

rapid inhale as she considered her thoughts. Looking inside herself for the answer, she added, "Maybe the energetic methods we talked about can help her."

Jamie was brilliant, thoughtful, and insightful. I sat staring at no one in particular for a moment as I considered her request. I did not feel compelled by Mona's spirit to make any changes in her life, although I did feel compelled to support Jamie, both in her work and in her life.

'YES' had become my daily mantra. I focused on saying yes as often as possible, so I could open myself to new experiences. Therefore, even though Mona's spirit did not beckon me, I agreed to see her, curious to learn what was possible.

As I considered the request, I realized the idea of working with her mother fit the journey I was exploring. Currently, my work had focused on cancer. Synchronistically, I was handed information from all directions—the universe had me running into doctors who were considering other forms of treatment for patients; I had several family members diagnosed with cancer who needed support; and people randomly asked me if I had found a way to heal cancer. I was indeed actively helping people with cancer find wellness. This request from Jamie, though, seemed to hold a different motivation from my work with cancer; it was not about prolonging her mother's life.

When Mona first came to my house, I found something unexpected in her physical energy. It pulled at my thoughts, causing me to reference a storybook character. This character, a troll, rescues a fairy, and at the end of the book is considered a hero.

From the way Jamie had described her, I had expected to meet someone much like Jamie herself—light and sprite-like, who could easily fly off to her next adventure. Instead, before me was a very dense, heavy, thick human body. Her face lacked emotion or shine. Her skin was clay-like, her mouth a straight line under her bulbous nose. This woman was in direct contrast to Jamie, who had a pert little nose which floated above an uplifting smile that lit up her whole face, even her tiny, slightly-pointed chin.

In addition, Mona was shorter, with thick ankles and wrists, her entire body a rectangle, completely absent of the curvaceous, joyful existence represented by Jamie. Mona appeared to be of the earth—heavy and solid like the ground, while Jamie appeared to be of the sky—flitting and floating along in her life. It appeared Jamie would float away if she were not held to the earth by some heavy, unseen weight. The weight was most likely her concern for her mother, keeping her grounded in this way.

Even with all the contrast and contradictions that separated them, I could see a direct, equal connection between their hearts. The connection felt awesome in size, overflowing with a purity of respect and love not often seen. Perhaps that was why Jamie saw her mother with such brightness and joy; it was the same way in which she saw herself.

I moved through the session, scanning Mona for what might be driving the recent change, my hands hovering an inch above her body. Surprisingly, I was not at all attracted to the infected area; her breasts and lungs seemed perfectly at ease with her life. I was repeatedly drawn to her head, where I eventually found a spot in Mona's brain behind her right ear.

"This is it. This is why she isn't doing well—this space in her brain." I paused to feel its energy again.

The way the spot pulsed was unique. The field of energy it formed cluttered Mona's thoughts, pressing her into confusion. Careful not to speak out loud, I listened to my thoughts: *This is the spot that will eventually be the cause of Mona's death, this tumor.*

Out loud to Jamie and her mother, I shared, "This space in your brain is much more urgent than the breast cancer." I wanted to be sure they understood the importance, so I added, "You're going to want to get it checked out much sooner than later. Tomorrow, if possible."

Jamie believed in me and what was possible, even before I believed in myself. Her proof came when she and her mother left that first session. Jamie was anxious as she experienced the oppressive feeling that something was terribly wrong with her mother, and she pushed Mona towards calling her doctor right away.

Mona, when confronted, admitted to Jamie that she knew about the spot. It was a tumor her doctors had found during her most recent MRI. Having noticed the anomaly, the idea was to keep tabs on it and check on it in six months when Mona would have her next full body scan.

The reason for watching its growth instead of simply operating was due to the tumor's location. Surgery would mean removing part of Mona's skull and brain, and possibly damaging her ability to function. Mona had advised her doctors, but not yet told her family, that she was done fighting through situations that took everything from her. She believed she had already given enough of herself to this world and was not afraid of the next world to come; she knew death was not the end.

More than a year later, Jamie lay stiff on my massage table. She appeared to be incapable of releasing the tension in her body. Her feelings of fear stood in the way of letting go of anything.

"But if I let go," she inhaled, using short upper chest breaths, "if I stop hanging onto these things," she paused again to breathe, incapable of taking a breath deep enough to finish her sentence, "maybe I'll lose the important things I need to keep."

I offered Jamie a tissue. She was coming to terms with her own fears surrounding the topic of death. She opted to dab her cheeks with the sleeve of her sweater instead; it was the sweater she had received as a gift from her mother.

It had been a year since Mona had passed. Jamie was afraid that if she did not somehow constantly refer to her mother's life with some public proclamation of support, Mona's twenty-plus years of battling cancer would fade into nothing, as if it had never existed. To Jamie, never existing was even worse than being forgotten. If Mona's fight never existed then Jamie would lose her mental support and the struggles of her own life would stagnate her.

## Echinacea Pupurea, or the Purple Cone Flower

Jamie spoke about her fears regarding her work. She minimized her value, allowing clients to underpay her for the same work she had created in the past for more money. I tried to focus on her questions about money, but they seemed hollow, as if she were using the distraction to avoid talking about her mother's death. I needed to deal with the elephant in the room, if only to assuage my own feelings of unfulfillment.

"Can you feel her?" I asked.

"Yes," she said.

*Hmm, only a simple answer. Should I press, or should I digress?*

Maybe I was the only one suffering under this pressure. Perhaps it was my own fascination that made me think it was important for Jamie to address her feelings regarding her mother's passing.

Then I saw it—a single, tiny tear fell from the outside corner of her left eye.

I placed a hand lightly on her shoulder and encouraged her to continue.

"I feel Mom all the time. I want to know what happened to her after she left her body. I can't ask myself; it just feels too difficult to deal with," she admitted.

"Let me help you." I offered. As soon as the words passed my lips my brain freaked. *This behavior is not mine! I never volunteer to address the dead for the living.*

I held reservations when it came to sharing the conversations I had with the other side. Energetically, I understand them very well; the vibrational exchange makes sense between the two of us. When the time comes to alter the translations so a third party can be included, the words I choose can throw us completely out of sync, grabbing focus with something I consider insignificant to the communication.

For instance, if I said 'dog' instead of 'cat,' it would create an issue of trust, which would get in the way of everything else. Persons listening would no longer be able to hear the essence of what I was sharing. In the past, the idea of harming someone, assuming they might feel misled, or solidifying my own fear of being misunderstood, would make me so uncomfortable I would have forgone the entire experience.

*This is too much,* I thought. *I have spent my entire life hiding who I am, and now...*I trailed off, letting my fear of transparency hold me captive. *Relax,* I thought. *This is Jamie. You trust her, and you want her to have this gift.*

Now it was my turn to inhale too many times. I realized I was willing to be vulnerable for her. I knew that to be effective, I had to strip away all my barriers. The more vulnerable and open I am, the more accurate I can be.

To be this vulnerable in front of someone else, well, that feels like standing on the stage with a full house in the Gershwin Theatre, naked, in front of people who are not expecting you to be naked! *VERY uncomfortable.*

I stopped my shallow breathing and pulled in a deep breath. It was amazing how easily this action pushed aside my fears. I closed my eyes and I opened to the space most people call 'the other side.' I had learned this space was not somewhere else; it was simply more awareness of the 'here,' without the 'now' connection.

*Mona.* I sent the vibration out, short, clear, and clean. I hoped to see where she was, or to at least connect to someone who knew where her transition had taken her.

*Hello,* Mona responded.

*Hello, it's so exciting to hear from you directly!* I said as a smile moved across my face, joyful in anticipation.

Mona immediately stood out as an anomaly to me. As our connection opened, the feeling of close proximity occurred. I was used to this feeling with the living. All the other departed souls I had communicated with until this point claimed they were moving upwards after they passed, rather than remaining on the Earth. The only time I felt this close proximity with the deceased, until now, had been when they had not yet transitioned. I tried to pull Mona in further to gain an understanding only to feel her energy flit away from me.

*It's been awhile.* I continued in my attempt to engage Mona. Many people kept in touch with me even after their passing. Mona was not one of them. When alive, she was private, barely sharing or connecting unless she was in my physical presence, and, even then, only in very limited ways. Since having passed, she had not changed that part of herself. I considered if I pushed too hard I would be intruding in her private space.

I pulled back and asked, *Where are you?*

*I am home.* She willingly showed me the sun about to rise. A crisp wind had settled up against the presence of the warmth created by the rising sun as it peaked along the horizon. Mona's excitement was focused on the expansive field of wild flowers sprawling out before her that would soon be waking under her tutelage.

*I am here with Jamie,* I said. *Can you tell us what you have been up to? She wants to make sure you are well.* I flashed the visual of Jamie in my home, reminding Mona of her own visit fourteen months prior.

*I don't remember you,* she said, mentally moving away from Jamie and me.

Her physical motion changed. In my connection to Mona, I felt her fly away, passing over the field of flowers. My balance changed with hers, my contact to the earth felt instinctive and true. I felt Mona, Earth, and myself simultaneously. We were one.

*I have work to do,* Mona chirped, as she flitted away.

*Wait!* I requested. I paused for a moment and considered how to get past her barrier. *Ah, my vibration! I can show you myself, as I am to Earth.*

Having received several vibrational gifts of identity,[23] I used these gifts in moments when others did not recognize me as someone to be welcomed. I pulled into my energy my gift received from Mother Earth, and embodied aspects of the gift while mirroring the essence of Earth herself.

*Ah, Shabnam*[24]*! I reference you as I do myself. You are of the Mother, Earth,* Mona's thought spilled from her energy with a tilted head.

---

23. An identity in this sense is a name that cannot be translated and which carries historic information to identify me and my relationship to Mother, Earth while in the space of Mother Earth. See footnote 27 for Mother, Earth.

24. One of the identities given to me by Mother, Earth to identify me as equal in my compassion to Earth's love for humanity. Literally translates to 'Morning Dew.'

Shabnam was a title I had received from prior communication with the spirit of Mother Earth[25]. This gift, this recognition as Shabnam, was given to me so others of the Earth could see me as Earth recognizes me; to understand and value me for more than my humanity, the part of me that extends past the limits of this body. It allowed those committed to Earth, as it did Mona, to reference me energetically as a presence preserving Earth's wellness, and to recognize me without my offering an explanation.

Mona, whose tilted head denoted her respect, continued the blessing with a vibration of love and gratitude for my connection to our Mother, Earth. *I know you in this realm as the one who pulls the heat from pain so the giving waters of life can condense and the weary can be fed. You are the cause of the dew that awakens my flowers to a fresh start! And yet, I know you beyond that.*

She paused as our current connection brought her a familiar regrouping of memories.

*I feel my daughter with me.*

She was then aware of who I was to her in this current moment, what our past experiences had been together, and memories of Jamie flowed in without effort.

*Please, tell my child I am Breena, living as Shea.*

I shared the phrase as spoken and then attempted to translate it, "In other words, she's working side-by-side with Mother Nature. Your mom says hello."

I half expected Jamie to balk at the strangeness of this entire situation, this being my initiation into what might be the fairy realm.

Super excited about Mona and what she had shared, and in an effort not to overwhelm Jamie, I telepathically pulled back. Because I pulled away from my intuitive truth, my brain and emotions were left with-

---

25. 'Mother, Earth' is an honorable way to address Mother Earth. This is not just a personification, rather it shows she has the same existence as a human being. The use of a comma shows a dimensional distinction; the fairy has a closer relationship to Earth as the actual mother, instead of how most people take her for granted and do not have this connection to her as our mother.

out the support from my intuition. This caused me to question myself. I wondered if I was making it up because of how I had previously viewed Mona as belonging to the Earth while she was alive. I mean, come on, I had already perceived her as resembling a fairytale creature!

"Is she happy?" Jamie asked without skipping a beat, oblivious to my mental discomfort regarding fairies. Maybe I did not sound as strange as I thought, or maybe it was Jamie's own enlightenment that kept her interested.

*I am well, here on Earth,* Mona answered. *I am in the dale.*

The picture I had received of the dale seemed to be of a familiar place, one connected to Jamie's heart.

Mona's presence was felt through me, amplified as if she was standing beside me, alive and incarnate. The amplification was part of Earth's gift to me as Shabnam. This connection opened a doorway to Mona's earthly dimension. Even with the strength of this connection however, Jamie could not hear her mother's words.

*What is your work?* I asked of her mother, trying to get more specific information.

Now, translating aloud, in real time, I shared what her mother said, knowing the risk of speaking without a filter.

*It is so wonderful,* Mona said to me. *My work is to raise the vibration of life. My job is to teach flowers to bloom. I love helping the flowers learn to look with their eyes, to openly receive the sunlight; with their mouths, to taste the dew. My mother, Nature, is teaching me to bring these miracles into their existence.*

Without any notice Mona flitted away, saying absently, *I have a lot to do.*

I felt Jamie raise out of her skin, energetically following Shea, her mother, as she moved away from us. Jamie was not quite ready to let her go. Aware of this, Shea turned abruptly to add one last thing before closing the connection, becoming more like Mona than she had during any other point of our communication.

*Tell my daughter that, to my greatest surprise, the purple flowers are the hardest to teach to bloom.*

Then she was gone.

As I shared this last bit with Jamie, she burst into tears.

I must have been insensitive allowing myself to forget this was once Jamie's living, breathing, loved one. I was completely wrapped up in our connection with Mona—now Shea—and I was fascinated with what I could see of her world. Earth was beautiful, magical even. I had forgotten that in front of me, Jamie was having her own experience with the communication.

Jamie took a moment to gain her composure. When she was ready, she shared the significance of her mother's last statement.

Her words came in a whisper. "It was too much for me to hope for, after all these years of her suffering, of her living with cancer, that I would find my mother in her happily ever after." She paused to wipe her face again, tears still streaming. Looking me in the eyes, she continued, "This is how I know you were communicating with her. She loved all flowers, but the purple ones were her favorite!"

I reached out and grasped her hand, both of us knowing there was no way I could have known that fact. I smiled, tears in my eyes, greatly moved by her sharing.

Jamie and I remained together and she shared animated tales about her mother including her love for nature, specifically for flowers. As Mona's sickness worsened over the years, she could no longer keep anything alive. All her energy was funneled into sustaining her own life. Her touch, seemingly tied to her health, had soured, leaving her unable to grow things as she had before cancer.

Jamie comically explained how the family had tried to keep the garden alive for her mother, but unfortunately, there was not a single green thumb in the bunch. Her mother was the one with the magic touch, the one for whom the flowers had bloomed.

"She's living her dream," Jamie said wiping away the last of her tears. "She is tending the gardens of the fairies. You know what she said about her name?"

I recalled Mona had said, 'I am Breena, living as Shea.'

"It's from a book Mom and I wrote when I was a kid, when I asked about her Celtic heritage. For us, it means she is living in the land of the fairies, being magic!"

"And the dale!" Jamie sounded even more excited. "I had drawn the picture of the dale from a photo of hers. We used to tell stories to each other about it at bedtime. In her later years, she had said if she could just have that back—her garden with her magic touch—it would be her Heaven on Earth."

Jamie, very much an enlightened being, can communicate with her mother herself; her grief and fears of the unknown blocked her mother's words. This is normal, based on our socialized beliefs about death. Having myself released these beliefs, I have a different experience with those who pass.

I am not unique in my ability, I am simply more open to it because of my firsthand knowledge about death. We can all hear and follow the lives of our loved ones as they transition and move on to their next adventures.

# Chapter Dedication

With gratitude for everyone who works without our knowing. Thank you for our beautiful world.

# Chapter Nine
## EVERY TIME AN ANGEL GETS HER WINGS

Las Vegas, September 2013

"How do you do it? How do you hear her?" Javi moved in closer to my face, his shoulders rising as he shifted his weight off his seat and onto his hands. I felt him searching even with my eyes closed. I was attempting to speak to Annabella, his aunt. Annabella was in a coma.

Communicating telepathically with the unconscious was easy. It gave me a clearer picture of the person's life without the everyday perception and focus issues that distracted me from their truths, like fear of loss or self-victimization.

"Well, since I haven't met her in person, I will use you to find her. First, I move into your energy to feel what she's like. Since each person is unique, all I have to do is recognize her vibration as you do, then I feel her; I know her." I gave a little shrug, not knowing what else to say.

"Vibration? You mean like a drum beat?" Javi's voice rose as he squinted in confusion. He often played the bongos at his family's gatherings and this did not make sense to him.

"I hadn't thought about it enough to be able to put it into words." I paused, and reached into my memories to see what thoughts and observations repeated when I used this method. "So, it's like this, each person has an identifying wavelength. Imagine your body made of light and nothing else. Your 3-D light form can be mapped and recognized for its unique code. It's like what science did, getting our DNA from our blood. If I mathematically translated what I experience, science could program it into a computer and create an image of the person. It's that specific."

I paused to let this new information sink in. Javi needed my support to accept my words. After I felt the necessary shift, I continued. "When I find her, I can say a face-to-face hello. She will see me in her mind's eye as I represent my energetic self."

Javi leaned back. "You have to feel my stuff before you can get to hers? Do you go through me the whole time?" Javi, already familiar with how it took a ton of energy for me to handle connecting to the energy of others, worried how it would drain me.

His concern was valid. Although I made the process look easy, it was complicated and would leave me weak for hours.

Working with healing energies brought a specific level of risk. In the moment of exchange, I connect to a person's past, present, and future as well as to his or her physical, mental, and emotional issues simultaneously. If I hung out solely in telepathic vibrations using my psychic abilities, there was no risk. If I stayed solely in observation of body, or only in listening to divinity, then I was without risk. When I connect with the intention of wellness, however, it is different.

The connection with intention creates motion in the stagnant energy system of the other person. My motivation is to observe their wellness prior to the imbalance. From there, I deliberately ignite change. It takes constant vigilance to maintain my individuality during a body, mind, and spirit communication.

In addition, creating some forms of wellness require the vibrations to be embodied by me for understanding, and then translated back to the person. In order to achieve wellness, the body, mind, spirit, and energetic system must realize the same truths simultaneously. For this type of embodiment work with the living, I access a person's DNA and translate a cell's photons—light packets—into words. It is this translation of the photons, while embodying a person's energetic vibration as my own, that puts me at risk of accepting their baggage as my own and losing my individuality.

So far, my experience had not moved me past this risk. Light, as a key component to creation, still has qualities beyond the comprehension of the human brain. It can, without understanding, create lasting change once experienced.

With my connection forming to Annabella, I was receiving into my consciousness information from my higher self that I believed she needed. I could already feel her divine need to understand this process of assimilating light. I opened directly into a conversation with her without a hello by sharing some of Earth's energetic history.

*Historically, mankind was designed to absorb light in the same fashion we currently absorb food—as a source of nutrition. A day came in our history when Earth and her inhabitants were separated from divinity. Disconnected from its source, our divine consciousness was at risk of perishing. We were forced to create the Universal Conscious Mind to survive. Without our divine connection, we started recycling light in our own system to hold onto it until the day it could be returned to the divine. Although this guaranteed no one would experience the final loss of existence[26], this constant recycling created a degradation of the souls' light energy.*

I felt Annabella's consciousness being drawn into me. She was, as I had been, timid when facing destiny. It was our sameness that allowed these words to come into my thoughts to be shared.

---

26. This is beyond what our common definition of death means: a person's energetic existence is not returned to divinity. The information created by their experience is gone. There is no record or connection. The only way a person would continue to exist would be through the memories of people who knew them.

I said, *At times, I push through the Universal Conscious Mind to connect directly to divinity. When I do this, I find myself living with a different light content than other inhabitants of Earth. I can clearly recognize how energy is displaced through obligation, how it drives suffering. Working from a place of divinity, I am omnipresence and balanced at all times. I can only view perfection in all things, including humanity. Confronted with humanity's desires to change, and knowing there is no need to change, creates an unmanageable gap.*

*There are too many missing steps between the advanced state of divinity and human existence. Trying to bridge that gap would be like trying to teach astrophysics to a two-year-old. The lack of knowledge and experiences is too vast.*

I paused and focused on Annabella. *You are going to need this next bit of information. When beings who already exist in divinity try to help humans, they do not recognize that there is something missing. After you cross over, you will no longer be influenced by the Universal Conscious Mind. You will no longer relate to humanity. Those on the other side look at us with an inability to understand that our freewill choices are driven from a place of loss or pain. They assume we can choose to be different as easily and completely as we choose to change our shoes.*

*Also, after you transition, you will work similarly to me. When working with humans, you will be unaware that there is a component of divinity missing in our Ketheric Templates for our Sacral Chakras. Hang onto this awareness.*

*What I am asking you to remember is that this missing component is necessary. Without it we cannot know all the details of another's light content. Because humans don't have this component, people must consume the light of others for understanding. This is why, when we bond with others, we accept a copy of their light as part of our own; it is in the consumption that we truly know each other.*

I thought about how consuming the light of others put me at risk of losing my individuation. In the beginning, it took days for this energy to dissipate and leave me. As an empath, when I resonated too strongly with the content of the light, I often found myself accepting it as my own. Now obligated to this energy, which was usually some kind of block, I had to work to release it again or else I would find myself holding symptoms of disease.

I explained, *The way I reduce the risk of losing my individuality is by simultaneously pulling in my own source of light while consuming the light of others. It is exhausting, but necessary to be able to return to the truth of myself.*

I considered our dilemma. Humanity was now unable to understand other's light content without consuming it. This had contributed to our loss of 'The Art of Relating'—the telepathic and energetic communications that keep us in constant contact with each other. Due to misuse, fear, and contamination, our awareness of these more metaphysical methods of connection died out. We were left without this divine, impassioned, universal conscious connection with one another.

*My willingness and ability to risk all that I am during this process has made me an expert at what I do. This open, vulnerable connection makes it possible to translate a unique resonance of vibration back to a person to be recognized and used for wellness. It also means that when I finish the process, I must spend a quantified amount of time adjusting and realigning myself with my truth. The obvious depletion can be seen all over my face. It is a kind of unavoidable exhaustion that presses me deeply into the need for rest.*

I felt Annabella's final alignment click into place with me, a fully conscious connection. I continued to express my work to her.

*When I work in this way, I consciously take on another person's energy. In a lesser form, most people do this every day without realizing that when they resonate with a person's story, they take on the energy of that person. The Art of Relating gives us a felt sense of what another person's experiences are before we know their story, and it opens us to an awareness that we would not have otherwise known.*

Javi put his fingertips on my hand. He knew when I drifted off because the look on my face changed from lively to flat, and he only needed to apply a very light touch to bring me back. He could not know I had already been communicating with Annabella, but he suspected as much.

Picking up the conversation with Javi, I replied, "It starts off going through you, yes. Once I know Annabella's energetic signature, I can ask for my own permission and connect directly."

This was the point in the process where most people got nervous and worried I would see too much—their insecurities, regrets, and embarrassing moments. Javi already knew his privacy was safe with me. Socially, I enjoyed the part of my personality that others considered to be nosey. Even so, snooping telepathically was a no-no. I found it to be impolite. I knew people lived with the relative expectation and belief that privacy was real and should be valued.

I had already released many of my false beliefs and reduced my need for privacy, knowing a day would come when this illusion of privacy would have to go. Until then, to help others feel comfortable, I taught myself to continuously hold the veil of privacy in place. As humans, we often fear the unknown because our brains have no idea what life would look like if all our baggage was out on the table.

"What do you do if she doesn't give you permission?" he asked.

"Then I continue to talk to her through you or I ask for a delegate. A delegate can be a being or an orb; it is an intelligence that has the right to represent the people who are unavailable or too far out of space and time to be reached. But, since you and I are friends, once she feels me, she'll feel our connection and likely be okay with speaking to me." I opened my eyes. "Really, it's more of a manners thing. I can recognize anyone, anywhere, anytime; we all can with practice. I just choose to do it from a place of respecting the views of privacy and with an invitation instead of an intrusion into their personal space."

This courtesy, which supported the social constructs in dealing with the living, was unnecessary with the comatose and the dead; the freedom to be me could be more completely expressed with them. Still, I had worked long and hard to perfect inviting people and energies to communicate with me, and I used these manners instead of stomping in like a heavy-footed ogre.

The universe, always a good teacher, kept me busy by making sure I mastered a gentle method of connecting, like the one involving Annabella in this moment.

I called to mind a student who arrived late to every class. She told me how horrible it was when I pushed telepathically into her head to see if she was coming or not. No one else in the group felt me as intrusive, and we realized it was her own fears about controlling her time and of being judged that made her feel me this way. My compassionate nature kept me ever vigilant when it concerned the experience of others. So, to avoid unnecessary interruptions by starting the class without her, I positioned myself to *ask* her telepathically instead of continuing to take the information from her thoughts. I realized, by holding my energy at half the distance, we became equal, thus eliminating the feeling of barging in which she disliked.

Through a myriad of those kinds of experiences, I mastered two-way telepathic communication and realized it was in the asking and then allowing the other person to answer that brought them into the conversation.

I closed my eyes again as Javi repeated his original question. "What do you think? Is my aunt going to be okay?" Annabella was the oldest of his mother's sisters. Even in her late eighties her family still prayed for her to live. I think it had something to do with their social conditioning—they believed that for a good life, one needed to fight to live for as long as possible.

Their conditioning left them unable to simply observe the experience of their loved one, and drove them to the opinion that death was something to be mourned, not celebrated. Instead of seeing death as a graduation, or as an opportunity to move into a reality without a physical body, they experienced death as a sign of personal failure. They rationalized death, creating concepts that superficially seem reasonable and valid but were unrelated to the truth, and created a stronger need for the stages of grief.

I realized that before the stages of grief were experienced, the answers I gave the living regarding the passing of a loved one often conflicted with their beliefs. This left them with a feeling of emptiness; whereas I, knowing what it meant to die, experienced satisfaction from observing and supporting their loved one's death process.

Due to the interference of grief and false beliefs, I was convinced that leaving out parts of a loved one's transition was necessary. I skipped over what I knew in my heart to be very important facts, because my brain believed I was sharing too much too soon with the living. My actions created a mental conflict in me as well.

I heard Annabella chime in, *Why do you do this? Javi is your friend.*

*I don't want to cause him suffering,* I told her. *I have seen the mental struggle that these kinds of truths create. He holds his false beliefs close to his chest, and I think he's better off without my confirming your upcoming death. Maybe Javi isn't ready to hear what we know.*

My gift of discernment made it possible to feel Annabella's chosen path—she was not going to live.

*When he realizes the truth, he will be happy for me.* I enjoyed that she had already accepted the idea of death without struggle. Those who embrace their passing have a fuller transition than those who became stuck in fear.

*Sharing what I know without having all the human answers to what happens to you next doesn't seem to be such a great idea. I mean, I know what's happening, but putting it into words for someone who is blocked with confusion and who considers death as loss, well, that doesn't make much sense. They just aren't ready! Javi doesn't know what he is asking—I do.* I had seen the reactions of others. Was I not responsible for his reactions if I told him things he could not understand?

Connected through Javi, I felt his burdens as my own. I prefaced my sharing with diplomacy and control. I could feel I was out of balance when I took away his freewill by choosing to withhold what I knew to be true. I did not give him a chance to be responsible; I decided for him. In this moment, my fear that I could harm him created a greater burden than the blessing my faith in truth supplied.

In some ways, I believed by not sharing I would no longer be responsible for people's feelings of despair; that I could remain blameless for sharing and they would awaken at their own pace. Even though I understood it was a person's need to push out that caused their reactions, I still stacked my beliefs to reflect my preference of Javi not experiencing pain or a sense of loss. I could have, instead, given my beliefs an order that filled me with strength and courage, but I did not. I remained in fear.

In that moment, while I considered my own perception about being responsible for other people's responses to information I delivered to them, I felt a gentle touch from Annabella. It was so slight that I easily could have overlooked it. Her touch hinted to a knowingness I lacked—something I had blocked as I held my beliefs of obligation. I believed I needed to meet the needs of others over my own.

*This feeling, I recognize it.* I grew excited as I realized the method she used. *This is my method! It's the same method I use to plant seeds in others who are not ready to hear what I know to be true in this moment. How masterful you are! These seeds are what make it possible for a person to eventually awaken to their truth. I always place them at the junction, where a habitual behavior can be looked at with new thought and eventually shift into freewill.*

Although it seems obvious looking back that I could have grown the seed she planted in that moment for understanding, I did not. I was not ready. I continued martyring myself by holding the suffering of others close to my heart, staying mired in my delusion. Later, from this single slight touch, I realized it was not my sharing that made me responsible for the reaction of a person, it was my own fear and belief that I could harm them that made me responsible.

Aware again of Javi's searching, I kept my eyes closed—not because it was necessary to see what I already knew, but to give myself space to consider my next step. I continued this in-depth conversation with

Annabella without including Javi. I still feared I could harm him, so my brain kept pushing out the details leaving me with nothing to share.

Behind the scenes, my discussion with Annabella moved to her swift transition that would follow her imminent death. I was not concerned about the amount of time the conversation took because the sending of information from one angelic being to another occurs in the flash of an eye. In person, there is often an awareness of this transfer, but when we are not in person we assume it is only our own thoughts, a sudden unexplainable lift in spirits, or a subconscious speculation that guides our contemplation.

When the right combination of circumstances arises, instead of a painful, vulnerable feeling of being exposed, the experience of connecting with a person energetically on an angelic level feels like magic. We rise and fall through the experience with a sense of euphoria. We can allow ourselves to understand the exchange in the moment, but more often, we reserve the reveal of the information the experience brought us for later, only sensing in the moment that there is something for us in the other person.

Annabella expressed that she was becoming her family's keepsake. Because of my fears around expressing the truth to Javi, my connection with Annabella came as a swift kick to the heart rather than as euphoria.

*I don't think the next step in your journey can be shared with Javi. How would I even begin to explain what a keepsake is?* I asked. I could feel what it was, but my brain had no words to bring about comprehension.

She replied, *I will be the family's Heritage Angel. I will remain on Earth.*

*Oh!* I thought. *Yeah, it won't be easy to tell Javi you are going to die, only to stick around as a ghost looking over your family's shoulders. Instead, I think I will settle for something bordering on truth that meets more of my needs.*

"She's not leaving this Earth any time soon," I told him bluntly. My internal hesitation left me feeling pressure as I moved away from my truth. This was becoming more and more obvious. *I can't leave things this way.* I decided to send the vibration of her eminent death directly to his energetic system. I bypassed spoken words with what I knew to be true. I wanted to save Javi from my misleading words and guarantee he would not suffer any trauma.

Still, I wondered the whole time why I was letting fear control me. *I am going to have to work through this.* I had too many beliefs standing between my thoughts and my actions. I wanted the same freedom with the living that I enjoyed with the dead.

Annabella felt me craft the vibration for Javi. She understood that death was okay and that his fears of such were unnecessary.

*That's a good vibration for him,* she shared, *since many in his life will be passing soon.*

*UGH! See what I mean? How can I share that with him? How can I kick him when he's down?* I told Annabella that this news would crush someone who did not know how to live in the moment.

*Christix...* I noticed Annabella's additional inflections used to personalize my name. These inflections, when translated to spoken word, made it possible for me to recognize who was communicating. *I want your ability to build a vibration. I often find I succumb to the vibrations of others and change who I am. It blocks my ability to self-create.*

*It is my acceptance of truth regarding my responsibility of freewill that allows me to build a unique vibration for others. After recognizing nothing is real, that everything is a choice, and that creation is our own, I work with my ego and take responsibility for my own balance. I can no more change a person's vibration than they can change mine, but if I understand the imbalances, I can offer them a vibration that restores balance and they will accept it. As long as I am in my truth, and acting from center balance whereby I speak the truth I feel compelled to share, I am not influencing anyone. A person's choice has nothing to do with me.*

I still remember thinking this clearly. A person's choice is his or her own, and yet I carried the belief that I was responsible for how they felt based on my behavior. Annabella knew this too, and yet my brain blocked the entire part of our conversation that would have allowed me to move forward in that moment and let go of that delusion.

*And how do you separate yourself after the vibration is built? Wouldn't it become part of you as well?* Annabella inquired.

This was a good point. If I were not in my own freewill, knowing I was not responsible for the emotions of others, it was likely I would take on whatever vibrations came in contact with me.

*Since I know clearly that I am a being of my own freewill, by releasing the burdens of obligation, false comfort, and delusion, I am able to see the separation between the vibrations of self and the ones I create for others.*

I relayed my response, knowing my process was part of the evolutionary path I had chosen when I accepted ascension of my angelic self into my physical form. *I still feel some conflict here that I can't quite work out yet, but when I came back into this body, I allowed for the greater good of this world to unfold into my heart, and then be reflected back to my head. When things don't completely make sense or they are still in conflict with beliefs I am working through, I fall back to my heart again to align my head. With the accurate communication from my heart to my head, I am whole. I can show you.*

I moved mentally into her space. *Here, let me take your hand and I will lead you.* Although I explain these things with physical action, in the ether there are no physical actions, only the motion of energy spilling out from me to others.

As I imagined myself taking hold of Annabella's hands, my own physical hands vibrated. I felt a slight tingle with pressure, warmth, and movement in my skin and muscles, even though I had done nothing more than think of our connection. With my thoughts, I gave Annabella an energetic imprint of my life that allowed her to witness my struggle with my own pain and how it had been resolved. It was in this vulnerable state of self, in my sharing and her receiving, where Annabella completed the cycle of love and compassion that I had learned during my own death. It was not through thought and understanding that she changed, it was through what I would later call 'I Become'—an energetic process that follows the I AM. Annabella, as my very first student to completely comprehend this level of compassionate relief, instantly became the part of humanity that makes the healing of others possible.

*Annabella, I want you to fully understand these exchanges were critical for my journey. At first it was the other side that pushed me with messages and feelings. They dropped them in suddenly to catch my attention. When I did not share the information I received, it became as much a body block for me as emotional pain was for others. As the block built up pressure, I felt more and more physical pain. Each time, the action of release left me feeling stronger, more stable and capable of sharing what I knew to be true. I was learning to be open when compelled. Over time I learned to recognize the energy of this on my own. Sharing, when compelled, was by far a more natural form of trust. Instead of trying to decide by beliefs and comparison when to be vulnerable, I waited until I was compelled to share the full expression of myself. I never have to trust if I am doing the right thing when I follow what I am compelled to do. It is not a thought; it is my natural state of being, an energetic process of interpersonal connections easily recognized when in a balanced state of being. It is a function of the Law of Attraction.*

For two days, I listened to Annabella share her endearing family stories, full of charm and innocent joy from her comatose place of residence. Though strange at first, witnessing the release of life through nonverbal communications—like this one with Annabella—had become normal. I heard things all the time by tuning into this band of vibrations. It was like listening to a radio; all I had to do was focus my thoughts while tied to the base of my core, and I could listen.

*I am excited to be the family's Heritage Angel,* I heard Annabella say as she returned to expand the concept of being a keepsake so I could understand it.

*Curious,* I met her statement with thoughts of comparison. *Will it be the same kind of angelic work I do helping people cross? Or maybe it is the same as the Guardians. Huh, I bet that's where people got the idea that family members are Guardian Angels! I bet they've been calling it the wrong thing for years.* I chuckled.

I was never more alive and free than when I was translating more and more of my energetic vocabulary, increasing my conscious awareness. Annabella, too, felt great joy as we realized we were the same; we were learning together, neither of us on our own.

*It is such a relief to have a confidant, someone who understands,* said Annabella.

I knew exactly what she meant. In general, my journey left me feeling separated from the world I once called mine. As my spiritual experiences appeared more unique and unreal to others, I felt what I shared distanced me instead of creating a connection. With the knowledge I had amassed, I was no longer relatable in casual conversations regarding spirituality. Knowing Annabella would not be alive in a body much longer did not even dampen our spirits. Having first met me before she transitioned into spirit, she helped me feel a greater connection to the living than I had felt in years. It was because of her willingness to communicate about these topics that I accepted the idea that I could find others still living who would be interested in sharing this journey.

Still smiling, I continued our conversation, *Please confirm my translation of the vibration. I want to be consciously aware of more.* I tugged gently at her physical body. It was an energetic form of play; the action helped me manage my humanity while I lingered so far energetically out of my physical body.

*I want to bring this awareness into words. I want to be able to explain the relationship between angelic abilities and vocations of the living.* I had known from a previous interaction with a Guardian Angel that they lived symbiotically with a human host and had never occupied a body or had a soul. Therefore, even if Annabella surrendered her soul to divinity upon death, she would not be the same as a Guardian since she had already occupied a body. Guardians connected to Earth through an existing, living human's earthly soul manifold[27]—which is basically a lesser copy of

---

27. The earthly soul manifold is a manifestation of our primary soul with some

our primary soul[28]. The earthly soul manifold gives Guardian Angels a portal to interact on Earth without a body or soul of their own to communicate from.

I waited to feel Annabella's defined vibration. Her response when translated into words was, *I have broken the chains that hold my family. There will be an end to our suffering.*

*Even more curious!* I sifted through everything I knew regarding our ability to bring an end to suffering; it was through enlightenment. By helping others see how they held themselves out of balance by not speaking truth or living in truth, they would realize the pressure of the energetic conflicts in their systems. If they paid enough attention, they would start to realize that this pressure was the precursor to energetic circular loops that kept them in patterns of suffering.

I nodded. *I get it! It's that whole 'acted upon by an outside force' concept. Once aware, we can bring healing light to their suffering. We end suffering by breaking repetition and obligation. We bring to their attention the need to release their narrowed focus. If they let go they can return to freewill.*

We, as humans, have very little desire to change anything unless we are acted upon by something or someone; without which, under the weight of our own pain, we might not even become aware that change is possible.

Annabella's action, her energy in existence, was the outside force that would begin the process of enlightening her family to the need for change.

*What an excellent idea!* I jumped up and down inside. *What if you can get people to see how they are holding back from being the full expression of themselves?* This was a major key to changing the world and ending suffering as we know it.

---

distinctions necessary to handle life on earth. The manifold is necessary to have a sensory experience and does not have the ability to destroy or damage the primary soul.

28. The primary soul is the soul created when we first separate from divinity. This is how we are created in God's image.

Becoming more and more aware of the implication, the light in my heart expanded. It reached a moment of expansion so great and exciting I thought I would burst. I had to let it go, and yet, I felt fear.

*It's okay,* said Annabella. *Release the belief that you need to keep your energy separate to maintain your identity.*

With her words, I realized I could be one with the world and still identify as me. No longer trying to constrain this light, I let it go. The light spread instantly out from me and enveloped the entire planet.

*And so it is!* Annabella exclaimed. *What a wonderful gift.*

I felt in agreement with her as she and I relaxed into the existence of this new light supporting the planet. This was a totally new and deliberate vibration I had constructed. Witnessing Annabella's generous gift to her family gave me a different courage, one I had not previously understood. It was the sacrifice of self without fear and it felt nice. The release of this vibration gave me a connection to others who had reached the same understanding. When Annabella moved on, I would draw the support here on Earth of others with like minds.

On the day of Annabella's passing, I asked if there was anything she wanted her family to know. I always hoped people would tell me things I could share; things that would in the moment make sense to their loved ones and give them comfort. To my dismay, free of the burdens while in their bodies, the dead often said things that seemed nonsensical to humanity, even though I could understand the information personally. Annabella was no different.

*Tell them that I am experiencing a lot of pain without my physical body.*

*Really!?* I thought, knowing no one would be happy to hear that. Not having had pain in my experiences of death or having seen it in the experience of any other death I had observed, her statement shook me. *Do you mean that separating from your body, being without a physical form, is causing you pain? Is the pain your own? I am going to need you to expand on that information if you want it to be shared.*

*No, it is not this person's pain I feel.* She was in transition now, her phrasing gave reference to the humanity of herself she was leaving behind. She was instead in the space of her full compassion referring to the pain she was now aware of in others. *I felt their windows of time and its burdens. I witnessed their whimsical feelings dissipate. Solamente para una nueva realidad (only for a new reality).* I felt the weight of her statement. I knew she was seeing the lives of her family pass before her, becoming aware of how they had given up their will in exchange for experiences of obligation. *They have no freedom.*

*Their narrowed focus, that's what you're witnessing.* I could feel the knot building in my third chakra. It was my memory of experiencing this same moment. It came two weeks after my return from death. I remember waking disconnected from the free-flowing love I had experienced with Alma. Annabella was seeing the suffering of her family without any filters. A unique part of the angelic existence, this feeling was raw and intense, the most unbearable experience many would ever have.

*Yes, they have come to a place in their lives where there is no reality other than a narrowed focus.* She flashed images of abandoned opportunity that forced each participant to experience less and less connection to faith, hope, and love in their lives, the energetics of which I now knew how to correct.

*I know,* I said. I attempted to share with her the internal support I had created when I had the same experience.

Her usually joyful connection had vanished. Her normal strength of will felt transitory. Annabella was falling into the trap of witnessing with attachment.

*It is why we are incapable of manifesting reality as we feel we should be able.* Though I had no personal connection to their issues, the world's sadness was as real to me as if I did. It was so real, I felt tears fall down my cheeks. *I have a beautiful life. I have an amazing understanding.* I was stating facts as I used what I knew to be true to pull us both back from the spiraling delusion of pain. *We need to be capable of connection with-*

*out attachment. We need to be separate from these feelings of damage that we each continually perpetrate on each other and ourselves.*

*Is there a reason you cry for this?* Annabella asked. She had shifted out of her sense of loss and was now on the other side of it. This meant she had reached the separation from suffering and was now capable of seeing the joy in everything. It was another understanding I had seen those first two weeks following my death. In this moment, I longed for that connection.

I felt a coolness wash over my left cheek as she waited for my answer, an answer that until now had eluded me. *Yes, I cry because I want to be free of this burden of wanting the world to change. I want to feel myself as whole without needing others to be different for this to be so.*

Overcome, I wept as I realized the pieces I was puzzling together would be an impossible fit into the beliefs I already held. I thought I had already released the need for the world to be different than what it was. For this need to be back again meant that another aspect of the same experience had to be addressed. I would need to go *through* this experience at another level. I could not jump over it or skirt around it. I knew I was ready for it, or it would not be here.

*How can I let go of all the fullness I experience from the interconnection of myself to others? There's no way to forget the connection and still feel the freedoms I know are possible.* Annabella and I both understood.

*I have a message for you.* I felt her words, quiet, gentle.

I knew why she had changed and what it meant. She was now the embodiment of her angelic self. All the most important messages I had ever received came in this form. I could not help but stammer even in my thoughts, knowing the challenge I often faced when handed these messages. *Yes? What is it?*

*I want you to know,* she paused to wait for my insides to adjust. Once I was peaceful and ready to handle the message, she continued. *There is not a way to feel without feelings.*

This message brought a clear understanding beyond words. It carried with it one of the original vibrations used to create humanity, a template of our core existence for me to embody. I felt the opening of energy inside my chest as I allowed myself to let go of the beliefs contrary to this light. As I edged closer to my body's release of these beliefs, I felt a sudden, sharp physical pain in my heart center. My brain, aware that I was letting go of beliefs that I used to maintain control and consistency in my life, fought against the action. My pain was my physical reaction to a fear that I could lose something. I did not know what life would look like without these long-standing beliefs, so I entered into fight or flight instead of allowing for the full release of the light's energy into my body.

Holding energy inside my body was a habitual response I resorted to when I feared vulnerability. Holding back made me think I could keep my identity as I saw myself. In the past, my reveal of my internal self led to the judgment and misassumptions of others. My vulnerable moments had ended with a sense of loss and a reduction in self-love, leaving me in fear.

Now fully aware of these patterns and habits and the fear they instilled, I felt again what it was like to be connected to humanity instead of divinity. Our fear bonded us together for survival; I held on to my familiarity to everyone and everything. In my brain, there was safety in what was familiar.

I had to ask. *What if I give up this part of myself, my external connections to my world, and I am left all alone?* I had witnessed this experience in so many, how they would find the moment of freedom but later revert to their former selves because they felt alone and unsupported with their new understanding. I knew the answer before the words were even finished. *If I give up all connections to the external world, I will no longer be alone. I will again be directly connected to the divine, and through the divine all things are one.* Still, my body shuddered and ached. *I can't make it! I can't release this burden.*

I sobbed again, recalling all the interpersonal moments I had experienced with others, feeling a connection to the beauty in our pain. It made us one. This feeling was as strong as my longing for the divine. *I have chosen to be obligated to experiencing life as the others have project-*

*ed it to me.* CRAP! THAT WAS IT! *OH MY GOD! That's what has been driving me this entire time.* My head was spinning out; I was flying out of my body as far into the universe as I could travel. *I constantly challenge myself to be the reflection I think they want to see. I do it out of protection for them and myself.*

With my realization, one that happened simultaneously with Annabella, I felt her pass. It was not without balance. She was helping me as I was helping her, a classic win-win. I sat in awe of the experience for hours, unable to move fully into my human existence. I hoped to capture into my body the impact of what I had witnessed through the expansion of myself.

One thing I enjoy about the other side, that some of us have here on Earth with our loved ones, is the ability to pick up a conversation as if it had never stopped. I smiled as I heard the familiar sound of Annabella in my ears, chittering on about her afterlife.

*So, how does a Heritage Angel exist?* I was curious as to the similarities there might be between our two vocations. I was attempting to move my acceptance of my role in the angelic realm into a place of consciousness that could be shared. *Are you more like Guardians, unaffected by freewill? Or more like me and subjected to the risk of losing clarity?* There was a constant battle I still faced in my work between indulging others in what they wanted to hear or have happen, or standing in the full expression of what I knew to be true.

Annabella, now on the other side, knew as I did that a Guardian's position was one of love; they are free from ever having experienced the burden of obligation humans had created here on earth. Guardians do not need to change anyone because they know we cannot make mistakes, that fear is not real, and that our lives are *our* journey and not the journey of others. Their clarity in these matters is without perception, attachment, judgment, or conclusion. From their vantage point, their support as advisors maintains a mastery that is immeasurable. Their ability to remain separated from control, as we have experienced it, gives them a space where they exist without accountability for our choices; Guardians required humans, who bare the consequence of their decisions, to be the final say.

This was different than in my work, where I was compelled to impress further upon the person what I knew to be true by sharing resonance—often by telling a story from my own life that contained the same vibration. When willing, a person's energetic system gathered an understanding from my example as to how to see his or her own situation with clarity instead of out of obligation. Although I never forced change, I was often excited when I experienced the awakening with another, their moment of reaching the 'aha!'

A Guardian did not need these moments of satisfaction, and I found that in the beginning, it was the satisfaction that gave me the courage to push on. As I am now with my work, more in the full expression of myself, I do not need confirmation or support to keep going; simply being me is enough.

*I see with clarity*, Annabella replied. *I am willing to share through my family's collective vibration an experience that can help those intimately connected understand at a greater level and release freewill choices that interfere with greater will. Unlike many on the other side who see only the macrocosm, and unlike the Guardians who are not personally invested, I am more like you—sharing from my position of clarity, not only a part of myself, but the view of my entire family.*

She showed me her very extensive family tree; her complicated connections surpassed the physical and existed beyond the obvious tangible relationships of cousins and children. Viewing this tree opened my thoughts to a reality of flowering connections through energetic bonds. These bonds included relationships that went deeper than birth and showed how love and thought tied people together as deeply as genetics.

*Without the beliefs of my life or the restrictions of my physical form, I can help others manifest miracles from the strength of their own hearts.*

There was a sense of satisfaction in what Annabella said. It was in this moment that I embodied a kind of freedom I had never felt before.

Even as a child I had been considered an old soul, unable to play and enjoy the experiences of life without pressure or intellectual calculations. While others played, I organized; while others laughed, I questioned the meaning of their laughter; and while others loved outwardly with forms of physical connection, I remained still and apart only feeling myself. Here, in this moment, I was finally aware of the thoughts of others who did not see the world as I did from a place of control and strain. This new comprehension of a childlike freedom was completely foreign. It was like being Alice and traveling through a looking glass to view a whole new experience that I previously felt must have been impossible.

Annabella continued. *Although these changes existed in the heart, it was not until I learned the value of the mind that miracles began occurring. It was not until after that first miracle that I, too, truly acknowledged my happening.* In our vocabulary, we referred to instantaneous change in others—where the room for change, timing in their lives, and the understanding of such possibilities cooperated within a single vibrational structure—to be 'the happening.' It was the happening that caused and created the love and existence for wellness.

Annabella's thoughts expressed to me what that first miracle had been. Once passed, she found her mother Marta, and Tio Rigo, her mother's brother, still existing on Earth.

Annabella, having known their lives to be loving and devoted to family, was surprised to find them still here, tethered and blocked from crossing. In general, when people have so much love they move on freely, so for Annabella and me this was new. *When I asked them of their suffering, it was easy to understand and I let them go.*

The visual of letting them go reminded me of when Gia and I had helped Nana pass. There were strings of light released from Marta and Rigo's forms that returned to the Earth to support Mother Earth with joy. Annabella explained that their love for Earth and Her ability to supply their families with all things needed to survive had not ended with their deaths. They had chosen to be forever grateful. Upon death, this tie of gratitude had remained and held them on Earth.

*All I did was enlighten them so they could finalize their passing.* It made sense that the light supplied by Earth sustained them and held their focus, keeping them here. To become enlightened was to be reconnected to divinity. This reconnection allowed them to return Earth's energy to her and gave them a connection to their new home, which allowed them to depart.

*Amazing!* I joyfully accepted this knowledge from Annabella.

I thought about the perfection that exists beyond our own creation of control, which chose this woman who had lived her whole life committed to loving her family to now have this as her afterlife. With her clarity, she would never fall subject to the manmade vibrations of fear or pain again. I had great respect for the idea that her genetic birth allowed her to carry a necessary piece of the puzzle through the vibration of her family. This connection would help them embody the work she shared with more ease. Using both the energy of the family's living souls and her connection to the transcended family members, she would have access to both the manifold and the eternal[29] soul of every family member.

On an especially hard day, when it felt like I was hitting a brick wall repeatedly, as everyone was upset and disappointed with life and unwilling to access the light as I shared it, Annabella cared enough to wander in and say hello.

*You resent a lot of people for having lost their way, and yet you hold them at a higher standard than you do yourself.* The standard she referred to was my belief that people knew themselves better than I possibly could since I had not experienced their entire life with them. I did not tell people they were wrong. I let them hold onto their painful beliefs. When I showed them the other way, they could see it was a benefit, and yet they kept returning to the idea of 'yeah, but' to justify their false beliefs.

*By holding back what you know and see, others will not discover their truths. If you don't challenge what they think and feel, then your truth*

---

29. The primary is the first soul to exist (see page 176). Once it gains experience it becomes known as the eternal soul.

*serves no purpose for them.* Her statement was strong. *I want you to share and be willing to tell each person their truth even when they can't hear it.*

I checked in with my feelings to see if what she said was true. *Yes, I do resent them,* I replied, surprised. My heart's only focus was love and it was my brain that carried the resentment. *I don't know how to help them and shouldering this constant pain has again left me feeling alone in this world.* I thought for a bit. *You know, I recognized Alma as love when I crossed. I have embodied that huge expansive feeling that does not exist in daily life on Earth. I know what's waiting for me on the other side, and yet three times I have chosen to come back.* I paused and remembered each of my deaths and my subsequent returns. *I know I want to be here, but I can't seem to bring that will and understanding back into this body. It feels like a futile exercise in constant conflict with the rules we humans live by.* I shook my head side to side as I recalled my third death, which I now refer to as my 'death of sorts.' *If I hadn't been made to beg during that one, I wouldn't even remember that I want to be alive. I would have tried again and again to be dead.*

Remembering those experiences restored my vibration of compassion. I shook my head again as I realized how easily hope could be forgotten. *Thank you for reminding me that others haven't had the experience of being free of all this darkness.*

With my heart feeling light again, I reached out to support humanity. Knowing suffering could end, I sent a shockwave reminder around the planet of what hope felt like. Hope, one of divinities' free flowing vibrations, supports love, along with faith and trust. It takes effort to hold love, as it is a lighter weight vibration compared to darkness, which is denser. It is like holding a gas without it being displaced by a solid.

As it was, communication with the other side tended to come across as vague, like fortune cookie answers. You know the ones that say, 'Look to the stars to find your prosperity,' or, 'A pleasant surprise is in store for you,' or the slightly encouraging, 'This may seem like the darkest night, but the dawn will soon come.' They speak from a macrocosm existence, without any of the details of our actual lives.

The other side sees all the details of our microcosm as our freewill choices—the ones we make to enjoy our experience here on Earth, such as choosing a book or a movie, having multiple partners or being monogamous, and so on. They do not see how important our freewill choices are to us and how we use them to symbolize a greater expression of self. When we are stuck in our focus of seeing the trees instead of the forest, it can be complicated to understand what their broad statements are referring to. The macrocosm concepts—like embodiment, control, and responsibility—shape us eternally and continue on past life as we know it, supporting our greater will and our personal growth in alignment with our souls. Once out of our human bodies, we forget how much the details in life meant to our existence as humans, how we use the details to shape the comprehension of our lives.

Annabella reminded me that being in a body gave me a perspective that the angelic realms did not have—the awareness of humanity's supersession of using freewill to override greater will. Prior to my partial angelic ascension, I had overridden my greater will with my freewill just as most people do.

There were clear moments when I knew I wanted to let go of the pain that greater will showed as unnecessary, but instead, I dug in with freewill and indulged in my fears. I allowed the negative aspects of my ego to take over. I reflected specifically on the moment I told Javi Annabella would not be leaving any time soon. This was not a proud moment for me. I had allowed fear and freewill to override what I clearly felt as my truth.

The difference between freewill and greater will is like putting your hand to the fire and watching it burn; as soon as you touch the flame and feel discomfort, you are encouraged to pull back. It is with freewill that you can override greater will and burn to death if you choose. You can lean face first into suffering and stay in freewill, or you can realize discomfort is the greater will's way of saying 'hello, I have something you might want to consider.'

I know greater will, as it is expressed on Earth, is comprised of contracts, agreements, and connections to our true selves. Greater will ties us to who we are outside of our bodies.

Later, when the Universal Conscious Mind was created during our disconnection from divinity, we moved freewill into a greater position of control. Freewill was previously designed to give our brain the authority to save life and limb when our intuitive connection to synchronicity was missing. Now, we can use freewill to decide if we want to stubbornly hold against what we know to be true, making it possible to seemingly harm others and ourselves.

Annabella continued the topic. *The only reason life lessons were created was to bring back balance between greater will and freewill.*

In many parts of my life I was learning to live with that balance. Once restored, life was more joyous and without many aspects of suffering.

*But in our folly, we learned to love it! This is what has been so confusing for most people.* With Annabella's words, I could clearly see the peril it created. We unknowingly prioritize experiences on Earth over the experience of our souls. It has moved us in a direction of death and disease, making full body ascension[30] impossible.

*Simultaneously, this freewill prioritization of experiences on Earth created a part of existence that does not occur elsewhere.*

*Yes, you're right!* I exclaimed. There was an intense chemical bonding that allowed the body, mind, and spirit combination to function miraculously, even at its own peril, to save the body and soul of another. *I mean, really, how else could someone run into a burning building to save the life of another? How else did we change from the animal instinct of only the strong surviving? Even with me, when I was sick and unable to take care of myself, I still had value.* This was the miracle that had been created. This was what made humanity so important in the universe.

Those who were out of body understood it was our imbalances of will that created this amazing devotion to humanity, our ability to be

---

30. Full body ascension is when all energetic aspects have come to reside permanently in the physical form, allowing for the potential emergence of esoteric capabilities.

selfless to our death. What they could not see was how our creation kept us unable to release suffering. Out of body, they were not aligned with our reality to give us the direction we were asking for—an ability to keep our creation of freewill with this higher level of control while still capable of holding knowledge of ways to eliminate our suffering. Those in body without an angelic connection may not even understand that we can have both freewill and a life without suffering.

As we hold delusion and truth side by side, we are unable to see the difference between them, blocking humanity's ascension. The power humanity has given freewill cannot be overridden, it must be surrendered, and our fear of being vulnerable makes that, for most, nearly impossible.

*Yet, we unknowingly give of our will and allow for our own subjugation, accepting other's beliefs over our own every day. This is the dilemma that has been created for all of us.* What Annabella said was spoken for both of us. It was enough to bring us momentarily to silence.

I thought about how, in my own work, I risked what the other side did not—the translation of the macrocosm into an individual's microcosm—in the hope of bringing humanity back on track to achieve our desired evolution of full ascension into our physical bodies.

*Annabella, I know what makes our work different from those on the other side. While the other side primarily speaks in terms that can be heard by those who have reached a level of ascension, we speak in terms that can be heard by those searching to reach ascension.*

When we returned to the conversation, Annabella's next words further intrigued me. *Unlike an embodied angel, Heritage Angels incur no drain of energy.* She was responding to the strain I currently felt as I contemplated ways to remain connected to the physical, spiritual, and energetic, while creating changes in the bones and muscles of others—including DNA alterations—without exhausting myself.

*In my work, I remain separate as myself while completely connected to everyone and everything; I am fully individuated.* Annabella's words in my thoughts were inspiring, yet they seemed too grand for my human brain to accept. Another seed was planted that would encourage me to work with the layers of individuation myself years later.

*Can you come down from that vibration to something that is more easily understood?* I asked.

Annabella began supplying me with fascinating images regarding the Heritage Angels' ability to impact the Universal Conscious Mind. *It takes quantity of thought, not quality, to make a change in the Universal Conscious Mind. The more people that think about a given topic, the more it becomes reality. Look at slavery. Once the mass consciousness accepted freedom as a possibility, it trickled into many areas of life. It even affected animals, changing them from sole property to companions.* Annabella's contact with her family, within the confines of the Universal Conscious Mind, would be used to create global change. The sheer expansiveness of her family tree gave her quantity to shift the unaware into awareness, whether in regard to releasing the control of judgment or a return to one's personal truth.

I reflected on her words and added, *With your family ties and effort, you could sway common beliefs back in the direction of greater will. People will start to understand how things like standing their ground through stubbornness to support an idea that is not even theirs doesn't help anyone. They'll start to see the win-win in every situation.*

This made sense to us both.

Her effort was definitely different than the stance I took. I was working towards helping people find their personal truth. For me, the Universal Conscious Mind was still being experienced much like a person's personal storm, full of obligation and codependency, which made it difficult to untangle the energetics and open the free flow of energy. Think of it like a really large game of Twister, each of us making a move with every spin while hoping to accommodate the moves of others. Each move and its wave of motion that followed had to be observed before change could successfully occur.

To avoid this, what I did during healing in relationship to the Universal Conscious Mind was go through it. I took people energetically above it to heal, making it possible for them and myself to exist for a moment without its control. With their new understanding and relationship to the choice of freewill, they could see a move as affecting only themselves without accommodating the assumed impact on others. Once they could achieve clarity of self, from that truth, they would then learn to reform healthy connections that allowed them to maintain their truth while being fully aware of others. This positioned them to look at the win-win in every situation. For many, the largest struggle is separating from the push and pull of the Universal Conscious Mind so they can see their own truth without the negotiation of holding the beliefs of others as more important than their own. With the understanding of one's personal truth, we as a group increase the light content on the surface of the planet. When we connect with the win-win the light increases exponentially.

Guardians deal with this issue by showing the purity of a situation. Basically, they help us to see when we wrongly follow our freewill. Well, maybe wrong is an incorrect word. It is more like this: Guardians offer assistance when someone looks for help to see when their freewill choices override their greater will.

*Freewill over greater will—I still see that one all the time.* I shared with Annabella how people get mad and hold a grudge when all they want is to feel loved. *They fear if they don't continually show they are upset, the person they are mad at won't learn. It's manipulation. We use our freewill to stay mad instead of using our greater will to find a win-win.*

Weeks later, Annabella popped in to share how she understood the Guardians' uses of the Earth's light energy[31] for the Earth and her inhabitants. *They are unable to absorb the light energy; they can neither remove nor exchange it like humans who have ascended can.*

She was referring to our ability to create unique vibrations, to understand our interactions through vibration, and to absorb vibrations. These

---

31. Light energy is produced by humans and released into our environment to be used by others. It is information that can be experienced at any time, and is brought into the body by intentional resonance.

new vibrations had not previously existed in the space of Earth. *Humans can hold as much or as little light as we choose. Without our connection to this light, the Guardians cannot move light on the surface of the planet or internally in humans.*

I recalled having met my friend Stella's Guardian Angel. Stella had become acquainted with her angel after finding herself at the bottom of her babysitter's pool. Stella, only three at the time, had stumbled into the pool and had no idea how to get out on her own. Still young enough to be connected telepathically to those out of body, she called out for help. The Guardian Jocelynn, whose name means 'she knows,' responded to the call. Once the connection was jointly accepted, Jocelynn could support Stella in a way that saved her life.

When I met Jocelynn, Stella was at my house giving me a massage. Stella, who felt called to support my transformation following my heart attack, had released a block in my left arm that brought up particularly painful thoughts regarding my relationship with Joseph. Jocelynn appeared following my inability to completely release the block.

At first, with her near, I felt only my own thoughts. The more stubbornly I held my pain and resisted forgiving Joseph, the more support of love I felt from the Guardian. Guardians support our truth. *My truth is love, so this pain is not in balance with who I am.* That's when I realized my fear was if I forgive Joseph he might mistake my forgiveness as an okay to treat me the same way again. The ability to acknowledge my fear with clarity was Jocelynn's gift to me, her response to my cry for help.

Myself not a devotee, the Guardians words were clear in my head, *I cannot change you. I can only witness as you forgive yourself.* It was a profound experience as Jocelynn related to my every thought, not with superficial support or beliefs, but with gratitude for my need to have the experience, compassion for how my fear trapped me, and support for my own freewill choice no matter what that might be. I found it interesting that in her support, unlike when we talk to friends and family, there was no guidance to make a choice. The effort of change was completely my own and yet with her support, what had felt impossible was now possible.

I realized that it was not my cry that brought her, rather it was Stella hearing my cry that brought Jocelynn to my aid. Jocelynn did not offer to be my Guardian, she only offered me support while I was with Stella.

For the average Guardian, three to five people are enough to care for. Jocelynn introduced herself to me as having the force and trust of twelve thousand living humans on her side. Her collective, who started tens of thousands of years ago with a handful of devotees, grew as each of their families grew. As each of their paths crossed with others who accepted this relationship with Jocelynn, it gave her the opportunity to expand and grow as a Guardian.

It is the Guardians' connection to our soul manifold that gives them influence over our light content in our realm and the ability to shift light and truth in any given situation through the agreement with their devotees. The Guardian, with this support, could spread this light energy to enlighten large groups at a time. With this kind of support, the people being enlightened by the Guardian did not have to be part of her devotees. With the groups' blocks temporarily displaced, the Guardian could work with the collective souls towards a win-win.

*Annabella, do you remember Michael? As far as I can see, he's one of the most well-known Guardians.*

*Yes, I know he never interferes with our existence without our request.*

*He's the one who explained to me how, once supported by enough souls, a Guardian rises to Archangel and lives in service to humanity and the Earth.* Guardians are connected and committed to the place of their births as an Archangel. For a Guardian, his acceptance of deciding to be of service is an eternal, pure love—a dedication. For Michael, his is Earth.

*It is the prayers and commitment of the living to these Guardian Angels, like Michael[32], that gives them their power to assist humanity in moments of need,* said Annabella. *If the souls were to forsake them, the Guardian*

---

32. We were first made aware of Michael in the bible and he is still active in the lives of believers today.

*Angel would lose control over planetary and internal light. They would lose their impact on Earth and her inhabitants.*

*Ha, that would surely put Michael in a difficult position. He'd be stranded, pushed off Earth, capable of only observing from the other side, having lost his portal!* I wondered if that might actually be a good turn of events. Michael and I had our differences. I sat opposed to his opinion that humanity needed to fail completely before being offered aid. I followed in the footsteps of Grace, my kindred, whose kindness is offered as the individual in need is searching for a connection to their humanity. Our support is given through the knowledge of our internal self, through our compassion and nurturing.

Michael, himself a compassionate and nurturing Guardian, is willing to use the 'last resort of will' to support an individual's current truth, even if it means harm will come to others. This occurs because the person is out of balance.

I always take the side of the win-win, helping an individual find their balanced truth before they harm others. Still, my resentment with which I begrudged Michael faded as I realized the impact his absence would have on his devotees.

*If Michael were separated from humanity, hundreds of thousands would lose his support of clarity.*

Annabella and I sat pondering the effect it would have on humanity. Finally, I communicated again to change the subject, *Do you think the Guardians would miss the experience of the living like we miss our dead?*

*Guardians' are different than me,* I continued with Annabella during her next appearance. *Instead of only offering clarity, I am driven to seek the perfect balance of freewill between the greater self and the soul manifold, while still living as a human. It's my remaining as a human that makes it difficult: being in a body, accessing divinity directly, and still feeling all humans as one, all the while creating change under the habitual and constant impact of the Universal Conscious Mind. Guardians already exist aware of balance without the impact of the Universal Conscious Mind or the habits of humanity. It is not an effort for them.*

My gift of discernment gives me the same embodied ability Guardians have—to see the macrocosm patterns related to greater will in our energy. This allows me to assist others to reach the same level of clarity. Since I have a soul, I can directly affect my external environment, sphere of influence, my physical form, and the physical forms of others.

During my ascension, I agreed to follow certain Universal Laws. This agreement allows me to craft vibrations that do not currently exist, from all forms of light[33]. Typically, non-ascended humans can only use the vibrations they were born into. It is my understanding that as more humans ascend to the level of embodied angels, death will cease to exist and life on Earth will become eternal. Earth will become our new Heaven.

The differences between each of our angelic presence seemed minor and specific. *But wait, you've occupied a body and kept your human soul. I wonder if connecting to your entire family tree connects you to the earth permanently, as are Archangels. Or did you give up your earthly soul?* I inquired, feeling perplexed, unable to complete the thought without more information.

*No,* she replied, in patience and kindness. She understood my struggle; she remembered how it felt to be unable to pull all of our divine information through the density into our bodies. She continued, *This is a special gift I will receive. The earth will not grieve for my loss[34], as I have not left. I gather strength, like a Guardian, by assisting my family, living or deceased. Unlike Guardians who are bound by the souls they guide, the list ever-changing, or you, guided by freewill, I am bound by heritage to my line, my infinite family, and can pass this to any number of them when I choose.*

---

33. Forms of light: my own internal light and the internal light of others, external light, the light of divinity, and photons (which are physical).

34. This literally means the release of the soul manifold.

Months had passed before I reached out to Annabella once more. I found her solidly rooted in her work, which gave us much to talk about. Her current priority focused on helping the living members of her family who were nearing the end of their physical lives.

*I help them understand how their confusion pulls them away from their pura vida ways.*

Being Costa Rican, Javi made it clear that historically, Annabella's family members were ingrained with a sense of fun and lightheartedness—a sense of freedom expressed through their communal way of life known as 'pura vida,' which means 'to live in joy,' having a pure life. It is a blessing they express to one another over and over, every day.

*This sense has been exchanged for other, more global views. It has slowly been lost and replaced with judgment and a need for control.* In the past, most Costa Ricans lived in what we would consider poverty, but were happy with their lives. Now, exposed to the wealth and possessions of their worldly neighbors through commerce and communication, they began to compare other's wealth to their own lack thereof.

*What was the result?* I asked.

*A craving in some, and depression in others.*

*Ah, that makes sense. I would expect it to show itself as symptomatic in their emotional behavior.*

*It did,* confessed Annabella.

This family, whose members lived mostly in the same city, began to go for long periods of time without seeing each other. They used to get together at least four or five times a year, but as the finger pointing started and one accused the other of not supporting his or her needs or beliefs, each saw the other as selfish and ungrateful. The family gatherings became fewer and the attendance smaller and smaller. Their absences solidified their judgments.

The change in their beliefs regarding work outside the home gained a higher priority over personal freedom. The need to gain more worldly possessions became much more important. These changes had begun to fray the threads that had previously held their family together through such close bonds.

She shared, *I grew up hearing stories about generations of families who had been torn apart by this work ethic, as it separated them first in body, then in mind, and finally in heart, which led to no more pure life. At first, my family could see how these new values were tearing others apart and they sought to avoid these same practices; but by the time I was dying, we too had fallen prey to the same splintering that was created by the 'work hard, earn more' credo.*

*So that's how it happened,* I said, beginning to see how the sense of shame connected to a distorted view of poverty made the desire for wealth and possessions a priority. *This desire occurred without the balance of love and compassion.*

*Yes,* she conceded. *When belongings are added to enhance a life already full of joy, there is balance. When belongings are added to enhance an unbalanced life, things are torn apart. In fact, that's how your young friend Javi ended up here in the United States. Javi wanted to provide his family with the western sense of wealth and abundance as he perceived it.*

We talked about the changes that occur for most at the moment of death. Her work, like Guardians and mine, was one of bringing clarity. When her family realized the damage their fears had done, she helped them heal their understanding of values in themselves, thus healing this understanding in their entire family tree. With each change, the family moved a step closer to their previous clean living.

Annabella continued. *My work is about enlightening the lives of others. It's not about being wrong or right. It's also never about spectacular creations—I work within the mundane. The influences we have—our truth shared with others—is about our lives and our own joy; it's the beginning of our existence to feel the experience of life. The divine has allowed us to exist here, not alone, but without interference. Because we have this freewill ability, there is a compassionate energy between humans. This energy keeps us from entering permanently into our darkness, the part of our selfishness that blocks us from others. It guarantees we have the possibility to return to our interpersonal connection. It's during our darkest moments, when our light is misunderstood by others because all they can see is our darkness, that this smaller, quieter connection can be ignited to create tremendous change. It's the most exciting thing I have ever seen.*

*I know exactly what you are saying. I watch people all the time who move off balance because of fear. If they have a fear of loss and they are giving to another, the other person feels it. I have seen it over and over. There is no connection to skewed balance. I see even for myself, no matter what my generous intentions are, if I am giving from a skewed balance of fear, others do not receive my gifts with gratitude. In fact, they often seem ungrateful.* I paused to consider my own experiences with this imbalance. *Like the time I was telling a friend that her relationship with her sister was unhealthy with all the bickering and she reacted to me with anger instead of being grateful that I wanted to help her see a change was possible. Her anger was because I told her this from a skewed balance; since I had my own issues with bickering, it wasn't clear that I was looking out for her best interest. I had been moving through my own layers of painful beliefs that bickering meant I was unloved, and this had been felt by her instead of feeling the care with which it originated.*

When the balance of a person's light content is low, he or she exists from a place of skewed reality. Instead of creating in life from his or her natural place of center balance, everything is created from a tangent, a skewed balance, missing its purity and truth.

*This repulsion to skewed balance is a safeguard. It occurs with every interaction between humans and makes the shift in our balance apparent so we can encourage and help others to shift back. It is part of the mirroring process. It is possible to learn this awareness of self; a commitment to our own truth is required to return from the skewed balance.*

The basic concept of mirroring is that we can only see what we know of ourselves in others. If I am annoyed by someone being late it is likely that I have a belief regarding tardiness, its expression of rudeness or disrespect, how it affects the plans of others, that it is a behavior to be avoided, or any other number of things I have concluded or have been told and accepted from others in my life. The mirror, when I am annoyed, is a direct reflection of my own beliefs and can reflect to myself that I am out of balance regarding responsibility, discipline, control, safety, trust, or ego in my own life. If I use this mirror to check internally, I can find my root issue, see I am out of balance, and begin to self-adjust.

Life is good.

If I instead look external for the root issue I will find confusion and often remain out of balance. This imbalance may be expressed in myself as judgment, assumption, conclusion, self-victimization, or anger with myself or the person I am interacting with.

I shook my head, recalling my own journey of understanding. The joy and light that was so easily obtained in my life today was centered on this one very important truth—*It is in our return to self that we consider ourselves to be whole.* On an energetic level when we are recognized as whole, life flows, our needs are easily met, and the win-win is our natural state of being.

I pointed out to Annabella how critical her effort was to the future of her culture and her family's freedom. *I believe it's possible to make those changes in the present; to be free of this suffering. I don't think we have to wait until death to realize this, either,* I said. *I still trust that suffering is a symptom that can be resolved.*

*I concur,* she said. *I have been assisting my loved ones with this very thing. My work with the already deceased is complete and I have begun influencing the living. My hope is to open them to their truth as their reality.*

*You have no idea what this means to me,* I said, as I wiped the tears of joy that leapt to my eyes. *You are supporting my dream!* I paused, showing my gratitude. *You give me hope. Your work, what you do for the living, it's everything I am fighting for.* I felt less alone knowing Annabella and others like her were taking up the fight.

Annabella extended her blessing as we said goodbye. *La esperanza es eterna (Hope springs eternal).*

Two years later I entered Javi's home and was pleasantly surprised to find his aunt in his space.

*Hola, Tia Annabella. ¿Cómo estás? (Hello, Aunt Annabella. How are you?)* I asked. I found it enjoyable that while conversing with Annabella in my head, my inhibitions about speaking Spanish vanished, making it far easier to communicate with her than when speaking out loud to the living.

*Como estas, mi bella hermosa! (How are you my beautiful one?)* She was excited to hear me. I gushed a little in return of her affection.

*Soy maravilloso. ¿Cómo estás? (I am wonderful. How are you?)* I asked her again, excited to hear what she had been up to. The room seemed brighter by her pure presence. There is such joy in maintaining the connection of a relationship after the energy has moved on from its body. I considered how satisfying it would be for Javi and his family to hear her like I did.

As I was over at Javi's to watch a movie, Annabella waited respectfully for me to catch up with Javi before going into details.

He talked about the vehicle that had previously been used for his family's transportation. It had belonged to another of Javi's brothers, Virgilio, who had recently sold it to purchase property so he could have his own family home.

"You know, I told my mom I would buy her a van for the three angels when I left Costa Rica twenty-five years ago. But since Virgilio had stepped up to share his, I didn't do it." Thoughts of his brother, Alex, caused him to pause. "I promised Alex, too." His eyebrows bunched up as he held back his deeper emotions. I had learned over the years that the grown siblings Javi called the three angels were those in the family who had mental disabilities which restricted their independence. They each required full-time assisted care, the weight of which bolstered Javi's commitment to his family. "I knew Mami and Papi couldn't get another van on their own and they would never have asked me to make good on my promise."

Alex was one of the angels. He was in his forties. Javi knew that as aging adults, the angels' weak feet and twisted ankles made all movements difficult. It was becoming harder and harder to get them outdoors and take them anywhere as a group. This made the importance of the van for each of their lives a necessity in Javi's heart and he moved forward with the purchase.

"I know spending the money now to keep that promise was probably the worst possible time for me to have done it, with my arm in a sling and having to have surgery, but it didn't even matter to me." His decision to buy the van at that time was huge because he would be out of work for more than sixteen months for recovery following the surgeries, so he would likely need that money for his own living expenses. "I feel better than I have in years! My entire heart knows it is the right time."

I watched with interest as he reflected on his decision.

"I think you're right," I chimed in as Annabella reached to tickle Javi's ear, which I saw him move to scratch. "Doing the things we truly feel, especially for those we love, can be more important than living with our fears. I understand it was probably scary, though."

I wanted to set him free. He was brewing drama in his thoughts as he reconsidered if what he had chosen was the right thing to do. I added, feeling his love for his family, "Things always tend to work out when we are in our truth."

While we watched the movie, Annabella and I continued our own telepathic conversation. She brought me up-to-date regarding her family and how Javi had been able to bravely make a choice that synchronistically met both his and his family's needs. *The win-win,* I chimed in excitement. *He did it with your support!*

By the end of our conversation, she brought me back to the memory of her death, when I had told Javi she was not going anywhere. She wanted my energy to be clean of this indiscretion, however slight.

*I understand,* I told her. I remembered how I had put a spin on the truth to make things easier for Javi, which only made it easier for me.

*I know. It never makes anything easier. All things must be brought into balance or released.*

Feeling uncomfortable, even with Annabella's support, I knew I needed to take responsibility for my actions in that moment. I knew that taking responsibility for myself changed me energetically.

*I am afraid because I do not know what life will look like once I make this change. Behaving this way is the only reality I have ever known or witnessed.*

*Keep up the good work*, said Annabella. Her words bolstered my internal strength.

*I can.*

In the original experience of sharing with Javi about his aunt, I had wanted to express my understanding that when death is imminent, people find peace. It is not an acceptance of death that brings this peace; it is the letting go of the beliefs used by the brain to maintain value in human survival of the physical body. Allowing this truth to come to the surface gave me a connection to what Javi had really wanted in that moment years ago. *He had wanted to let go of his fear!* I realized we all did. I could clearly see the balance between two people in that moment. It was not in our holding that we became capable of center balance—it was in our release. *My holding back of who I am in my truth never helps anyone.*

Tentatively, I began speaking aloud to Javi. "Do you remember when I said Tia Annabella wasn't going to leave the earth anytime soon, but then she passed two days later?"

He nodded. "Definitely. That was a big moment in my life."

If I had not been so distracted with my own fears of being revealed, I would have noticed the softness as it took over Javi's face. I would have felt the shift of energy in his fingertips as his usually stiff, strong hands became relaxed with a sense of peace. I might even have noticed the tenderness in his heart as he fondly recalled that time in his life.

"I knew then what was happening to her. In fact, I knew you would be losing many family members and friends in the following five years as well." My heart ached as I spoke. I knew it was my own fear of how sharing this information would affect him that caused the clenching in my throat. I knew it was the fear that I could be wrong or make a mistake that caused the feeling of acid burning inside my esophagus.

"I was afraid if I shared what I knew to be true, I could harm you." I paused as snapshots of all my fears flashed through my mind, my brain further aware of what I believed I could lose. "I was afraid of so many things back then, and even though that was years ago, I realize that this fear is still in my life. If it is in one area of my life it is in all. If I don't remove it, then I am still holding it." I had started babbling a bit. Still, with the first words out of my mouth, I was less nervous.

I shared my entire experience with him, including how I had sent the vibration to help him feel death as I knew it to be true, instead of having to experience it from a painful place of loss. I struggled after that reveal, my ego unraveling as I considered my own false belief that I could interfere with the freewill of another by sharing my truth. Even though I saw humanity's version of death to be twisted and conflicted, folding in on itself with so many misunderstandings, I was not sure if that gave me the right to interfere with a person's freewill choice by sharing my own version of reality.

Still, I had witnessed how Javi had changed regarding his response to death after that day. Each death in his family had been met with a sense of understanding instead of with overwhelming sorrow. He no longer related to the grief of others.

"Did I steal something from you? Did I leave you without a connection to what you needed by giving you this change?" I asked.

Javi was sincere in his response. "I don't think you could. I remember that day. I remember feeling something different, and after you left, I sat thinking about the ideas of life and death, wondering which idea I wanted to believe. My family's beliefs were painful. I remembered, too, what you had told me about delusion—that pain is the heads-up we are going down the wrong path. So, I backed up. I stopped thinking every thought that brought me pain and I rested, knowing everything was okay. The next day when I woke, I felt a sense that my aunt was with me. I doubted it at first, but I also remembered that you had told me about how it felt and what to look for. I didn't think about what she would say; I just listened without my thoughts and with my body. It was a very interesting time. So, did you steal something from me? I don't think so. Instead of feeling a sense of loss, I felt a deeper sense of love."

I added, "I am sorry I held back part of my truth because of my fear. I'll do my best to never do it again." I felt Javi's energy shift. He remained silent. Even though our friendship had grown through these past years, my own thoughts and fears regarding his silence, and the serious look on his face, led me to a fearful place, thinking maybe he was not okay after all. I considered I was being too vulnerable, too open.

*That's what you are talking about!* I said, touching Annabella again. I was able to recognize how my own fear, whatever was showing on my face, was going to make and create this moment. Instead of staying in my fear, I took a breath, and with it, I released all my tension. Instead of fear, I chose my friendship, its love, and the faith that every challenge in my life was present so I could experience more of my personal truth.

As I relaxed into myself again, I saw the pain in Javi's eyes lessen. If I did not support pain, he would have to do twice as much work to hold onto it. The examples I set in my life impact those around me. After a little longer, he finally answered.

"I am good. It is okay." We locked eyes and I was aware that information flowed freely between us; so much pain released that had nothing to do with this moment. I could see how our pain had controlled us, keeping us in this uncomfortable place. It felt like an hour, although I know the experience lasted only seconds.

Then, when the moment was over, he spoke. "I knew in my heart she was going." He looked at me, still serious. "When I talked to you that day, I was looking to you for my confirmation more than anything. If I had known I was right, I would have felt so much better." He paused and nodded. "Then, when she passed two days later, I finally knew, I am right and Christine is wrong," Javi burst out laughing, unable to hold back his mirth.

Socking him playfully in the arm at his humorous attempt to release my suffering, we crumpled against each other, laughing. I relaxed into the idea of knowing I could protect him less and be more myself in all aspects of our relationship. Relieved, I also knew without a doubt that the freedom we were both experiencing in this moment would not have been possible if it had not been for the love of his Tia Annabella.

Javi's family was being healed through the deep-rooted love of their very own Heritage Angel.

# Chapter Dedication

To Javi and his family, for the joyful jubilation, the complete acceptance into their culture, and the full embrace into their pura vida life.

# Chapter Ten

# THE LIGHT

Las Vegas, August 2016

*I* sat reflecting back on August of 2009. After my first series of classes at the library, I clearly remember asking Joseph for help. I was struggling with my skepticism, as my old patterns of logic were clashing with my now-personal experiences.

"What if it isn't real? What if my perception of all this is truly my own imagination and I am crazy?"

He thought for a moment, giving the question serious consideration. When he was moved to answer, he asked me something unexpected.

"What if you are? What if you are crazy?" He paused, then asked, "Are you doing anything to hurt people? Are you taking something from them, or trying to manipulate them?"

"No, of course not!" I said. Even the idea of such a possibility startled me.

"Are they getting better? Are their lives changing in a good way?"

I was beginning to see a light. "Yes!"

"Well, if that's the case, then does it matter if you're crazy?"

"No," I said, my eyes wide open above my smile. I shook as my mind realized this extreme truth for the first time. I was very much like a child who had just been told that all the presents under the tree on Christmas morning were mine!

"Well then, I think as long as you aren't hurting anyone, and you aren't stealing from them, it doesn't matter if you're crazy or not."

Looking back, I laugh. I did not realize then that Joseph never said I was not crazy! What I took from that moment was the freedom to keep going, to find the faith and conviction to put one foot in front of the other each day on this completely unknown path before me. At the time, I did not have any examples to follow and the only thing that felt good was my new commitment to a goal of being of service. Like every doctor and every humanitarian, I have taken an oath within myself, before my God and my universe: 'Above all, do no harm.' That was the easy part, as I believe we all live with this core part of our humanity. What came after was harder.

I had to learn and accept that in each person there exists a right to his or her personal journey. No matter how much or what we know to be true, it is not our job to steal their journey from them, nor force them to join ours. Knowing how to heal a person's life does not give me the right to demand they heal. Sadly, this means watching people harm themselves. I often have an up close and personal front row seat to others' self-destruction. It takes belief and faith in something greater than myself for me to dig deep and offer support and guidance to them from a place of their own choosing. At times, this process has been hard, and has stretched the very fibers of my being.

Standing patiently, I have watched as people digest my experiences and reorganize what I share from a place of their own misconception. I understand it can be difficult to adapt to these new insights. The comfort of being human, as we are, slightly corrupted with beliefs that are not ours, creates our personal struggle. It is indeed a false comfort that must be resolved. My experience demands I release these things and encourage others to do the same. Allowing people their strife and knowing their responses have nothing to do with my sharing—all that has been hard for me.

It would have been easier to pull back and stay in a place where life had no friction, to remain in my own comfort zone where nothing pulled me from my peace and balance. I chose, instead, to discover that another person's process is never about me, and to see how their own experiences can mirror my own needs for growth and change. I live, knowing that without the contribution of what is uniquely me, the change they are asking for cannot be found, and the change I need will not be revealed. It is the intertwining of the real—each of us with our unique selves—with the victorious nature of our never-ending souls that has kept me strong and willing to stay on this path less traveled.

As difficult as it has been to endure, the upside to this grand adventure is my own change. Like a caterpillar, I have shed beliefs that were not my personal truth. I now fly free of the cocoon that encased me, forever changed, having been witness to the power of the human mind and spirit. I am awed!

The contribution of each and every person to my life is far-reaching and life-affirming. I look forward to opening to more vast, incredible experiences than even my very creative mind can guess are possible. As I connect to all of you—each of you having a unique piece of this divine puzzle—we can create a pathway that other human beings have yet to walk.

## Chapter Dedication

Keep up the good work everybody.
Keep creating your unique space in this world.

# Final Thoughts

"I am glad to see you made it; we've been waiting for you!" In the same way the Native American extended this hope to my life, I hope your experience in reading this has brought you a little further into my world where, surprisingly, everything is possible and everything is experienced as a win-win. It is done without compromise, without the overriding beliefs of others, and without disruption of joy. It is a place where we all work and live together as one while maintaining our individuality.

With that said, let me go over a couple of things I believe you may want to know. Having had so many experiences with the dead, I expect you wonder whether my stories are true to life or altered. I work to make sure, in the limited space and time I have for sharing, everything is communicated with the same spirit as when the story was experienced by me. My many varied experiences make it impossible to express each one individually. In some instances, multiple experiences have been combined for the sake of getting to the heart of the lesson. Other, less entertaining parts, have been set aside for the story to make sense.

A transition that did not fit in this book is *why* I started working with people in bodies. Out of fascination, I started comparing the dead to the living. As I brought the information I gathered from observing the dead into conversations with friends and family, I began to see similarities between the two. In one such exchange, a friend was less than inspired when I pointed out that by changing her communication skills she would not have the same problem as a dead guy I spoke to. She suggested instead that I should look at my own life and fix myself. Her generosity in pointing out that I was lax in regard to doing all the same work in myself was well received. I immediately stopped helping others and focused on helping myself by applying the same tactics and information to understand the 'why' and 'how' of my existence. This brought rapid change and growth to my own life in the same way it had for the dead. My suffering came to an end. I began sharing what I had learned with others, and this time, I was living proof!

This particular group of stories represents my shift from skeptic to believer. Learning to trust myself gave me the space to experience the vulnerability I hid from the world. Next, I had to become vulnerable enough to have in-depth, intimate encounters with the living that this type of healing work requires. It became obvious that the end goal of everything I learned was to work with the living to end suffering on earth.

My day-to-day life is not centered around death. Rather, I deal more with the science of energetics. The geometrics and physics are what drive my inclination towards these experiences and keep me engaged. By learning how things worked and what was possible, I found that once each little piece was put together, my life became amazing. I could finally see the whole picture. Though my research started out being for my own experience, the fact that it is sought after and is spilling out into the lives of others, gives me hope for the day we will work in groups regarding wellness.

Although fun, my ability to experience the visions, information, synchronicities, and confirmations from the other side has not changed who I am. I have always been and will always be me. The experiences only shed light on more of the parts I had previously hidden behind the veil.

The knowledge does not clear the veil; it is the actions I take that create my changes.

There are support workbooks for the Death: Awakening to Life series. These workbooks include, in great detail, concepts, methods, examples, and practices to be used as support for what you may want in your own life, opening doors for these extraordinary changes I have expressed while sharing my story.

There will be two more memoirs to follow that deal with specific themes. Animals, plants, children, and miscarriage will be the focus of the second book. Book three will be about my experiences with large-scale traumatic events. In all three books, I hope to convey that we can absolutely break through the veil that protects our brains by reaching a level of readiness for things we cannot currently comprehend.

When I pushed past the veil with force, I found myself in a place of fracturing. I can tell you this: we all live our lives knowing what we know. If you want to learn something but, by doing so, you cannot live with your revelations, the veil will keep it hidden.

My personal wish, now that you have completed this book, is that you realize you can absolutely communicate with your loved ones after they have passed. Keep in mind, the dead are *not* everywhere all the time; they also have busy existences. Do not give up if you do not get them the first time you call.

My hope is that you experience these stories with a depth and emotion that brings them close to your heart, that you are as inspired as I have been to seek out what is uniquely you. I tell my apprentices, "If you try to take something I've shared and apply it to your life as a template and fall flat on your face, don't come back to me saying, 'But you said it would work!' because I didn't." What I have said is we are each responsible for the actions we take, and though I am happy to share my journey with you, only you can do the work that will create your extraordinary life.

As I write this and look back at my journey, I realize I could not have lived my life up until the moment of my death without the veil. I would have always been striving to get to that feeling of love and connection I now know exists and is waiting on the other side for all of us. The veil has been used to blind me to this love so I can more easily choose to live and love here in this moment as I am. Even now, I can no longer recall clearly the feeling I had experienced with Alma other than knowing it was the largest such feeling and connection of my entire life.

Each step of the way, when I did not die, I was encouraged to rise to a new life experience. I have always believed in the basic good of humanity—that in our core we all intend to do no harm. This drove me, challenged me, to stick up for the underdog not only to help them, but also to save their attackers from experiences they too would find impossible to endure as life progressed.

By helping both sides, I felt the support for my cause grow. Each time, another welcomed, willing participant chose to bare the cross of hope with me. With each challenge, I have begun to realize my entire journey has been like someone leading me, holding my hand. Each step had a well-placed hint, a string of breadcrumbs leading me to the presence and support to learn every amazing detail that would make it possible for me to someday add to the wellness of my world. Every value, every heart break, every moment of boredom, stress, heroism, fear of loss, every single experience of joy was necessary in that moment of my death to create my clarity. Each of us, as we look at our own lives with this intention, can see for ourselves how we have been led.

Experiencing the brink of death, and my desire for so much more than a quiet life of desperation, drove me not to settle. It drove me, and still drives me, to fight for life—to fight for what I know is possible. I strive to embody my individuated self and to help others live their truths, not only for my own sake, but to ensure we all, upon our deaths, Awaken to Life.

# ACKNOWLEDGMENTS

*J* would like to thank the team at Winterwolf press: Arleen Barreiros, Teresa Kennedy, John Dixon, Elisa Cantu, Wendy Scott, and special guest editor Randy Peyser. It has been a pleasure working with such an excellent team of professionals.

My unending gratitude for Russ Thompson, writing consultant, for drawing the story out of me when I had no idea how to bring it to the page; and for Laura Jones, my most favorite of editors and a kindred spirit. Your support and friendship made the work process more of a party than a chore. I waited with baited breath for each and every response.

To my dear friend and fellow author Laura C. Cantu, who sought me out and connected me with this wonderful team at Winterwolf Press because of her belief in me. I am ever so inspired by your ability to reach past what most people think is already the end of the process.

To my personal team of Beta Readers: your belief in the book's merit encouraged me to fully understand that the world needed my story with all its vulnerable truths. I worked harder to meet your expectations and used your faith as my litmus test.

I would like to express my adoration for Sergio Diaz, for wrangling the yahoos and managing every other detail of the important things in my life while I focused on the writing process. Without you, it would have taken two years instead of one. Much love.

Thanks from my heart to each of those on the other side who answered the call when I could not remember the details of our experiences together from the place of my human brain.

*Christine Contini* is on a mission to bring joy, empowerment, and knowledge to the world. Her goals are to awaken the sleepers and to unveil the many miraculous advances in human evolution that we all can achieve. Through sharing her own experiences, she can illustrate what is possible and introduce slight adjustments to familiar concepts so they become life changing realizations. Christine delights in inspiring people to recognize their own innate power and to learn to completely embrace themselves as enlightened human beings. "We are all participating in this grand adventure together, and not only are we more effective when we work in groups, but it's more fun too."

# Winterwolf Press

We hope you have enjoyed *Death: Awakening to Life* by Christine Contini. Would you like to read more titles from our library?

## CHECK OUT A WHIMSICAL TALE FROM WINTERWOLF PRESS

Join Noah and his friends as they race against time and plunge headfirst into the unknown to save a dying faerie.
    Written by Laura Cantu.

## CHECK OUT A DARK FANTASY FROM SHADOW WOLF PRESS

After witnessing something dark and strange, Zephera– a nineteen-year-old assassin– is forced to accept a seemingly impossible quest to save her world.
    Written by Aubrie Nixon.

www.winterwolfpress.com /Social Media Handle: WinterwolfPress

CPSIA information can be obtained
at www.ICGtesting.com
Printed in the USA
LVHW05s1551230618
581686LV00023B/345/P